Consul Willshire Butterfield

An Historical Account of the Expedition Against Sandusky

under Col. William Crawford in 1782: with biographical sketches, personal reminiscences, and descriptions of interesting localitie

Consul Willshire Butterfield

An Historical Account of the Expedition Against Sandusky
under Col. William Crawford in 1782: with biographical sketches, personal reminiscences, and descriptions of interesting localitie

ISBN/EAN: 9783337324551

Printed in Europe, USA, Canada, Australia, Japan

Cover: Foto ©ninafisch / pixelio.de

More available books at **www.hansebooks.com**

AN

HISTORICAL ACCOUNT

OF THE

Expedition against Sandusky

UNDER

COL. WILLIAM CRAWFORD

IN 1782

WITH

BIOGRAPHICAL SKETCHES, PERSONAL REMINISCENCES, AND
DESCRIPTIONS OF INTERESTING LOCALITIES

INCLUDING, ALSO, DETAILS OF THE DISASTROUS RETREAT, THE
BARBARITIES OF THE SAVAGES, AND THE AWFUL
DEATH OF CRAWFORD BY TORTURE

C. W. BUTTERFIELD

CINCINNATI
ROBERT CLARKE & CO
1873

Prefatory.

CRAWFORD's campaign was one of the most notable of the distinct military enterprises of the Western Border War of the Revolution. Nevertheless, it has heretofore found but little space upon the page of American History. This, however, is not surprising, when we consider that its most striking incidents occurred within a brief space of time, and beyond the bounds of western civilization.

On account of the paucity of authoritative published statements relating to the expedition, I have been compelled, from the commencement, to depend, to a considerable extent, upon authorities in manuscript. Nor can this be regretted, as it has caused the pushing of investigations, whenever practicable, to fountain sources. I have relied upon traditions, only when better testimony was wanting; and not even then, without careful consideration and the closest scrutiny. It is believed, therefore, as much reliability has been attained as could well be, concerning events transpiring mostly beyond the extreme western frontier of our country during the turbulent period of its struggle for independence.

The melancholy fate of Crawford caused a profound sensation throughout the United States. Washington was greatly affected by it. He made it the subject of a special communication to Congress. So prominent a soldier and citizen had not, during the Revolution, met such a cruel death. It took a strong and lasting hold upon the sympathies of the people. Pennsylvania and Ohio—each, in naming a county in honor of him—have done signal justice to his memory. "The fate of this unfortunate officer has excited, and will continue to excite, so long as the history of the West shall be read, the most painful interest and the liveliest sympathy." I have attempted faithfully to record the leading incidents of his life, and to narrate, with particularity, the circumstances attending its close.

To James Veech, Esq., of Allegheny, Pennsylvania; Hon. William Walker, of Wyandotte City, Kansas; Dr. William A. Irvine, of Irvine, Warren county, Pennsylvania; John D. Sears, Esq., of Upper Sandusky, Ohio; and Robert A. Sherrard, Esq., of Steubenville, Ohio, I beg to express my sincere acknowledgments for their unremitting endeavors to aid me. To the many friends who have in various ways kindly assisted me, I take pleasure in tendering my warmest thanks. The custodians of the public archives at Washington and Harrisburg have furnished valuable materials; as also have the officers of the Western Reserve Historical Society at Cleveland, and the Librarian of the State Library at Columbus.

In the preparation of this work I have sought to give the real motives which actuated the patriotic borderers in marching into the wilderness; and have endeavored, by untiring effort, to bring before the public such particulars of the campaign as seemed worthy of perpetuation. It will be seen that it was not an unauthorized expedition—a sudden and wild maraud; but was set on foot by the proper authority, and carefully and considerately planned; that, instead of unfurling the black flag and marching with an intention to' massacre inoffensive Indians, as has been so frequently charged, it moved under the banner of the United States, and for the sole purpose of destroying enemies, not only of the western frontier, but of our common country, thereby to give ease and security to the border.

C. W. B.

BUCYRUS, CRAWFORD COUNTY, OHIO, *May*, 1873.

PORTRAIT OF IRVINE AND THE IRVINE PAPERS.

The portrait of Brigadier-General William Irvine, facing the title-page of this work, is from an oil painting by B. Otis, a celebrated portrait painter of Philadelphia, after one by Robert Edge Pine, an eminent English artist, who came to America in 1784. The original was taken in New York, when Irvine was a member of Congress,—aged forty-eight.

Extracts from letters of Irvine, in the following pages, are from originals, or from copies in his own handwriting or that of Lieut. John Rose, his aid-de-camp—with few exceptions, which are noted. Quotations from letters *to* Irvine are from originals, unless otherwise stated. Most of these letters are in the collection of Dr. William A. Irvine, grandson of the General.

CONTENTS.

CHAPTER I.—War upon the Western Border of Pennsylvania and Virginia. 1777—1781, ... 1

CHAPTER II.—Brigadier-General William Irvine in Command at Fort Pitt—Affairs in the Western Department. October, 1781—April, 1782, ... 16

CHAPTER III.—An Expedition Projected in Western Pennsylvania against Sandusky. April 4—May 7, 1782, ... 49

CHAPTER IV.—Rendezvousing and Organization of the Sandusky Expedition. 15-24th May, 1782, ... 62

CHAPTER V.—Biographical Sketch of William Crawford. 1732—1782, ... 81

CHAPTER VI.—Sketches of the Officers under Crawford, . . 121

CHAPTER VII.—March of the Army from Mingo Bottom to Sandusky. 25th May—4th June, 1782, ... 136

CHAPTER VIII.—Preparations by the Enemy to Repel the Americans, ... 157

CHAPTER IX.—Sketch of Simon Girty, the White Savage, . . 182

CHAPTER X.—Battle of Sandusky—June 4, 1782, . . . 202

CHAPTER XI.—Retreat of the American Army. June 5-6, 1782, 214

CHAPTER XII.—Battle of Olentangy—Return of the Americans. June 6-14, 1782, ... 233

CHAPTER XIII.—Alarm of the Border—Determined Spirit of the Bordermen, ... 258

CHAPTER XIV.—Personal Incidents and Sketches, . . 281

CHAPTER XV.—Stragglers Captured by the Savages, . . . 311

CHAPTER XVI.—Captives in the Wilderness—Indian Barbarities, 327

CHAPTER XVII.—James Paull—His Escape from Death—His Subsequent Career, ... 362

CHAPTER XVIII.—Dr. John Knight's Escape through the Ohio Wilderness. 13th June—4th July, 1782, ... 369

CHAPTER XIX.—A Race for Life—Escape of John Slover from Mac-a-Chack, ... 375

CHAPTER XX.—Awful Death of Crawford by Torture. 11th June, 1782, ... 379

COL. CRAWFORD'S
Expedition against Sandusky,

IN 1782.

CHAPTER I.

WAR UPON THE WESTERN BORDER OF PENNSYLVANIA AND VIRGINIA. 1777—1781.

AT the commencement of the struggle of the American colonies for independence, the scattered settlements west of the Allegheny mountains had little to fear from the hostile armies of Great Britain. Their dread was of a more merciless foe. Nor were their fears groundless; for the Indians of the Northwest, influenced by British gold and the machinations of English traders and emissaries, soon gave evidence of hostile intentions. Explanations by the Americans that the questions in dispute could not affect their interests, were made in vain. It was to no purpose that they were exhorted to take part on neither side. Painted and plumed warriors were early upon the war-path, carrying death and destruction to the dismayed borderers—the direct result of a most ferocious policy inaugurated by

England—"letting loose," in the language of Chatham, "the horrible hell-hounds of savage war," upon the exposed settlements.

The warfare thus begun was made up, on the side of the savages, of predatory incursions of scalping parties; the tomahawk and scalping-knife sparing neither age nor sex, while the torch laid waste the homes of the unfortunate bordermen. As a natural consequence, retaliatory expeditions followed. These were not always successful. At times, they were highly disastrous. Occasionally, however, the foe received a merited chastisement. At this day, it is difficult fully to appreciate the appalling dangers which then beset the frontiers; for, to the natural ferocity of the savages, was added the powerful support of a civilized nation, great in her resources, whose western agents, especially at the beginning of the war, were noted for their brutality.

The center of British power and influence, in the Northwest, was at Detroit, where Henry Hamilton, "a vulgar ruffian," was in command; succeeded, however, before the close of the war, by Arentz Schuyler de Peyster, who, although carrying out the policy of the British government, did so in the spirit of a "high-toned gentleman." Indian depredations received their inspiration and direction from this point. It was here the Wyandots from the Sandusky—a river flowing north through Sandusky Bay into Lake Erie—were enlisted in the interests of Great Britain. It was here these Indians and the Shawanese from the Scioto and Miami rivers—northern tributaries of the Ohio—received aid to murder, pillage, and destroy on the border settlements of Pennsylvania and Virginia. It was here other tribes were made close allies of Great Britain, for the express purpose of turning them loose upon peaceable settlers—upon unarmed men, and helpless women and children.

The important post, however, of Fort Pitt—Pittsburg—was, from the commencement of hostilities, in the possession of the Americans, and the center of government influence and interest west of the Alleghenies. At the very beginning of the war of the Revolution, John Neville—afterward famous as a victim of the "Whisky Insurrection"—took possession of the dilapidated fort, at the head of a body of Virginia militia, and held it until superseded by a Continental command. His Indian policy was one of strict neutrality; powerless, it is true, with all the western tribes except the Delawares, who were located upon the Muskingum,[1] a northern affluent of the Ohio. In holding this tribe in check, he was aided by George Morgan, congressional agent of Indian affairs in the West, and by Moravian missionaries who had gathered together many of these Indians in establishments upon that

---

[1] So called, at that period, below the mouth of Sandy creek; afterward, however, known as the Tuscarawas, above the confluence of the Walhonding.

river, in what is now Tuscarawas county, Ohio, where they were taught the blessings of civilization and Christianity.

The frontiers of Pennsylvania and Virginia suffered terribly by this irregular warfare—legitimate, from the stand-point of the savages, but murderous and wanton in its instigators. On the 27th of July, Hamilton, at Detroit, had already sent out fifteen parties of Indians, consisting of two hundred and eighty-nine braves, with thirty white officers and rangers, to prowl on the borders. In September, Fort Henry—Wheeling—was furiously attacked; but, after a gallant defense, the assailants were repulsed, and withdrew across the Ohio.

In the spring of 1778, there appeared upon the theater of conflict a new element of destruction to help on the work of devastation and death—tories, outlaws, and deserters from the States; renegades among the Indians—"of that horrid brood," wrote Hugh H. Brackenridge, of Pittsburg, in 1782, "called refugees, whom the devil has long since marked as his own."[2] These desperadoes and go-betweens came well nigh

---

[2] *Narratives of a Late Expedition against the Indians; with an Account of the Barbarous Execution of Col. Crawford; and the Wonderful Escape of Dr Knight and John Slover from Captivity, in 1782. Philadelphia: Printed by Francis Bailey, in Market street. M,DCC,LXXIII.*, p. 23, *note*. An X in the date, as will be seen, is accidentally omitted. This work is referred to in the following pages either as "Knight's Narrative," or "Slover's Narrative."

changing the neutral policy of the Delawares to hostility against the Americans; frustrated, however, by the prompt action of Brigadier-General Edward Hand, who had succeeded Neville in command at Fort Pitt, and by the undaunted courage of the missionaries upon the Muskingum. Other tribes were inflamed to a white heat of rapacity against the frontier settlements by the wiles of these wicked men.

Pennsylvania and Virginia now began to bestir themselves to protect their distant settlements. A force was raised to garrison the advanced posts upon the western borders. Congress also determined to make common cause with these suffering States. The new-born nation aroused itself to chastise the savage allies of Great Britain in the West. In May, 1778, Brigadier-General Lachlin McIntosh, of the Continental army, succeeded Hand in command of the Western Department, of which the headquarters was Fort Pitt. He brought with him a small force of regulars, for the defense of the frontier and ulterior operations. Congress, in the meantime, having received official information of the real cause of the great activity of the western Indians, determined upon an expedition against Detroit; rightfully concluding that the reduction of that post would be the quickest and surest way of bringing ease to the suffering border.

McIntosh, therefore, was ordered to move upon Detroit—the neutrality of the Delawares having meanwhile been assured, at least for the present, by a treaty at Fort Pitt, on the 17th of September. He descended the Ohio with a force of regulars and militia, in the month of October, to the mouth of Beaver,[3] a northern tributary of that river, where, on the present site of the town of that name, about thirty miles below Pittsburg, he erected a fort, which was called, in honor of the projector, Fort McIntosh. It was a small work, built of strong stockades, and furnished with bastions mounting one six-pounder each—the first millitary post of the United States established beyond the frontier settlements, upon the Indian side of the Ohio.

From the expensiveness of the undertaking, Congress was reluctantly compelled to abandon the expedition against Detroit. In lieu thereof, McIntosh was ordered to proceed against any Indian towns, the destruction of which, in his opinion, would tend most effectually to intimidate and chastise the hostile savages. After due consideration, McIntosh decided to move against Sandusky—a Wyandot town upon the upper waters of the river of that name—and contiguous villages and settlements. For that purpose, he marched into the wilderness westward, with a thousand men; but, upon reaching the Muskingum, it was decided to proceed no further until spring. A halt was accordingly called, and a fort built near the site of the present town of Bolivar, in

---

[3] MS. Order-Book of General McIntosh: Irvine Collection.

Tuscarawas county, Ohio, on the west bank of the river, and called, in honor of the president of Congress, Fort Laurens. Leaving a garrison of one hundred and fifty men, under the command of Colonel John Gibson to protect the post, McIntosh returned with the rest of his army to Fort Pitt.

Colonel Gibson, at Fort Laurens, soon found himself in an uncomfortable position. In January, 1779, several hundred British Indians laid siege to the fort, and continued its investment for six weeks, reducing the garrison to the verge of starvation. The savages were then compelled to return home, as their supplies had likewise become exhausted. Soon after the raising of the siege, McIntosh arrived with provisions and a relief of seven hundred men. Colonel Gibson was succeeded by Major Frederick Vernon. McIntosh having again returned to Fort Pitt, was afterward relieved by Colonel Daniel Brodhead, who now took the command of the Western Department.[4]

Fort Laurens, the first military post erected by the American government on any portion of the territory now constituting the State of Ohio, was finally evacuated in August; not, however, until the garrison had again been reduced to terrible straits. With the abandonment of this fort, ended the first campaign undertaken against Sandusky from the borders of Pennsylvania and Virginia. Its failure was due not so much

---

[4] Col. Brodhead's Order-Book: MS. From the Irvine Collection.

to the want of men, as to the lack of means—the sinews of war were wanting. Fort McIntosh was also soon after abandoned, together with several smaller works of defense near the Ohio.

The withdrawal of all forces from the Indian country caused great alarm and indignation in the settlements on the border. Early in 1780, a meeting of citizens was held in Westmoreland county—the then western frontier county of Pennsylvania, including all of the State west of the Laurel Hill—and resolutions passed requesting the re-occupation of the abandoned forts. But the pressure of the war upon the Atlantic States prevented this; and nothing was left the borderers but to protect themselves as best they could. Small parties frequently pursued the Indians into the wilderness with good success; but now, to add to the general dismay, the Delawares, who had so long withstood the influences and threats of the British and their savage allies, declared for war—only a small band remaining friendly to the Americans; the residue joined the Confederacy of the Northwest.

Informed of the disaffection of the Delawares, Colonel Brodhead organized an expedition against them. Nearly half his force was volunteers. Their rendezvous was at Fort Henry—Wheeling. They numbered about three hundred. They crossed the Ohio, and made a rapid march, by the nearest route, to the principal Delaware village upon the Muskingum. It occupied the site of the lower streets of the present town of Coshocton, Ohio. The army reached the point of destination on the evening of the 19th of April, 1781, completely surprising the Indians. Their town was laid waste, and fifteen of their warriors were killed and twenty taken prisoners. Another village, two and a half miles below, on the east bank of the river Muskingum, was also destroyed. Brodhead then proceeded up the valley to a town, the present site of Newcomerstown, Oxford township, Tuscarawas county, where he met some friendly Delawares who were then occupying the place. These Indians, placing themselves under the protection of the United States, accompanied the army on its return to Fort Pitt.

Before leaving the Muskingum, Brodhead sent for the Moravian missionaries, whose establishments were at no great distance up the valley, to confer with them upon the existing state of affairs. There were three villages of the "Christian Indians"—New Schönbrunn, Gnadenhütten, and Salem, all situated within what is now Tuscarawas county. The missionaries from these contiguous villages soon made their appearance at Brodhead's camp, where they met a cordial welcome. The American commander advised them, in view of the hostile attitude of the Delawares, their peculiar situation— "between two fires," and the increasing jealousy of the belligerents, to break up their establishments and accompany him to Pittsburg. This they declined doing, and they were left to their fate.

The failure of McIntosh, in his designs upon Detroit and the Wyandot towns upon the Sandusky, greatly discouraged further attempts in that direction. The heroic George Rogers Clark, however, under authority of Virginia, aided, to some extent, by Pennsylvania, now undertook the task of getting together a sufficient force to justify an attempt against the western Indians and Detroit. Brodhead, at Fort Pitt, was ordered to aid him, with arms and ammunition, to the extent of his power The troops were to rendezvous at the falls of the Ohio—Louisville; the Wyandot towns were to be the special object of attack.

Much enthusiasm was manifested in the Western Department in aid of the expedition. The Pennsylvania force of one hundred and seven mounted men, under command of Colonel Archibald Lochry, the prothonotary and lieutenant of Westmoreland county, on their way down the river to join Clark, was attacked by the Indians, from an ambush, about eleven miles below the mouth of the Great Miami river, in what is now the State of Indiana, and all killed or captured. This most unfortunate affair occurred on the 24th of August.[5]

---

[5] *McBride's Pioneer Biography*, vol. i, p. 273. A small stream, called Lochry's creek, perpetuates the memory and locality of this event.

Clark was reluctantly compelled to abandon the expedition.

Without waiting the result of Clark's campaign, an expedition had been, in the meantime, concerted against Sandusky—Upper Sandusky, as it was sometimes called, to distinguish it from Lower Sandusky, a Wyandot town where Fremont, the county town of Sandusky county, Ohio, now stands—by Colonel Gibson, who had succeeded Brodhead in temporary command at Fort Pitt—so eager were the oppressed people of the border to destroy that most prolific hive of mischief to the frontier settlements. Extensive preparations were made, and troops ordered to rendezvous at Fort McIntosh on the 4th and 5th of September. A large number of volunteers was enrolled, leading citizens of the Western Department taking an active part in the project and offering their services to Colonel Gibson for the campaign. But the borderers were doomed to disappointment. There were insurmountable obstacles in the way. The scheme was therefore abandoned.

The western frontier was now menaced with a British and Indian invasion from Canada. The Department of the West was in confusion. Fort Pitt was little better than a heap of ruins. The regular force was wholly incompetent to the exigencies of the service. It consisted of the remains of the Eighth Pennsylvania and of the Seventh Virginia regiments. A dispute between Colonels Gibson and Brodhead, as to the command, added greatly to the disorder. The garrison was in want of pay, of clothing, of even subsistence itself. The militia of the Department was without proper organization; and, when called into service, destitute, to a great extent, of military knowledge and discipline.

The civil government of the country was even in a worse state than the military. A controversy had long existed between Pennsylvania and Virginia as to the ownership of what is now Southwestern Pennsylvania, including Pittsburg. Each asserted and exercised an organized jurisdiction. This had seriously embittered many individuals of the two States against each other. Nor was this personal and private excitement the worst consequence attending it. Public bodies of both States were affected by it. Violence and indecorum marked their conduct. Officers of each commonwealth acted oppressively. The people were divided in their allegiance. Arrests and counter-arrests were the order of the day. The controversy, however, as between the two governments, ended in 1780; but the people, to a certain extent, had come into open disrespect of their own State from having long contemned the authority of a neighboring one. Hence, there was a general restlessness, and a desire on the part of many to emigrate into the wilderness, beyond the Ohio, to form a new State.

Such was the disorder—the confusion—which beset the Western Department at the moment of the threatened invasion. Washington fully appreciated the difficulties. Something must be done, and done quickly. Above all things, a commander was needed at Fort Pitt, possessed not only of courage and firmness, but of prudence and judgment. The commander-in-chief, with great care and concern, looked about him for such a person. His choice for the position, after due deliberation, fell upon Brigadier-General WILLIAM IRVINE, of Carlisle, Pennsylvania, then at the head of the Second brigade of that State—a corps of great and merited distinction.

Washington having communicated his decision to Congress, that body, on the 24th of September, ordered General Irvine to repair forthwith to Fort Pitt and take upon himself the command of the garrison at that post, and of the Western Department, until further orders. He was empowered by Congress to call in, from time to time, such aids of militia as would be necessary for the defense of the post under his command and the protection of the country. The executives of Virginia and Pennsylvania were requested to direct the proper officers of the militia in their respective States to obey such orders as they should receive from General Irvine for that purpose.[6]

At this period, the president of the Supreme Executive Council of Pennsylvania—a body constituting the supreme executive power of the State—was *de facto*, as well as *de jure*, the governor of that commonwealth.

---

[6] Extract from Minutes of Congress, by Charles Thompson, Secretary: MS.

That office was held by William Moore, the councilor for Philadelphia, who notified the lieutenants of Westmoreland and the new county of Washington—officers having a general command and supervision of military affairs therein—that, as the Council was disposed and had resolved to pay due respect to the requisitions of Congress and afford General Irvine all the assistance in its power; they should call forth, agreeable to law upon his requisitions, such militia as might be necessary for the defense of Fort Pitt and the protection of the country.[7]

Benjamin Harrison, governor of Virginia, did not, however, issue like orders to the lieutenants of Monongalia and Ohio—border counties of that State—until in the following May; and when issued, were practically inoperative, on account of an existing law, prohibiting the removal of the militia of Virginia beyond its limits. Moreover, the extended frontiers of these counties, as they then existed, reaching from the northern end of the " Pan-handle "[8] to the waters of Middle

---

[7] MS. Instructions: October 11, 1781. Irvine Papers.

[8] "Tradition, in accounting for the strip of land driven in wedge-like between Ohio and Pennsylvania, constituting what is called the Pan-handle, states that it was owing to an error in reckoning that the five degrees of west longitude reached so far to the west, and that much dissatisfaction was excited when the result was definitely settled, as great importance was attached to the command of the Ohio river by the authorities of either State.

"When the State of Ohio was formed, in 1802, the Pan-handle first

Island creek, required all the able-bodied men of their sparse and scattered settlements for home protection.

---

showed its beautiful proportions on the map of the United States. It received its name in legislative debate, from Hon. John McMillan, delegate from Brooke county, to match the Accomac projection, which he dubbed the Spoon-handle."—*History of Washington County. By Alfred Creigh, LL.D.* App., pp. 36, 37.

CHAPTER II.

BRIGADIER-GENERAL WILLIAM IRVINE IN COMMAND AT FORT PITT—AFFAIRS IN THE WESTERN DEPARTMENT. OCTOBER, 1781—APRIL, 1782.

WILLIAM IRVINE, who had been ordered to the command of the Western Department, was born near Enniskillen, county Fermanagh, Ireland, on the 3d of November, 1741. His ancestors originally emigrated from Scotland. His grandfather was an officer in the corps of grenadiers, which fought so gallantly at the battle of the Boyne. Of his parents we know less than we could wish, but enough to show that both were highly respectable.. Not less so was the early life of William himself, which gave evidence of good character and superior abilities.

Young Irvine's elementary education commenced at a grammar school in Enniskillen, and was completed at the College of Dublin. Having come to an age when it was proper to select a profession, his own choice led strongly to that of arms; and a friend of the family—Lady Cole—went so far as to procure for him a cornetcy of dragoons; but, owing to a quarrel with his colonel, he resigned his position. His parents then entered him a student of medicine and surgery, under the celebrated Cleghorn. That the pupil was worthy the preceptor may be fairly presumed from the fact that, on closing his studies, he was immediately appointed surgeon of a British ship of war.

The incident last mentioned took place during the long contest between France and England, which began in 1754, and terminated in 1763, "when Wolfe and Amherst conquered Canada," and " the vast but frail fabric of French empire in the West crumbled to the dust." It was in the course of several years of hard and constant service, that, becoming acquainted with the condition of society in this country, he took the resolution of seeking a professional establishment here; and accordingly, within a few months after the declaration of peace, arrived in America, followed subsequently by two brothers—Captain Andrew Irvine and Dr. Mathew Irvine, the celebrated "fighting surgeon" of Lee's Legion.

Attracted by the number and character of his countrymen, who had located themselves in the interior of Pennsylvania, he made his way thither; and, in 1764, became a citizen of Carlisle.[1] Nor was he long in this new situation, until, by diligence and skill, he was able to recommend himself to general confidence, despite of manners habitually reserved, and sometimes seemingly

---

[1] Irvine married Anne Callender, daughter of Captain Robert Callender, of Carlisle, who was largely engaged in the Indian trade, and who served in Braddock's campaign with credit and distinction. The result of this marriage was a family of ten children—five sons and five daughters.

austere, and which utterly excluded the use of those gossiping and parasitical means so often and scandalously employed in giving birth and currency to medical fame.

Irvine's personal ascendency, resting on foundations so little liable to change, continued unabated until, in 1774, he was called to take part in the great political controversy which terminated in the independence of the colonies. To pilot Pennsylvania through the political breakers, now foaming and dashing around her, safely into the Union, required great prudence, activity, and perseverance. There was the mischievous tendency to overcome of *religious scruples*, which disaffected more than one important sect of the community. So, too, *national prejudices* had to be combated, which were inseparable from a population made up of different nations, habits, and languages. But, lastly, there was a *proprietary influence* to be overpowered, which, operating through the multiplied channels of friends and agents, addressed itself alike to the hopes and fears of the whole community.

That Pennsylvania was able to overcome all these mischievous tendencies was due to the wisdom and energy of a few patriotic men, mostly of Scotch-Irish descent, of whom Irvine was one.

As a first step in the right direction, it was agreed that a meeting should be held in Philadelphia, to be followed, in rapid succession, by similar assemblages in the eleven counties of the province. The meeting took place in Philadelphia, on the 18th of June; and on the 15th of July a provincial convention came together in that city, which promptly concurred in recommending the selection and sitting of a general congress. It denounced the Boston port bill as unconstitutional, expressed its sympathies with the sufferers under it, and declared its willingness and determination to make any sacrifice necessary for the support of American rights. Of this convention Irvine was a diligent and active member.

In January, 1776, Irvine was appointed to raise and command a regiment which became the Sixth of the Pennsylvania line, though afterward numbered the Seventh. The activity put into this new service was highly creditable to the commander and his subordinate officers; as, in less than five months from the date of his instructions, we find the regiment raised, clothed, and equipped, and marched to the mouth of the river Sorrel, in Canada, and on the 10th of June uniting with Thompson's brigade in the unsuccessful attempt made by that corps to surprise the vanguard of the British army, then stationed at Trois Rivieres.

In this enterprise, the commanding general and Colonel Irvine, with about two hundred subordinates and privates, who formed the head of the attack, were made prisoners and carried to Quebec—a misfortune sufficiently great in itself, but much aggravated, in the present case, by the fact that though there were prisoners of commensurate rank ready for exchange, yet, from some misunderstanding between the two governments or their agents, Colonel Irvine was not exchanged until the 6th of May, 1778, although released on parol on the 3d of August after his capture. To compensate him, in some degree, for a mortification, so severe and long continued, he was promoted to the command of the Second Pennsylvania brigade; and, on the 12th of May, 1779, was commissioned brigadier-general.[2]

From the date of Irvine's exchange as a prisoner of war his career was a highly honorable one, both as patriot and soldier. He saw considerable active service in the army, especially distinguishing himself at Monmouth by an advance through Lee's retreating troops—concerning which history has been unjustly silent; his march, the night after Arnold's treachery became known, to the defense of West Point, shows the great confidence reposed in him by Washington. He had already acquired a knowledge of the traitor's character, and had not been backward in giving information concerning it to the commander-in-chief.

---

[2] *Rogers' Amer. Biog.*, p. 252; *Drake's Dic. Amer. Biog.*, article *Irvine*; *The Olden Time*, vol. ii, pp. 479, 480. The article in the first of these authorities was written by Gen. John Armstrong, author of the "*Newburgh Letters*" of 1783. He was Secretary of War in 1812–13, and a historian of the war of 1812–15.

He was the preference of Washington for the command of the Pennsylvania troops to be sent South, but Wayne, being his senior, was placed at the head of the corps, although most of the men had been recruited and got together by Irvine's exertions. He was, however, too sincere a patriot to complain; but he often said, afterward, that he would have infinitely preferred the southern command to the isolation and comparative inaction at Fort Pitt; yet, as we shall soon see, his prudence there was of as much value to the common cause as perhaps his activity would have been in the southern campaign.

Immediately after General Irvine's appointment to the command of the Western Department, he repaired to Fort Pitt and began the task of putting that work in a tolerable state of repair, to meet the emergencies which might arise in case of an attack by the enemy. New pickets were prepared; and, to encourage the completion of the improvements proposed, Irvine aided in the labor with his own hands. This had a happy effect. Every officer followed his example. The greatest activity prevailed. In a short time the fort was put in a much better condition for a successful defense than it had been since 1764. It was probably this which induced the abandonment of the contemplated invasion from Canada, as Fort Pitt was to have been the objective point of the invaders.

General Irvine next addressed himself to the task of

reforming the regulars under his command. He had been ordered, by Congress, to arrange the troops in such a manner as to retain no more officers than were absolutely necessary for the number of non-commissioned officers and privates, and to arrange the staff-departments so as to retain no more officers or persons than the service demanded. He, therefore, now began the work. The Eighth Pennsylvania regiment was so reduced that only two companies could be formed from it. These he called "a detachment of the Pennsylvania line." Colonel Gibson had, some time before, been ordered to reform his regiment, the Seventh Virginia, into two companies, which had been effected previous to the arrival of General Irvine. The supernumerary officers of the Pennsylvania troops were ordered to repair forthwith to their proper regiments in the Pennsylvania line; and orders had been issued, by Colonel Gibson, to the supernumeraries of his regiment, to return to Virginia; "but the officers were so distressed, for want of clothing and other necessaries," wrote Irvine to Washington, on the 2d of December, "that they were not able to proceed!" The writer adds: "however, they are now making exertions, and, I hope, will soon set out."

If such was the condition of the superior officers, what must have been the plight of the rank and file! We will let General Irvine answer. In his letter to Washington, just mentioned, he said: "I never saw troops cut so truly a deplorable figure. No man would believe, from their appearance, that they were soldiers; nay, it was difficult to determine whether they were white men!" But the commander did not despair. Under his supervision there was an immediate improvement. "Though they do not yet come up to my wishes they are some better," is his hopeful language. The quartermaster's department next engaged his attention. The contractors were also called to account. And then, for the first time, was there a chance for the general to turn his attention to the state of the border.

The post at Wheeling (Fort Henry) was found to have a garrison of one Continental officer and fifteen privates. Irvine did not see how he could spare any of the soldiers at Fort Pitt for their relief. The latter were so few and so ill provided for, so irregular, and, in every respect, so unlike soldiers, that it seemed absolutely necessary they should be kept together as much as possible for the present. Neither did the commander desire to make haste to draw out the citizens of the different counties for tours of military duty. He would try whether enough volunteers could not be obtained to take the place of the men at Fort Henry. In case of failure, however, he resolved to call out, for that purpose, according to law, a sufficient number of the militia.

On the 18th of November, Irvine wrote to James Marshal, lieutenant of Washington county—which then comprehended all the territory west of the Monongahela and south of the Ohio, to the State line—asking him to engage, if practicable, "one discreet, intelligent subaltern officer, with six or seven men," to march to the relief of the garrison, at Wheeling, "to take charge of the post by the 1st of December, at furthest, and to remain there till the 1st of March, unless sooner discharged or relieved—they to be allowed for it as having served a tour of militia duty, and every other emolument and allowance, agreeable to law." If this force could not be engaged as volunteers, then Marshal was to order out one subaltern, one sergeant, one corporal, and fifteen privates of the militia; and, when ready to march, they were to be sent to Fort Pitt for instructions.

"I can not comply with your requisition," was the answer of Marshal, two days after, "of engaging a number of men for the defense of Fort Wheeling, as I am heartily tired out with volunteer plans." But he was ready and willing to obey orders: "I shall order out, according to class, the number of militia you have demanded, and order the officer to wait upon you for instructions." Marshal made good his word. Lieutenant Hay waited upon General Irvine; and, on the 28th, received his orders "to proceed to Wheeling with the detachment under his command, there to relieve the garrison of Continental troops—taking upon himself the charge of the post."

These instructions of Irvine evince the thoughtful care he was already beginning to exercise over the border: "I do not apprehend any danger of an attack, during the winter season, of any considerable number of the enemy; notwithstanding, you ought to be vigilant, and guard against surprise, which a few skulking savages might effect if you should prove unwatchful, and which would not fail of bringing disgrace on you, and might be attended with fatal consequences to the inhabitants of the settlements, the protection of whom is the main object of your being posted there."[3] The officer was enjoined, in case of an attack, to maintain his post to the last extremity, and to give the earliest notice possible to the country, that the citizens might come to his support.

General Irvine now turned his attention to the condition of the country generally. He found the people, on account of the failure of Clark's and Gibson's expeditions, in the greatest consternation and utmost despair; particularly in Westmoreland county, Lochry's party being all the best men of their frontier. In his letter to Washington, of December 2d, Irvine said: "At present, the people talk of flying, early in the spring, to the eastern side of the mountain; and are daily flocking to me to inquire what support they may expect." It was very generally believed, and the

---

[3] MS. Instructions: Irvine to Hay.

commander himself shared in the opinion, that the failure of Clark and Gibson would greatly encourage the savages to fall on the frontiers with double fury, in the coming spring.

Irvine soon found that a favorite scheme, over all the country, was an attack on Detroit. He, therefore, set at work to investigate the subject. He gave to his commander-in-chief, in the letter already mentioned, the information he had obtained and his views upon the propriety of the undertaking: "It is, I believe, universally agreed that the only way to keep Indians from harassing the country is to visit them. But we find, by experience, that burning their empty towns has not the desired effect. They can soon build others. They must be followed up and beaten, or the British, whom they draw their support from, totally driven out of their country. I believe if Detroit was demolished, it would be a good step toward giving some, at least, temporary ease to this country." In a pecuniary point of view the project commended itself to the judgment of the commander, and he further explained to Washington: "I have been endeavoring to form some estimate, from such information as I can collect; and I really think that the reduction of Detroit would not cost much more, nor take many more men, than it will take to cover and protect the country by acting on the defensive." The answer of Washington, written the 18th of December, was but a reflex of Irvine's views: "I am convinced that the possession or destruction of Detroit is the only means of giving peace and security to the western frontier." But he added: "When we shall have it in our power to accomplish so desirable an end I do not know." And again, on the 21st, he wrote: "Whether we shall or shall not be in a condition to prosecute an enterprise against Detroit, in any short time, I do not know."

As it was now December, and the cold weather had fairly set in, no more trouble was apprehended from the Indians until the early days of spring. Irvine, therefore, saw no necessity for calling out any more militia for the present. He had fully informed himself with regard to the condition of affairs in his department, and had communicated freely with Washington, also with Congress, and the Board of War, concerning the most important matters. Nevertheless, there were many measures deemed weighty, concerning which Irvine believed it would be better to confer directly with Congress and his commander-in-chief. As early, therefore, as the 3d of December, he wrote to the former: "I think proper measures would be better concerted by my being present, either with Congress or General Washington; as there are many things which, on such occasions, can not be so well committed to paper." He had already informed Washington that he was pretty certain it might be of use for him to go down to Philadelphia, in order the better to communicate with the government. He thought the succeeding three months could be well employed by him there—better than at his post in the Western Department. The commander-in-chief, in a letter of the 21st, notified Irvine that permission had been granted him to repair to Congress, that the benefit of his advice might be had in digesting measures for the security of the frontier. So he made preparations for setting out.

On the 10th of January, 1782, Marshal, of Washington county, was ordered by Irvine to call out one subaltern, one sergeant, and fifteen privates of the militia, to relieve Lieutenant Hay and his garrison at Fort Henry, by the 1st of February. He then sent the sub-lieutenants of Westmoreland—Edward Cook and others—also the lieutenant, of Washington county, a circular letter, informing them that he was to go down to Philadelphia on public business connected with his department; that he was not certain what length of time he might be detained there; and that, during his absence, Col. Gibson would have command. As he was apprehensive there might be a necessity for calling out the militia before his return—especially as his garrison must continue to be employed in repairing Fort Pitt—they should, on the requisition of Gibson, who would be the best judge when such necessity might arise, order out such numbers as he should call for, not exceeding fifty, for one tour of duty; the tour not to exceed one month's time. "I hope," said Irvine, "to return by the 1st of March, before which time I presume there will not be much danger of any damage being done; at the same time, I think it most prudent to take every proper precaution." On the 15th, Irvine issued his last order before setting out on his journey: "As the General will be absent some time, he requests Col. Gibson to use every exertion to put the post in as good a state of defense as possible. For this purpose he will employ the garrison whenever the weather will admit."[4] This was a wise precaution, as it was afterward ascertained that the Indians had concerted, at their villages, during the winter, an expedition against Fort Pitt; but learning, by two deserters from the Falls of the Ohio, of the state of its repairs, they abandoned the project. The commander then left for Philadelphia, taking Carlisle on his way, for a visit to his family.

Colonel John Gibson, put in command of the Western Department, by General Irvine, was born at Lancaster, Pennsylvania, on the 23d of May, 1740. He received a classical education, and was an excellent scholar at the age of eighteen, when he entered the service. He made his first campaign under General Forbes, in the expedition which resulted in the acquisition of Fort Du Quesne—afterward Fort Pitt—from the French. At the peace of 1763 he settled at this post as a trader.

---

[4] MS. Order-Book of General Irvine: Irvine Collection.

Shortly after this, war broke out with the Indians, and Gibson was taken prisoner, at the mouth of Beaver creek, together with two men who were in his employment, while descending the Ohio in a canoe. One of the men was immediately burned, and the other shared the same fate as soon as the party reached the Kenhawa. Gibson, however, was preserved by an aged squaw, and adopted by her in the place of her son, who had been killed in battle. He remained several years with the Indians, and became familiar with their language, habits, manners, customs, and traditions. At the termination of hostilities he again settled at Fort Pitt.

In 1774, Gibson acted a conspicuous part in the expedition against the Shawanese, under Lord Dunmore; particularly in negotiating the peace which followed, and which restored many prisoners to their friends after a captivity of several years. It was upon this occasion, near the waters of the Scioto river, in what is now Pickaway county, Ohio, that Logan, the Mingo chief, delivered to Gibson the celebrated speech so renowned in history.

The particulars of this memorable affair, as afterward given by Gibson, were, in effect, that when the troops had arrived at the principal Indian town, and while dispositions were making preparatory to an attack, he was sent in with a flag, and authorized to treat for peace. As he approached the spot where the chiefs of the hostile tribes were assembled, he met Logan, whom he at once recognized. On opening the business to the assembled warriors, he found them sincerely desirous of peace; but the Mingo chief did not join in the conference. While the discussion was going on, Logan came up and beckoned Gibson aside. The former led the way to a copse at some distance. Here the two sat down, and the chief delivered the speech in his own tongue,[5] desiring that it might be conveyed to Lord Dunmore. It was accordingly translated and delivered immediately afterward.[6] "This brief effusion of mingled pride, courage, and sorrow elevated the character of the native American throughout the intelligent world; and the place where it was delivered can never be forgotten, so long as touching eloquence is admired by men."[7]

On the breaking out of the Revolutionary war, Gibson was appointed to the command of one of the Continental regiments raised in Virginia, and served with the army at New York and in the retreat through New Jersey. He was then employed in the Western Department, where Irvine, upon his arrival at Fort Pitt, found him in temporary command of that post.

---

[5] This has been questioned, *American Pioneer*, vol. i, p. 18; but, in view of the fact that Gibson spoke the language of Logan fluently, I see no reason for doubting the statement.

[6] *Howe's Hist. Coll. of Ohio*, 407; *Rogers' Amer. Biog.*, art. *Gibson;* *Jefferson's Notes on Virginia.* Boston: 1829, pp. 66, 240, 248.

[7] Discourse by Chas. Whittlesey, Columbus, 1840.

Before the arrival of Irvine, an incident occurred which strikingly illustrates Gibson's bravery and intrepidity. A few settlers on the Monongahela, near the mouth of Decker's creek, had been cut off by a war-party of Delawares. Of those captured was Thomas Decker, from whom the creek derives its name. Only two or three of the settlers escaped; and one of these, making his way to Redstone Old Fort (Brownsville), gave information of the catastrophe. The commandant, Captain Paull, dispatched a message to Fort Pitt, conveying intelligence of the visitation, and notifying Colonel Gibson of the probable direction taken by the savages in their retreat.

Gibson, leaving the command of the garrison in the hands of a subordinate, passed rapidly down the river, hoping to intercept the savages. In this, however, he failed; but came accidentally upon a small party of Mingoes, encamped on Cross creek. Little Eagle, a distinguished chief of that tribe, commanded the party; and discovering the whites about the same time that Gibson saw them, he gave a fearful whoop, at the same instant discharging his gun at the leader of the whites. The ball passed through Gibson's coat, but without injuring him. With the quickness of a tiger he sprang upon his foe, and, with one sweep of his sword, severed the head of Little Eagle from his body! Two other Indians were killed; the remainder escaped, and reported that the captain of the whites had cut off the head of their chief with a *long knife*. This was the origin of that celebrated and fearfully significant term, "Long-knives," applied thereafter, by the Indians, to the Virginians, and finally to the Americans and whites generally. Gibson was ever afterward known among the savages as the " Long-knife Warrior."[8]

The month of February, 1782, was one of unusual mildness. War-parties of savages from Sandusky visited the settlements and committed depredations earlier than usual on that account. From the failure of the expeditions against the western Indians in the previous autumn, there had been a continued fear—a feverish state of feeling—during the winter, all along the border; and now that the early melting of the snow had brought the savages, at an unwonted season, to the settlements, a more than usual excitement upon such an occasion prevailed.

On the 8th of the month, Henry Fink and his son John were attacked by Indians at the Buchanan settlement. John was killed.

On the 17th, one of the savage bands—Delawares—attacked the house of Robert Wallace upon Raccoon creek, in the northern part of Washington county, during his absence, and carried off his wife and three children. Wallace, upon his return home in the evening, finding his wife and children gone, his home broken up,

---

[8] *De Hass' Hist. Ind. Wars W. Va.*, pp. 215, 216.

his furniture destroyed, and his cattle shot and lying dead in the yard, immediately alarmed the neighbors, and a party was raised that night, who started early the next morning in pursuit; but, unfortunately, a snow fell, which prevented their coming up with the savages, and the men were obliged to return.

With their prisoners, consisting of Mrs. Wallace, her little son Robert, two and a half years old, another son ten years of age, and an infant daughter, and what plunder they could carry off, the savages made their way toward the Ohio; but finding the mother and her infant somewhat troublesome they were tomahawked and scalped. The two boys were carried to Sandusky, where the elder died. Robert was then sold to the Wyandots, by whom he was held in captivity about two and a half years. His father hearing of him, sent a man to the Wyandot town, after peace had been declared, giving him a certain mark by which the boy could be recognized; and by that means he was rescued and restored to his friends.

About the time of the attack upon Wallace's house, John Carpenter was taken prisoner, from the waters of Buffalo creek, in the same county, by a party of six Indians—two of whom called themselves Moravians, and spoke good Dutch—and hurried across the Ohio. His two horses, which they took with him, nearly perished in swimming the river. The savages, as well as their captive, suffered severely before reaching the

Muskingum. The two Moravian Indians treated their prisoner with particular indignity.⁹ In the morning, after the first day's journey beyond that stream, Carpenter was sent out to bring in the horses, which had been turned out in the evening, after being hobbled. The animals had made a circuit and fallen into the trail by which they came the preceding day, and were making their way homeward. He immediately resolved to attempt an escape. This was a very hazardous undertaking; as, should he be retaken, he well knew the most cruel tortures awaited him. However, he made the effort and was successful—coming in to Pittsburg by the way of Forts Laurens and McIntosh.

On the 8th of March, as William White and Timothy Dorman and his wife were going to, and within sight of Buchanan fort, they were shot at by savages. White was wounded in the hip, fell from his horse, and was tomahawked, scalped, and mutilated in the most frightful manner. Dorman and his wife were taken prisoners. The people in the fort heard the firing and flew to arms; but the river intervening, the savages escaped.

The different parties of the Indians striking the settlements so early in the season, greatly alarmed the people, as has already been mentioned, and but too plainly evinced the determination of the savages to harass the border with much more than their usual

---

⁹ *The Penn. Packet* (Philadelphia), April 16, 1782.

ferocity and perseverance. The borderers came to the conclusion that a quick and spirited exertion was necessary to save the country.

Gibson, in temporary command at Fort Pitt, found himself beset with many difficulties. His garrison, owing to neglect and destitution, were in a mutinous condition. He could do little to cover and protect the frontier. His power to call out the militia was more ideal than real. The absence of Irvine was felt to be a misfortune by the country people. His presence was needed on this trying occasion.

When Brodhead visited the Muskingum, in the month of April of the previous year, most of the hostile Delawares had drawn back from that river and set up their lodges in the country of the Wyandots, among the Shawanese, and further west, leaving the whole country between the Sandusky and Scioto on the west, and the border settlements on the east, an uninhabited region except where the Moravian missionary establishments dotted the wilderness. The clustering villages of the peaceable and inoffensive Moravian Indians had become objects of suspicion to both sides. Brodhead warned them of their danger. Their leaders seemed to covet destruction, by clinging to a passive neutrality when even an armed one would have been an absurdity. On either side there was a determination to break up the establishments. The British and their savage allies were beforehand with the Americans in the work. In September, just previous to the arrival of Irvine at Fort Pitt, the villages were sacked and the missionaries and their families, with all the "believing Indians," carried to the Sandusky.

Ignorant of these events, David Williamson, a colonel of militia in Washington county, marched, some time afterward, to the Muskingum with a detachment of men, to compel the missionaries to remove farther away from the border; or, in case of a refusal, to take them prisoners. Upon their arrival in the valley they found their task anticipated by the enemy. They captured a small party, however, who had returned from the Sandusky to gather corn left standing in the fields; and with these they returned to the settlements. These "Moravians" were immediately set at liberty by General Irvine.

Soon after the capture of the family of Wallace, upon Raccoon creek, and of Carpenter, upon the waters of Buffalo, Colonel Williamson again led a squad of about ninety men into the Indian country, to overtake the savages, and, if possible, to recover the captives in their hands.[10] He pushed forward to the deserted missionary villages of the Moravians upon the Muskingum, from which the party of Indians who had been depredating upon the frontier had just retreated, which he reached on the 6th of March. Here

---

[10] *Penn. Packet*, April 16, 1782.

a considerable number of Christian Indians, from their camp in the Wyandot country, were found, who had returned to gather corn which was still standing in the fields.

Williamson, it seems, had been informed that these Indians had not left the Muskingum, as had been reported;" and his party, it is said, determined, as a part of their plan, to surprise their towns. Colonel Gibson sent an express from Fort Pitt to warn these converts of their danger, but the messenger came too late. Of the one hundred and fifty men, women, and children at work in the fields, over ninety were put to death before the return of Williamson's force. The residue escaped.[12]

The expedition of Williamson to the Muskingum did not allay the excitement upon the frontier; it was now prevailing all along the border. On the 24th of March, a party of borderers attacked a few friendly

---

[11] This intelligence, though erroneous, was brought by Carpenter, who had been taken by the Indians and made his escape, as previously related. He was deceived by the presence of these "Moravians."

[12] This occurrence was afterward generally spoken of, upon the border, as "the Moravian affair." It is perhaps best known in history—especially Moravian history—as "the Gnadenhütten Massacre;" as the killing was done at the middle village upon the river, which, as we have seen, was called Gnadenhütten. The Indians who escaped the massacre, and their associates remaining behind in the Wyandot country, constituted "the remnant of the Christian Indians upon the Sandusky," hereafter frequently mentioned.

Delawares who were living on a small island at the mouth of the Allegheny—known as Smoky or Killbuck's island, since gone—just opposite Fort Pitt. Several of the Indians were killed, including two who held commissions in the service of the government; the remainder effected their escape into the fort, except two who ran into the woods and succeeded in eluding their pursuers. Even the life of Colonel Gibson was in jeopardy, who, it was conceived, was a friend to the Indians—so great was the agitation throughout the western country. And it is not to be wondered at—savages were making their way into the settlements; the settlers were threatened, on all sides, with massacres, plunderings, burnings, and captivities. There was alarm and dismay in every quarter.

The people of the border were forced into forts which dotted the country in every direction. These were in the highest degree uncomfortable. They consisted of cabins, block-houses, and stockades. In some places, where the exposure was not great, a single block-house, with a cabin outside, constituted the whole fort. For a space around, the forest was usually cleared away, so that an enemy could neither find a lurking place nor conceal his approach.

Near these forts the borderers worked their fields in parties guarded by sentinels. Their necessary labors, therefore, were performed with every danger and difficulty imaginable. Their work had to be carried on with their arms and all things belonging to their war-dress deposited in some central place in the field. Sentinels were stationed on the outside of the fence; so that, on the least alarm, the whole company repaired to their arms, and were ready for the combat in a moment.[13]

It is not surprising that there was a deep and widespread feeling of revenge against the hostile and marauding savages. The horrid scenes of slaughter which frequently met the view were well calculated to arouse such passions. Helpless infancy, virgin beauty, and hoary age, dishonored by the ghastly wounds of the tomahawk and scalping-knife, were common sights. When the slain were the friends or relatives of the beholder—wife, sister, child, father, mother, brother—it is not at all a wonder that pale and quivering lips should mutter revenge.

From Pittsburg south, including the valleys of the Monongahela and Youghiogheny, and the territory west of these to the Ohio, was a scope of country having, at this time, a considerable population; nevertheless, there were few families who had lived therein any con-

---

[13] Notes on the Settlement and Indian Wars of the Western Parts of Virginia and Pennsylvania from the year 1763 until the year 1783, inclusive. Together with a View of the State of Society and Manners of the First Settlers of the Western Country. By the Rev. Dr. Jos. Doddridge, Wellsburgh, Va. Printed at the office of the Gazette, for the author; 1824. pp. 117, 139.

siderable length of time that had not lost some of their number by the merciless Indians.[14]

On the 8th of March, General Washington sent instructions to Irvine, then at Carlisle, for his guidance upon his return to the West: "You will proceed with all convenient dispatch to Fort Pitt, the object of your command; and you will take such measures for the security of that post, and for the defense of the western frontier, as your Continental force, combined with the militia of the neighboring country, will admit.

"Under present appearances and circumstances," continues the commander-in-chief, "I can not promise any further addition to your regular force than a proportion of recruits for the Virginia and Pennsylvania regiments, which are already upon the western station; consequently, offensive operations, except upon a small scale, can not just now be brought into contemplation. You may, however, still continue to keep yourself in-

---

[14] "It should seem," says Doddridge (*Notes*, 268), "that the long continuance of the Indian war had debased a considerable portion of our population to the savage state of our nature. Having lost so many of their relatives by the Indians, and witnessed their horrid murders and other depredations upon so extensive a scale, they became subjects of that indiscriminating thirst for revenge which is such a prominent feature in the savage character." But, to say that "a considerable portion" of the people of Southwestern Pennsylvania and Pan-handle Virginia, was, in 1782, "debased to the savage state of our nature," is altogether too harsh a criticism.

formed of the situation at Detroit and the strength of the enemy at that place.[15]

General Irvine returned to Fort Pitt on the 25th of March, and assumed the chief command of the post.

Colonel Gibson remained at the fort during the war, in command of his regiment. He was a member of the convention which framed the constitution of the State of Pennsylvania in 1790, and was subsequently a judge of the court of common pleas of Allegheny county, and also a major-general of militia. In 1800, he received from President Jefferson the appointment of secretary of the Territory of Indiana, an office held by him until that Territory became a State.

Colonel Gibson, at this time, finding that the infirmities of age were thickening upon him, and laboring under an incurable cataract, retired to Braddock's Field, the seat of his son-in-law, George Wallace, where he died on the 10th of April, 1822, having borne through life the character of a brave soldier and an honest man.[16]

General Irvine's arrival at Fort Pitt was most opportune. He found the country people in a frenzied condition to all appearance. Anarchy and confusion would soon have reigned supreme. The regular troops were in a mutinous condition. It seemed, at first, as

---

[15] *The Writings of George Washington. By Jared Sparks*, vol. viii, p. 248. The original Instructions are in the Irvine Collection.

[16] The late Chief Justice Gibson, of Pennsylvania, was his nephew.

though the whole country must be given up to the enemy, the fort evacuated, and the bounds of Canada extended to the Laurel Hill. However, in a few days things were in a more favorable condition.

For some weeks after the general's return, courts-martial were almost constantly sitting for the trial of mutineers and deserters. Several suffered the death penalty. "One hundred lashes, well laid on," was a common sentence. Cleanliness in and around the fort was rigidly enforced.[17] The troops were reduced to obedience; and the commander then turned his attention to the protection of the country. He immediately resolved to call a convention of the lieutenants of the several counties and the principal field officers of the militia, as well as of citizens of note, in the Western Department, to devise ways and means for the defense of the border.

Edward Cook, a former sub-lieutenant under the lamented Colonel Lochry of Westmoreland county, had been promoted to a full lieutenancy. To him Irvine addressed a letter on the 28th of March. "You are already acquainted," wrote the commander, "with the resolution of Congress, and orders of the president and council of Pennsylvania, respecting my command in this quarter; in addition to which, I have received instructions from his excellency, General Washington.

---

[17] Irvine's MS. Order-Book.

As making arrangements to cover and protect the country, is the main object, and, as it is to be done by a combination of regulars and militia, the business will be complicated. And, further, as there will be a diversity of interests, I think it of the utmost importance, that, whatever plan may be adopted, it should be as generally understood as the nature of the service will admit." Irvine continued: "You will conceive that I shall stand in need of the counsels and assistance, on this occasion, of some of the principal people of the country." He then added: "I wish, therefore, to see you and at least one field officer of every battalion in your county; for which purpose I request you will be pleased to warn such as you may think proper, to attend at this post, on Friday, the 5th of April next. Punctual to the day will be necessary, as I have written to Colonel Marshal, and others, in Washington county also, to attend on that day."

To John Evans, lieutenant of Monongalia county, and David Shepherd, lieutenant of Ohio county, Virginia, similar letters were sent; but to each was appended these words: "Whatever difference local situations may make in sentiments respecting territory, a combination of forces to repel the enemy is clearly, I think, a duty we owe ourselves and our country." It was thus the skillful commander poured oil upon the troubled waters of the boundary controversy.

The convention of the 5th of April was well attended. Marshal, however, was absent; his official duties were such as to preclude his attendance. The principal post on the Ohio, below Fort Pitt, at the mouth of Yellow creek, had been evacuated for want of provisions. To fill up that station and supply the men with rations, kept him away "to prevent the frontiers in that quarter from breaking," is his language, in a letter to Irvine of the 2d of April. "However," he adds, "I shall most heartily concur in any plan that may be adopted for the good of the country." Evans, of Monongalia county, was not at the convention; but wrote Irvine that the number of effective men in his district did not exceed three hundred; that they were so scattered as to form a frontier of eighty miles. He begged the commander, in the most earnest manner, to assist him with men, arms, and ammunition.

Shepherd, of Ohio county, was at the meeting, and reported that he could not aid in a general defense of the frontier with any men, as nearly all, in his district, were enrolled in Pennsylvania. Colonel Cook, lieutenant, and Colonel Campbell, sub-lieutenant, represented Westmoreland county. In place of Marshal, from Washington county, came Colonel Vallandigham, sub-lieutenant; also Colonels Williamson and Cook, and Major Carmichael, of the militia, and James Edgar, Esq., citizen and member of the State legislature. Major McCulloch, also of the militia, was present from Ohio county, Virginia.

The principal questions discussed at the convention were as to the mode of defense and the number of men necessary to be called out in each district. The officers of Monongalia and Ohio counties had received no instructions from the executive of Virginia to call out the militia upon Irvine's requisitions, as had the lieutenants of Westmoreland and Washington counties from the governor of Pennsylvania. It therefore rested entirely upon these last-mentioned counties to insure the proper protection of the frontiers, as only volunteers could be had from the former counties, and they were not to be depended on. A full and free interchange of views was had at the meeting. Irvine was placed in full possession of all necessary information touching the different forts, stations, and block-houses upon the frontier; the number and condition of the men in actual service; when their tours of duty would expire; how they were supplied, and to what extent, with provisions, arms, and ammunition; and many other important details. The number of men to be called out in Westmoreland and Washington counties was agreed upon, and all present pledged Irvine their warmest support in his endeavors to protect the country.

The plan agreed upon was to keep flying bodies of men constantly on the frontiers, marching to and from the different places. The regular troops were to remain in Fort Pitt and Fort McIntosh. Westmoreland agreed to keep sixty-five men, formed into two companies, constantly ranging along the frontier from the Allegheny to the Laurel Hill. Washington county stipulated to keep in actual service one hundred and sixty men, to range along the Ohio from Montour's Bottom to Wheeling, thence some distance along the southern line, under two field officers.[18]

The commander now applied himself energetically to the task of placing the frontiers in as complete a condition for defense as the means at his hands would admit. The garrison at Fort Pitt continued work upon that post. A supply of provisions was sent to Fort McIntosh, where there was a garrison of about thirty-five men. This post had been occupied for some time previous to Irvine taking command of the Western Department. The militia of Washington county were formed into four companies; two of these were placed so as to patrol the Ohio from Pittsburg to near Wheeling. Every precaution was taken to guard against surprises of the enemy. Nevertheless, it was well understood that a defensive policy, with whatever care plans might be laid, would prove ineffectual against occasional inroads of the wily, prowling savages, who, in spite of every precaution, frequently crossed the Ohio, fell suddenly upon helpless victims, and then quickly recrossed that river into the wilderness beyond. Hence it was,

---

[18] From a MS. memorandum in the handwriting of Irvine.

that, notwithstanding the exertions and success of Irvine, in covering and protecting the borders, the belief was very prevalent in the Western Department that positive security was to be obtained only by carrying the war into the Indian country.

CHAPTER III.

AN EXPEDITION PROJECTED IN WESTERN PENNSYLVANIA AGAINST
SANDUSKY. APRIL 4—MAY 7, 1782.

THE war of the Revolution was now virtually ended. The Western border war, however, which it had evoked, was still raging with undiminished fury. Lord Cornwallis had surrendered, and the murderous forays of the Indians of the north were at an end; but, in the west, there was no cessation of predatory incursions of the savages. On the 27th of March, Mrs. Walker, living on Buffalo creek, Washington county, was taken prisoner, but made her escape. On the first day of April the savages captured Mr. Boice and family, consisting of eight persons, and hurried them into the wilderness. The day following a man was killed near Washington county court-house by Indians.

On Easter Sunday, Miller's block-house, on the Dutch fork of Buffalo, in Washington county, was attacked by a party of about seventy Shawanese. On this occasion, more than the usual amount of heroism was displayed by the occupants of the post. The savages arrived during the previous night, and lay in ambush around the fort. Within the inclosure were three men and several women and children. Two of the men going out in search of an estray, were killed by the

Indians, who immediately afterward surrounded the block-house. Quite an old man was the only male left inside. But the courage of one of the women, who boldly fired upon the savages, kept them at bay until the post was relieved by three men, who broke through the enemy's lines, and got into the block-house unharmed. The Indians then disappeared.[1]

It had been some time known upon the border that the project of attacking Detroit had been abandoned by the general government. For the borderers to attempt its reduction was, of course, out of the question. But it was a very general opinion than the Indian towns and settlements, between that post and the Ohio, could be assailed with a fair prospect of success. The feasibility, as well as necessity, of this was strongly urged, notwithstanding the excellent arrangements inaugurated by Irvine for the protection of the exposed settlements.

"This is most certain," wrote Marshal to Irvine, on the 2d of April, "that unless an expedition be carried against some of the principal Indian towns early this summer, this country must unavoidably suffer." This sentiment found an echo in the minds of most of the settlers of Washington county. The same view was generally entertained in Westmoreland county, and in the two border counties of Virginia. And notwithstanding previous failures, there were still very many who believed that a volunteer expedition might be or-

---

[1] *His. Washington County*, App., p. 46-50.

ganized against Sandusky, of such magnitude as would promise almost a certainty of success, if united and zealous efforts were put forth.

Volunteer enterprises, however, had come to be looked upon, very generally, with disfavor. The citizens of Washington county were mostly favorable to the drawing out of the militia for all military undertakings.

Marshal, on the 4th of April, again wrote Irvine: "The bearer hereof, Colonel Williamson, is now prepared for a voyage down the river, with about thirty thousand weight of flour. But, from a real love to his country, he proposes not only to carry an expedition against Sandusky, with the militia of this county, together with what volunteers might be raised in Westmoreland, but offers to advance such part of the flour as might be necessary for the occasion." He added: "The people in general on the frontiers are waiting with anxious expectation, to know whether an expedition can be carried against Sandusky early this spring or not." The writer approved the scheme: "I could therefore wish that Colonel Williamson would be countenanced in this plan, if with propriety it can be done." This letter, and the arrival of the bearer of it at Fort Pitt, brought the subject of a proposed expedition against Sandusky, fully and officially, to the notice of General Irvine.

The authority conferred upon the commander of the

Western Department by Congress, to protect the country, carried with it, by necessary implication, the use of such force, and in such a manner as his own judgment should dictate; in short, *how* the country was to be protected, was largely a matter of discretion with him. However, it was plainly his duty, and this he fully appreciated, to direct whatever forces might be, from time to time, under his command, in the most effectual manner for covering the frontiers, and giving ease and safety to the border settlements. It was clearly seen that a defensive policy alone, however much it might be governed by prudence and discretion, afforded the country but an indifferent protection. The matter of an offensive warfare, including especially the proposed scheme against Sandusky, received, therefore, Irvine's most careful attention and consideration.

The commandant was already committed against the policy of visiting Indian towns—as being, usually, void of beneficial results, unless their occupants could be followed up and beaten in battle; yet, as the general voice of the people was in favor of an enterprise against the Wyandots, he resolved to obtain all the information possible, of their strength and intentions; whether any white men were among them; and especially whether any regular British troops or rangers were at Sandusky. Captain Uriah Springer, of the Virginia line, with three soldiers and as many Indians, was sent to reconnoiter. But the Indians proving too timid for their advance all the way, the party returned without accomplishing anything.

Besides the question as to the condition of the enemy, there were other important ones to engage the serious deliberations of Irvine, before authorizing an expedition to march into the Indian country. There was another kind of enterprise then agitated in the settlements, and much talked of; which was, to emigrate beyond the Ohio and set up a new state. "This scheme is carried so far," wrote Irvine to Benjamin Harrison, governor of Virginia, on the 20th of April, "that a day is appointed, by advertisement, to meet, for the purpose of emigrating."

It was the belief, however, of the commandant that, although a considerable number had serious thoughts of the matter, yet they would not be able to put their plan into execution. "Should they be so mad," he continued, "as to attempt it, I think they will either be cut to pieces, or they will be obliged to take protection from, and join the British. Perhaps some have this in view; though a great majority are, I think, well-meaning people, who have, at present, no other views than to acquire large tracts of land."

At all events, Irvine regarded the new state scheme as a dangerous one; and he must be satisfied that, in the proposed undertaking against Sandusky, there was no covert design to promote it. The fact that the *same day* was appointed for the meeting to be held at Wheeling, of those who proposed to emigrate, as was suggested for the rendezvous of the expedition, was calculated to excite suspicion.² Certain it is the good management of Irvine prevented what might have become a serious revolt of the people, and perhaps a severance of the region of the Alleghenies and its annexation to Canada. Had such an event transpired, the commissioners on the part of the United States in the treaty with Great Britain securing American independence, would almost certainly have failed to carry the western boundaries of the country beyond the Ohio.

It was before the return of Irvine to Fort Pitt, as previously mentioned, that Williamson led his second expedition to the Muskingum. That affair made a deep impression upon the mind of the commander of the Western Department. He had been uniformly kind to the missionaries and their converts.³ In a let-

---

² Wills De Hass (*His. and Ind. Wars, W. Va.*, p. 189) has *combined* the efforts for the meeting at Wheeling, with those put forth to further the expedition against Sandusky. He says: " Every inducement was held out to join the expedition [against Sandusky]. Placards were posted at Wheeling, Catfish, and other places, of a new State that was to be organized on the Muskingum, and no effort left untried that could excite either the cupidity or revenge of the frontier people." The two schemes, however, were in nowise connected. I do not find that the Sandusky expedition was placarded at all.

³ *Loskiel's His. Miss.*, P. iii, p. 175; *Heckewelder's Narr. Miss.*, p. 298; *Doddridge's Notes*, p. 262; *Schweinitz's Life of Zeisberger*, pp. 531, 535, etc.

ter to Washington, of the 20th of April, he characterized the killing of those inoffensive Indians—men, women, and children—as an outrage.

Irvine wrote, on the 8th of May, to the Moravian bishop, Rev. Nathaniel Seidel: "I believe the missionaries are safe, and I can assure you it will always be pleasing to me to be able to render them service. I hope (and think it probable) they have removed farther than Sandusky—that being now a frontier, and one of the British and Indian barrier towns; they can not rationally expect to be safe at it."[4] A messenger of the Mission Board of the Moravian Church, who had been sent to Fort Pitt to make inquiries, reported to the authorities at Bethlehem, Pennsylvania, about the last of May, that the commandant, as well as a majority of his officers, and many intelligent citizens, did not approve of the affair at Muskingum, and would do all in their power to protect the remnant of the Christian Indians.

That the resolutions of Congress appointing Irvine to the command of the Western Department, and the powers therein granted, authorized the calling out of the militia, upon such an occasion as the proposed expedition, if the commandant deemed it necessary for the protection of the country, was not for a moment

---

[4] I do not find a copy of this letter among the Irvine papers. The reader will find it printed entire in *Schweinitz's Life of Zeisberger*, p. 575.

doubted. Irvine proposed not to exercise this authority, however, even though he should finally conclude to favor the enterprise.

All must *volunteer* for the campaign, and place themselves under his orders as militia, to be, in all respects, subject to the military laws and regulations for the government of the militia in actual service, the same as if *drawn out* according to law, upon his requisition. The moment, then, they took up their line of march, they would be liable to the rules and articles of war for regular troops.

The number of men necessary for the proposed expedition was carefully considered by Irvine. It should be so large as to give a reasonable assurance of final success. From all the information he had been able to obtain of the enemy's forces upon the Sandusky and vicinity, and their facilities for concentration in the event of being attacked, he was of the opinion that the army should number not less than three hundred; fewer men would place the lives of all in jeopardy; a greater number would increase the chances for a favorable termination of the enterprise. The expedition would have to be not only respectable in number, but, to warrant success, must be conducted with the utmost secrecy and dispatch. It would be indispensably necessary, therefore, that all should be mounted.

It would be out of the power of the commandant to furnish any material aid to the expedition, either of arms, provisions, or equipments of any kind. He had not a horse to spare. A limited supply of ammunition and a few flints were all he would be able to give.[5] Each volunteer, therefore, would have to supply himself with a horse and equipments, with a rifle, with rations, and other necessary articles, at his own expense. Nor could he promise any remuneration from the general government for losses or services during the campaign.

Such were the conclusions of the commander of the Western Department concerning the proposed undertaking against Sandusky. They strikingly illustrate the two prominent traits of his character—prudence and judgment. In the meantime the country people became clamorous. On the 1st of May, Marshal wrote Irvine: "Since I had the honor of consulting you on the expediency of an expedition against Sandusky, I have met with the officers and principal people of this county, and find that, in all probability, we shall be able to carry forward the enterprise." He made a request, also, that instructions to the officer who should be appointed to command should be forwarded by the first opportunity. On the 7th of the month, a number of the principal people of the department made application in person to Irvine for his consent to the

---

[5] Ammunition was also furnished by the lieutenant of Washington county—James Marshal; not by "the lieutenant-colonel of Washington county," as Doddridge has it —*Notes,* 269.

project. Dorsey Pentecost, a resident of Washington county and member of the Supreme Executive Council of Pennsylvania, was present at the meeting. The scheme was discussed fully and unreservedly.

Satisfactory explanations having been made and assurances given, Irvine finally gave his consent to the proposed expedition, but upon these express conditions: that the people did not mean to extend their settlements, nor had anything in view but to harass the enemy, with an intention to protect the frontier; and that any conquests they might make should be in behalf of and for the United States; that they would be governed by military laws as militia; that they must collect such numbers as would probably be successful; and, lastly, that they would equip and victual themselves at their own expense.[6]

There was a general desire expressed that Irvine should command the expedition; but he did not feel himself at liberty, consistent with instructions from the commander-in-chief, to become the leader of the enterprise. He would assist, however, in its organization, and would issue instructions for its direction and guidance.

It was arranged that the volunteers were to select their own officers, and that each one should receive a

---

[6] Irvine to Washington, 21st May, 1782: *Sparks' Corr. Amer. Rev.* iii, 509. I do not find a copy of this letter in the Irvine Collection. The reply of Washington is, however, among those papers.

credit for two full tours of military duty, providing he furnished himself with a horse, a gun, and one month's provisions. It was also agreed that any one having been plundered by the Indians, should, if he volunteered, have his plunder again if it could be found, first proving it to be his property. Horses lost on the expedition, by unavoidable accident, were to be replaced by others taken from the enemy.[7] The 20th of May was the time fixed upon for the rendezvous; the place, Mingo Bottom, a point on the west, or Indian side, of the Ohio, about forty miles by land, and seventy-five miles by water, below Fort Pitt. The name of a prominent citizen was mentioned by Irvine in connection with the command. The suggestion was favorably received.

Pentecost wrote to Moore, president of the Supreme Executive Council, on the 8th: "I hear there is great preparation making for a descent on Sandusky, to set out on the 20th of this month, which will be conducted by a gentleman of experience and veracity."[8] On the next day Irvine also wrote to Moore: "A volunteer expedition is talked of against Sandusky, which, if well conducted, may be of great service to this country." "They have consulted me," he adds, "and shall have every countenance in my power, if their numbers and arrangements promise a prospect of suc-

---

[7] *Knight's Narrative* (ed. of 1783).
[8] *Penn. Arch.*, vol. ix, p. 540.

cess." "We confide in your zeal and prudence," responded Moore on the 30th, "to direct the force which may be in your power, in the most effectual manner for covering the frontiers."

The project against Sandusky was as carefully considered, and as authoritatively planned, as any military enterprise in the West, during the Revolution. As a distinct undertaking, it was intended to be effectual in ending the troubles upon the western frontiers of Pennsylvania and Virginia. The scheme was not irruptive in its origin, but smooth and steady-flowing. Its promoters were not only the principal military and civil officers in the Western Department, but a large proportion of the best known and most influential private citizens.

Nor was there any difference of opinion as to the necessity for the expedition. That most of the scalping-parties prowling upon the frontiers came from Sandusky, was well known; not, however, that *all* the savages depredating upon the settlements were Wyandots; but that their town was the grand rallying-point for the British Indians before starting for the border. The pressing need, therefore, for its destruction, none failed to appreciate. On a line running nearly north and south from near the mouth of the Sandusky river to the head of the Miami, were located Wyandots, Shawanese, Delawares, and Mingoes. On this line, about equally distant from the two extremes, was the objective point of the proposed expedition, within the limits of what is now Wyandot county, Ohio.

No very energetic effort was necessary to induce volunteering for the expedition. The constant inroads of the savages operated, to a great degree, as a sufficient stimulant. On Sunday, the 12th of May, John Corbley, a Baptist minister, a resident of Washington county, was, with his family, surprised by the Indians while on his way to public worship. His wife had a sucking child in her arms. Both were killed and scalped, as were also a son about six years old and a daughter. The other daughters, the savages supposed they had killed, but, although scalped, they afterward recovered. The father made his escape.[9]

---

[9] Old Red Stone. By Joseph Smith, D.D. Philadelphia: 1854.

CHAPTER IV.

RENDEZVOUSING AND ORGANIZATION OF THE SANDUSKY EXPEDITION. 15-24 MAY, 1782.

UP and down the Monongahela and Youghiogheny, and westward to the Ohio, in nearly all the settlements, there was now an unusual stir, as it became known that the expedition against Sandusky was to go forward. As the day fixed upon for the general meeting—Monday, the 20th—was close at hand, volunteering was very brisk. The proper place for assembling had been carefully considered at the conference at Fort Pitt. Fort McIntosh had several advocates. This point was of easy access, especially for those living down the rivers, in the vicinity of Pittsburg. For prudential reasons, however, it was finally determined not to rendezvous at that point; as ever since the beginning of the war, the country west to the Muskingum was constantly infested with war-parties of the enemy. The expedition would run a great risk of an early discovery, by passing through a portion of the wilderness, so generally traversed by the savages. A point further down the Ohio would be more desirable. Besides, it would be nearer on a line from a majority of the settlements to Sandusky; hence it was that Mingo Bottom was chosen.

The spot where the volunteers were to assemble is still a somewhat noted locality. It is in what is now Steubenville township, Jefferson county, Ohio, about two and a half miles below the town of Steubenville. Mingo Bottom is a rich plateau, on the immediate bank of the Ohio, in the south half of section twenty-seven, of township two, range one, of the government survey, extending south to a small affluent of the Ohio, known as Cross creek. Opposite the upper portion of Mingo Bottom is Mingo Island, containing about ten acres, although much larger in 1782. It supports a scanty growth of willow bushes only; but within the recollection of many now living, it was studded with trees of large size, particularly the soft maple. Cross creek, on the Virginia side, flows into the Ohio about three-fourths of a mile below. Before the great flood of 1832, the island contained not less than twenty acres. The usual place of crossing was directly from shore to shore across the head of the island. At the landing on the west bank, the vagrant Mingoes had once a village—deserted, however, as early 1772. Their town gave name to the locality. The Ohio has been forded at this crossing, in very low water. The bluffs of the river are below the island, on the Virginia side; above, on the Ohio side. Mingo Bottom contains about two hundred and fifty acres.

So eager were some of the volunteers, that, by the 15th, their arrangements were all made, and they were on their way to the place of rendezvous. There were not a few, however, who were unable to equip themselves for the campaign, though willing to risk their lives in the enemy's country. However, in nearly every instance, a friend was found in time, to loan a horse or furnish supplies for the occasion. It was not doubted by any one that the State of Pennsylvania would reimburse all who should sustain losses. Many, therefore, from this belief, as well as from a spirit of patriotism, materially aided the enterprise, who did not, or could not, volunteer.

There was much enthusiasm in the settlements, preparing for the campaign; nevertheless, there was, generally, a due appreciation of the desperate nature of the project. A march so far in to the enemy's country as was now proposed, had not been made in that direction, from the western border, during the war. The venture, therefore, required stout hearts and steady nerves, when looked fairly in the face. It is a tradition—nay, an established fact—that many, aside from the ordinary arrangements necessary for a month's absence—not so much, however, from a presentiment of disaster as from that prudence which careful and thoughtful men are prone to exercise—executed deeds "in consideration of love and affection;" and many witnesses were called in to subscribe to "last wills and testaments."

It was generally understood that, when the army should begin its march from Mingo Bottom, it would press forward with all practicable speed to effect a surprise, if possible; the best horses, therefore, in the settlements were selected for the enterprise. In their trappings, as might be expected, nothing was sacrificed to show—to mere display. Bridles of antique appearance, and saddles venerable with age—heir-looms in not a few instances, brought over the mountains—were put in order for the occasion. Pack-saddles also were called into requisition for carrying supplies. These were, as a general thing, exceedingly primitive in their construction. Some furnished themselves with extra rope halters, in expectation of returning with horses captured from the enemy.

The volunteer, in his war-dress, presented a picturesque appearance. His hunting-shirt, reaching half-way down his thighs, was securely belted at the waist, the bosom serving as a wallet. The belt, tied behind, answered several purposes besides that of holding the wide folds of the shirt together. Within it, on the right side, was suspended his tomahawk; on the left, his scalping-knife. He wore moccasins instead of shoes upon his feet. His equipage was very simple. Strapped to his saddle was the indispensable knapsack, made of coarse tow cloth, in which were several small articles, placed there, perhaps, by a loving wife, or a thoughtful mother or sister. From the pommel of his saddle was suspended a canteen—a very useful article, as the weather was unusually warm for the season. Flour and bacon constituted his principal supply of food. His blanket, used as a covering for his saddle, answered also for a bed at night.

Of his weapons of defense, the volunteer relied mainly upon his rifle. Trained to its use almost from infancy, he was, of course, a sharp-shooter—frequently a dead-shot. Taking his trusted weapon down from the hooks, where it was usually to be seen suspended beneath the cross-beams of his cabin, he carefully cleaned it, and picked the flint anew. His powder-horn was then filled, and securely fastened to a strap passing over his left shoulder and under the right. His leather pouch, either fastened to his belt or thrust into his bosom, was first filled with bullets, bullet-patches, and extra flints. The edge of his tomahawk was made a little keener than usual; and his scalping-knife was carefully examined before being thrust into its leathern sheath.

The moment of leaving was, in many cases, a trying one to the volunteer. There are many incidents still lingering in the memory of the aged, who, in their youth, were told the tales of these parting scenes. "My father was one of the volunteers," writes Joseph Paull, a citizen of Fayette county, Pennsylvania, "and at that time was young and unmarried. When he determined on going he told his widowed mother. She was greatly distressed. 'Why, James,' said she, 'you are not well enough to go; you are sick.' 'I can ride,' was the response, 'and I can shoot.' 'But,' interrupted the mother, 'suppose you lose your horse?' 'Well,' said James, 'I have made up my mind to go.' And go he did, leaving grandmother in great grief, as he embraced her and bid her good-bye. He was very sad when he mounted his horse and rode away. Once with his comrades, however, his sadness soon wore off."[1] Usually, however, the soldier took leave of home without ceremony. A common mode was to step out of the door of the cabin, discharge his rifle, and immediately march off, without looking back or saying a word. Hand-shaking, parting words, and kisses were too trying to his feelings!

The volunteers were mostly of Irish or Scotch-Irish descent—young, active, and generally spirited. Many were from the Youghiogheny and around Beesontown (Uniontown), in Westmoreland county. Most of these came on to Redstone Old Fort (Brownsville), on the Monongahela, where they were joined by many from the settlements around, and from the "forks of Yough." They then proceeded to Catfish (Washington), in Washington county. After the accession of a considerable number from this vicinity and Ten-mile, the whole moved westward, adding a few to their numbers in "Pan-handle" Virginia.

As the volunteers threaded their way toward the

---

[1] Notes to the author, 1872.

Ohio, along the bridle-paths, their course was mostly through dense forests; only here and there was there a lonely cabin, or, perchance, a fort or stockade. As they passed these, they were sure to be cordially greeted by the borderer; and matrons, in linsey petticoats, with home-made handkerchiefs as the only adornment for their heads and necks, standing barefoot in front of their doors, waved onward the cavalcade with many a "God speed you, my brave lads!" Many, however, were dilatory in their arrival at the Ohio; so that all were not gathered opposite Mingo Bottom when the crossing began—indeed, some crossed the river above and others below the appointed place, traveling along the west bank of the stream until they reached the site of the old Mingo town.

But little difficulty was experienced in crossing the river; and no accident happened worthy of note. The water was unusually low in the stream for that season of the year.

On the 20th, the day set for the meeting, there were many who had not yet reported.

On the 21st, Irvine wrote Washington: "The volunteers are assembling this day at Mingo Bottom— all on horseback, with thirty days' provision."[2] "If their number exceeds three hundred," continued the writer, "I am of opinion they may succeed; as their

---

[2] *Sparks' Corr. Amer. Rev.*, iii, 509. A copy of this letter, in the handwriting of Irvine, is in my possession.

march will be so rapid they will probably, in a great degree, effect a surprise." In a postscript, Irvine adds: "The volunteers have sent, requesting my instructions (which I will send) for the officer who may be appointed to command." They were dispatched, the same day, to Mingo Bottom, and were directed "*To the Officer who will be appointed to command a Detachment of Volunteer Militia on an Expedition against the Indian town at or near Sandusky.*" These instructions, or "positive orders," as Irvine afterward termed them, in a letter to Washington, of the 16th of June,[3] clearly evince the careful consideration of one having a just appreciation of the object in view; and forcibly exhibit the elevated character of their author.[4] They are as follows:

"Where an officer is detached, though he may have general instructions, yet much must depend on his own prudence. On such an expedition as the present, where a variety of unexpected events may take place, I think it would be vain to attempt being particular. In general, however, it is incumbent on me to give such ideas as I think may be of use.

"The object of your command is, to destroy with

---

[3] The words of Irvine are: "They had my advice, and, indeed, positive orders." The letter is on file in the Department of State, at Washington.

[4] I have before me a copy of these instructions, in the handwriting of Irvine.

fire and sword (if practicable), the Indian town and settlement at Sandusky, by which we hope to give ease and safety to the inhabitants of this country;[5] but, if

---

[5] The fictitious story of the bloody design of the volunteers against the remnant of the Christian Indians supposed to have been upon the Sandusky, had its origin in the publication by a New York newspaper (the city then being in possession of the *British*), some time after the Gnadenhütten affair, of a report that Williamson and his band had been prevented, at that time, from proceeding to the Sandusky from the Muskingum, to destroy the remnant of the Moravian congregation. *Therefore*, reasoned the Moravian missionaries (who were then at or near Detroit), when an army *did* come to the Sandusky, it must, forsooth, have been the *same band*, come for the purpose of *murdering the rest of the Christian Indians!* Dr. Jos. Doddridge, in 1824, following the Moravian Heckewelder, puts this down as an *historical verity;* but adds: "The next object was that of destroying the Wyandot towns on the same river."—*Notes*, p. 269. In all examinations of the correspondence of those projecting the expedition against Sandusky, and of those who took part in that enterprise, as well as of papers and documents of that period relating thereto, and of cotemporaneous publications, I have not met with a single statement or word calculated to awaken a suspicion even, of intended harm to the Christian Indians upon the Sandusky. Whenever the objective point of the expedition is mentioned, it is invariably given as *Sandusky* or the *Wyandot* town or towns. "Against the Wyandot towns."—*Knight's Narr.*, p. 4 (ed. 1783). "Against Sandusky."—Irvine to Washington, 21st May and 16th June, 1782. "For Sandusky."—Marshal to Irvine, 29th May, 1782. Even to the present day, the *real* object of the enterprise, strange as it may seem, is not understood by the Moravian historians. So firmly grounded in the belief of the bloody design is the Rev. Edmund de Schweinitz, in his *Life of Zeisberger* (p. 576), that when he discov-

impracticable, then you will doubtless perform such other services in your power as will, in their consequences, have a tendency to answer this great end.

"Previous to taking up your line of march, it will be highly expedient that all matters respecting rank or command should be well determined and clearly understood, as far at least as first, second, and third. This precaution, in case of accident or misfortune, may be of great importance. Indeed, I think whatever grade or rank may be fixed on to have command, their relative rank should be determined. And as it is indispensably necessary that subordination and discipline should be kept up, the whole ought to understand that, notwithstanding they are volunteers, yet by this tour they are to get credit for it in their tours of militia duty; and that for this and other good reasons, they must, while out on this duty, consider themselves, to all intents, subject to the military laws and regulations for the government of the militia when in actual service.[6]

---

ers Irvine to have been a friend to the Christian Indians—heartily disapproving of the massacre at Gnadenhütten—he declares it evident that the Sandusky expedition "was undertaken without the knowledge of General Irvine, or that he was unable to hinder it!" This writer speaks of the expedition (p. 564) as a "second campaign against the Christian Indians!" referring to the Gnadenhütten massacre as the first one.

[6] In a letter from Irvine, dated Carlisle, November 10, 1799, (for which I am indebted to Hon. Charles Foster, of Fostoria, Ohio, who obtained leave to withdraw it from the files of Congress,) directed to

"Your best chance of success will be, if possible, to effect a *surprise;* and though this will be difficult, yet, by forced and rapid marches, it may, in a great degree, be accomplished. I am clearly of opinion that you should regulate your last day's march so as to reach the town about dawn of day or a little before, and that the march of this day should be as long as can well be performed.

"I need scarcely mention to so virtuous and disinterested set of men as you will have the honor to command,[7] that, though the main object, at present, is for the purpose above set forth, viz., the protection of this country,[8] yet, you are to consider yourselves as as acting in behalf and for the United States. That, of

---

John Lyon, of Uniontown, Pennsylvania, I find this sentence relative to the expedition against Sandusky: "In looking over my instructions to the officer who should be appointed to command that expedition, I find he was enjoined to regulate rank of officers before he took up his line of march, and to impress on their minds that the whole must, from the moment they march, be, in all respects, subject to the rules and articles of war for the regular troops." He adds: "All the troops, both regulars and militia, were under my orders."

[7] In striking contrast with this language are the animadversions of the Moravian writers: "Gang of murderers."—*Loskiel, Hist. Miss.,* P. iii, p. 188. "Gang of banditti."—*Heckewelder, Hist. Ind. Nations,* p. 120.

[8] "Undertaken," says Doddridge (*Notes,* 278), "with the very worst of views—those of murder and plunder!" A statement as erroneous as one could well be.

course, it will be incumbent on you especially who will have the command, and on every individual, to act, in every instance, in such a manner as will reflect honor on, and add reputation to, the American arms—always having in view the laws of arms, of nations, or independent states.

"Should any person, British, or in the service or pay of Britain or their allies, fall into your hands—if it should prove inconvenient for you to bring them off, you will, nevertheless, take special care to liberate them on parole, in such manner as to insure liberty for an equal number of our people in their hands. There are individuals, however, who, I think should be brought off at all events, should the fortune of war throw them into your hands. I mean such as have deserted to the enemy since the Declaration of Independence.

"On your return, whatever your success may be, you will please to make report to me. I very sincerely wish you success."

On Friday morning, 24th of May, all had crossed the river, and were present at the place appointed for the general meeting. "Our number," wrote John Rose,[9] from Mingo Bottom, that evening, to Irvine, at Fort Pitt, "is actually four hundred and eighty men." Of these, about two-thirds were from Washington county; the residue, except about twenty from Ohio

---

[9] An aid-de-camp of Irvine, with the rank of lieutenant in the Continental army.

county, Virginia, were from Westmoreland—mostly from that part included the next year (September 26, 1783) in Fayette county.¹⁰ Great activity prevailed among the men in preparing for the march; as it was given out that the afternoon would be spent in organizing the army, by the election of the proper officers, and that the march would begin early on the morrow should some powder arrive in time, which had been sent for the day previous, to Fort McIntosh.

Under the spreading boughs of the sycamore and sugar-maple, which, in the rich soil of the bottom, grew uncommonly large, active preparations were going forward. The black and white walnut, the water-elm, with here and there a hickory, hackberry, and white ash, threw grateful shadows upon the busy multitude grouped along the margin of the Ohio. All were in high spirits. Everywhere around, there was a pleasurable excitement. Jokes were bandied, and sorrows at parting with loved ones at home quite forgotten—at least, could outward

---

¹⁰ "The troops were volunteer militia, part Pennsylvanians and part Virginians, and a few Continental officers whom I sent."—Irvine to Lyon, 10th November, 1799: MS. letter. A letter from Marshal to Irvine, 29th May, 1782, says: "I have not yet ascertained with exactness the number of men from the different counties, but I believe they are nearly as follows: Westmoreland about 130; Ohio (Va.) about 20, and Washington 320." Upon this subject, Doddridge (*Notes*, 269) makes a surprising blunder. He says: "They were all volunteers from the immediate neighborhood of the Ohio, with the exception of one company from Ten Mile, in Washington county."

appearances be relied upon. Nevertheless, furtive glances up the western hill-sides, into the deep woods, kept alive, in the minds of some, the dangerous purpose of all this bustle and activity.

The volunteers assembled at one o'clock, to elect their officers. They then distributed themselves into eighteen companies, chosing their captains by vote.[11] The policy of forming such small companies was a wise one, as it brought together, as a general thing, those only who were acquainted with each other; besides, so few men could be much more easily directed, than a large number, in the Indian mode of warfare, where skulking, treeing, tomahawking, and scalping were practiced. Names of some of the captains have been preserved. "Many of them, I have often heard mentioned," writes Nathaniel Ewing, of Uniontown, Fayette county, Pennsylvania, "but their names have faded away in the long course of seventy years."[12] Among those chosen were McGeehan,[13] Hoagland, Beeson,[14] Munn,

---

[11] *Knight's Narrative*, p. 5.

[12] Communication to the author—1872.

[13] Application of James Ross for a pension, June 19, 1833.

[14] "The captain of my company was named Beeson; he was from that part of Westmoreland which soon after became Fayette county. Beesontown—afterward Uniontown—was named in honor of him."— *Philip Smith's Recollections of Crawford's Expedition*. Mr. Smith was one of the volunteers. A grandson, Albert M. Smith, of Centreville, Wayne county, Indiana, has kindly written down and placed at my disposal whatever of these Recollections have been preserved in the family.

Ross, Ogle, John Biggs, Craig Ritchie, John Miller, Joseph Bean, and Andrew Hood.

One lieutenant and one ensign were chosen by each company. An old narrative of the expedition, in rhyme, recites:

> "There was Ensign McMasters, another as brave;
> He fought many battles his country to save:" [15]

and James Paull remembered, fifty years after, that the lieutenant of his company was Edward Stewart.[16]

In the election of the general officers there were four hundred and sixty-five that voted. There were chosen one colonel commandant, four field majors, and one brigade-major. Considerable interest was manifested in the choice of the first officer. General Irvine had taken some pains to bring forward a candidate—one in whom he reposed great confidence. But David Williamson was also a candidate; was very popular, and had numerous and obstinate adherents. A strong argument in his

---

[15] The "poem" from which these two lines are taken is entitled "*Crawford's Defeat.*" It begins—

> "Come all you good people wherever you be,
> Pray draw near awhile and listen to me;
> A story I'll tell you which happened of late,
> Concerning brave Crawford's most cruel defeat;"—

which "story," it may be premised, contains much more history than poetry. It was long after a favorite song upon the frontier—sung to various tunes. Its echoes are remembered to have been heard even at a late date, and as far west as the valley of the Sandusky.

[16] Application of James Paull for a pension, January 15, 1833.

favor was the circumstance of his being a citizen of Washington county, which had sent out twice as many men for the expedition as Westmoreland, where his opponent resided. However, upon counting the votes it was found that two hundred and thirty had been cast for Williamson, and two hundred and thirty-five for his opponent, WILLIAM CRAWFORD.

The four field majors elected to rank in the order named, in command under Crawford, were David Williamson, Thomas Gaddis, John McClelland, and Major Brinton.[17] Daniel Leet was elected brigade-major; John Knight was appointed surgeon; John Slover and Jonathan Zane, pilots. John Rose went as aid to the commander-in-chief. Knight and Rose were officers at Fort Pitt under Irvine, and were specially detailed by him for this service.

NOTE 1.—The important letter from Rose to Irvine is in the Irvine Collection. It was written just upon the eve of the departure of the expedition from Mingo Bottom, and immediately after its organization. It contains the only complete list of the field majors, with their relative rank, that I have seen. Nothing is said, however, about the election of Daniel Leet as brigade-major. This, and other interesting information, I have obtained from the declaration for a pension, made on the 3d of October, 1832, by Francis Dunlevy, then a resident of Lebanon, Warren county, Ohio, since deceased; and from his MS. notes of the

[17] Rose to Irvine, 24th May, 1782. Major Brinton's full name I have never seen. Knight, in his Narrative (p. 5), speaks of him as "Major Brenton;" so also the "song" just referred to: "There was brave Major Brenton," etc.

campaign, kindly furnished by his son, A. H. Dunlevy. In an affidavit appended to an application for a pension, made by James Workman, March 29, 1833, Hugh Workman also speaks of Leet as having had a command as major in the expedition.

There was, doubtless, a roll and roster of the expedition, but it has since been lost. It may have been sent, for some purpose, to Philadelphia, then the seat of the Pennsylvania government. These are conjectures only. Certain it is that no copy or original, in print or MS., is now known to exist. Mr. Hazard, the careful compiler of the "Colonial Records," of Pennsylvania, and "Pennsylvania Archives" did not find any, as nothing of the kind appears in those voluminous and valuable publications. So far as attainable, from varied sources, all the persons in any way belonging to the expedition are named in these sketches.

NOTE 2.—That it was the intention of the expedition against Sandusky to destroy the remnant of the Christian Indians, is an error widely circulated. I have in my possession manuscript Recollections of some of the volunteers, in which are indignant denials of the accusations made in Heckewelder's Narrative and Doddridge's Notes concerning the *animus* of the campaign. There seems to have been considerable feeling aroused in Western Pennsylvania and Virginia upon the publication of these calumnies. In justice, however, to Doddridge, who, as has been stated, early gave this error currency, it must be said that the Moravian writers, Loskiel and Heckewelder, were the *first* to assert it *as truth:*

"The same gang of murderers, who had committed the massacre upon the Muskingum, did not give up their bloody design upon the remnant of the Indian congregation, though it was delayed for a time."—*Loskiel's His. Miss.*, P. iii, p. 188.

"Not satisfied with this horrid outrage [the massacre at Gnadenhütten], the same band not long afterward marched to Sandusky, where, it seems, they had been informed that the remnant of that unfortunate congregation had fled, in order to perpetrate upon them the same indiscriminate murder."—*Heckewelder's His. Ind. Nations*, p. 281.

This is repeated, in substance, by the last-mentioned writer, in another work soon after published (*Narr. Miss.*, pp. 337, 338, etc). Doddridge then took up the refrain (*Notes*, p. 268), and his followers are legion; some giving, as he, the fictitious purpose along with the true one; others copying Loskiel and Heckewelder, stating only the fiction; as will be seen by such extracts as the following:

" Depredations still continuing to be made, from time to time, on the settlements, after the return from the Moravian campaign, it was determined a force should be raised and marched against the Sandusky Indians, who seemed the most active in keeping up the warfare; when an opportunity would likewise be had to come up with the remaining Moravians."—*His. of the Backwoods. By A. W. Patterson*, Pittsburgh, 1843, p. 254.

" Flushed by this success [the Moravian affair], a new expedition of four hundred and eighty men marched . . . . . to complete the destruction of the Christian Indians by assailing Sandusky."—*His. of the United States. Hildreth*, vol. iii, p. 423.

" It was in the month of March, 1782, that this great murder [the killing of the Moravian Indians upon the Muskingum] was committed. And, as the tiger, having once tasted blood, longs for blood, so it was with the frontier-men; and another expedition [Crawford's] was at once organized to make a dash at the towns of the Moravians, Delawares, and Wyandots, upon the Sandusky."—*Annals of the West. By James H. Perkins. St. Louis*, 1850, p. 261, 262.

" The signal success attending the expedition against the Moravians, induced many who had been engaged in that atrocious affair, to get up a second one, on a more grand and extensive plan, against the Indian settlements at Sandusky. This was the ostensible motive, but some believed it was merely intended to finish the work of murder and plunder upon Moravians. Such, at least, is said to have been the object with some who composed the expedition; with the majority, however, it was regarded as an expedition to punish the Wyandots for their many and long-continued depredations upon the whites."—*His. Ind. Wars W. Va. Wills De Hass*, p. 189.

"It [Gnadenhütten affair] was immediately followed by active preparations for a volunteer expedition against the new settlement of the Christian Indians, and the Wyandot and Delaware towns, on the head waters of the Sandusky."—*His. of the State of Ohio. By James W. Taylor. Cincinnati*, 1854, p. 378.

"The success of the expedition of Williamson [the Gnadenhütten massacre] excited the borderers to prepare another invasion of the Indian country, to finish the destruction of the Christian Indians by the massacre of the fugitives at Sandusky."—*Annals of the West. By James K. Albach. Pittsburgh*, 1857, p. 380.

"The campaign of 1782 [Crawford's] . . . . may be regarded as a repetition of the Williamson Moravian expedition."—*Red Men of the Ohio Valley. By J. R. Dodge. Springfield*, O., 1860, p. 285.

CHAPTER V.

BIOGRAPHICAL SKETCH OF WILLIAM CRAWFORD. 1732—1782.

WILLIAM CRAWFORD, elected by the volunteers assembled at Mingo Bottom to command the expedition against Sandusky, was born in the year 1732, in Orange county, Virginia.[1] His parents were of Scotch-Irish origin. His father, a respectable farmer, died when William was four years old, leaving another and younger son, Valentine. His mother, Onora, was a woman of uncommon energy of character, possessed of great physical strength, yet kind in disposition, and very attentive to her children. She married again; her second husband was Richard Stephenson, with whom she lived ten years, when he died. William had five half-brothers: John, Hugh, Richard, James, and Marcus, and one half-sister, Elizabeth. The latter died young.[2] The seven boys were all remarkable for their size and strength. They all lived with their widowed mother, when, in the year 1749, they became acquainted with the youthful George Washington, surveyor, at that time, to Lord Fairfax.

---

[1] In 1738, the legislature of Virginia erected out of the territory of Orange two counties; one was called Frederick, within which was the place of Crawford's nativity. It is now in Berkeley county.

[2] Communicated by Dr. Alfred Creigh, of Washington, Pa.

It was while Washington was surveying in the valley of the Shenandoah, that his acquaintance with Crawford began, which ripened into a friendship never broken until the death of the latter They were both of the same age. There are many traditions concerning the athletic sports of Washington with the Crawford and Stephenson boys while the former was stopping at the widow Stephenson's. When his daily toils were ended, a fine lawn, in front of the house of his hostess, was, on bright evenings, the scene of many encounters at wrestling, running, and jumping. Washington was as tall as any of the boys, but not so heavy. In their frolics to see which was "the best man," it often happened that, in wrestling, the young surveyor was worsted. But in running and jumping, he was generally victorious. These manly sports were often continued until late in the evening. When, in after years, fortune and fame smiled upon Washington, he did not forget the sons of the widow Stephenson.[3] They were the recipients of many favors at his hands. Especially did he prove the steadfast friend of William Crawford.

The childhood home of Crawford was the home of the pioneer. He was cradled among rude scenes, and reared upon a rough but generous diet. His education was limited; his knowledge was more of men than of books. Living almost at the verge of the settlements

---

[3] *Weems' Life of Washington*, pp. 28, 29.

in the west, he knew but little of the refinements of polished society. He grew to manhood apt in expedients, generous in disposition, strong in body and mind, cool and collected under excitement, and possessing the most undaunted courage in the face of danger. Having learned the art of surveying in his companionship with Washington, he made that his vocation up to about the age of twenty-three, when not engaged in the duties appertaining to a farmer's life. During the year 1755, he gave up his double occupation of surveyor and farmer; forsook the compass and the plow for

> "The pomp and circumstance of glorious war;"—

receiving from the governor of Virginia a commission as ensign, and joining a company of riflemen destined to augment the army of the ill-fated Braddock, in his march against Fort du Quesne, afterward Fort Pitt.

The war then raging was a contest between England and France for the vast region between the Alleghenies and the Rocky Mountains. "This extensive territory had been explored, mapped out, and, in a good measure, occupied by the French. Their forts, missions, and trading posts—the centers, in some cases, of little colonies—were scattered throughout the valley of the Mississippi, and on the borders of all the great lakes."[4] It was against one of these forts, Du Quesne, situ-

---

[4] Francis Parkman. *Preface to Robert Clarke & Co.'s reprint of Bouquet's Expedition.* Cincinnati, 1868, p. 11.

ated at the junction of the Allegheny and Monongahela rivers, that the British army under Braddock was marching through Virginia, when joined by young Crawford and his company of riflemen.

The march of Braddock to the vicinity of Fort du Quesne; the battle of July 9th, with the French and Indians who had ambuscaded their enemy; and the overwhelming defeat of the approaching army and death of Braddock, are the principal events in the history of that campaign. Ensign Crawford was a participant in the battle, and, for gallantry displayed upon that disastrous occasion, was promoted, the following year, to a lieutenancy.

The western frontier settlements of Pennsylvania, Maryland and Virginia, were now, for the first time, visited with the horrors of savage warfare. The deadly foe "moved with stealth and mystery, only to be traced by its ravages and counted by its foot-prints." These irruptions continued until 1758, when diplomacy and the triumph of the British arms over the French brought about a general peace with the western Indians; but not until the valley of the Shenandoah—the home of Lieutenant Crawford—had become almost a solitude. During all this time Crawford had been employed in garrison duty, or as a scout, at the frontier posts of Pennsylvania and Virginia, learning much of the best methods of fighting savages.

But the time had now come for another attempt at

the reduction of Fort du Quesne. The command of the expedition to effect this, was given to Brigadier-General Forbes; his army to consist of regulars and colonial troops. Washington was now commander-in-chief of the Virginia troops, which were to make a part of the army of General Forbes. His force consisted of two regiments of one thousand men each—one led by himself, the other by Colonel Byrd. Upon the authority of the governor of Virginia, Washington now promoted Crawford, obtaining for him the commission of captain. Thereupon Captain Crawford recruited a full company of hardy, stalwart farmers and hunters, from his own neighborhood, to augment the regiment of Washington, his friend and benefactor.

The rendezvousing of Crawford's company, preparatory to marching his men to join the force under Washington, disclosed the fact that there was a want of transportation. Here was a dilemma. Fortunately, however, there happened to be at the place where the company was encamped, a teamster who had stopped to rest and feed his horses. In such an emergency, Crawford felt no hesitancy in pressing the wagoner into his service, and accordingly announced to the stranger his determination.

The owner of the team was in no humor to submit patiently to what he considered an oppressive act. But how could it be avoided? He was alone, in the midst of a company of men who were ready and strong enough, at a word, to enforce their captain's orders. Remaining a short time silent, looking sullenly at the armed men, as if measuring their strength with his own weakness, he finally observed to Crawford, that it was hard to be forced into the service against his will; that every man ought to have a fair chance, and that he was taken at a great disadvantage, inasmuch as the odds against him were so great as to deprive him of the power of self-protection.

He thought the captain was taking advantage of circumstances, and he would now make a proposition, which the commander certainly was bound in honor to accede to: "I will fight you," said he, "or any man in your company. If I am whipped, I will go with you cheerfully. If I conquer, you must let me off." From what has been said of Captain Crawford's personal activity and strength, it will not be a matter of wonder to learn that the challenge of the doughty teamster was at once accepted. Both began to strip; the men prepared to form a ring, determined to show fair play, and to see the fun.

At this moment, a tall young man, who had lately joined the company, but a stranger to most of them, and who had been leaning carelessly against a tree, eyeing the scene with apparent unconcern, now stepped forward and drew Crawford aside. "Captain," said the stranger, "you must let *me* fight that fellow, he will whip *you; it will never do to have the company whipped!*"

A few additional words of like import overheard by the men—with the cool, collected, and confident manner of the speaker—induced them to suggest to Crawford, that perhaps it *would* be prudent to let the stranger try his hand. The captain, having done all that policy required, in accepting the challenge, suffered himself to be persuaded by his men; and it was agreed that the youth should be substituted in his place.

By this time the wagoner was stripped to the buff and ready for the fight. He was big, muscular, well filled out, hardened by exposure, and an adept in pugilistic encounters. His air was cool and professional; his mien, defiant and confident. When the youthful-looking stranger, therefore, walked into the ring, clad in his loose hunting-shirt, and looking slender and a little pale, the men had not the utmost confidence in *his* success. However, there was fire in his eye; and, as he threw aside his garments, a stalwart frame was disclosed of enormous bones and muscles. The spirits of the company immediately revived.

Preparations being finished, the word was given. The youth sprang upon his antagonist with the agility and ferocity of a tiger! The blood followed at every blow of his tremendous fists. The contest was short and decisive. The teamster was completely vanquished. The hero of this, his *first* fight for his country, was afterward Major-General Daniel Morgan, of Revolutionary fame! [5]

The Virginia forces, under Washington, which Captain Crawford and his company now joined, having formed a junction with the troops under Forbes, the whole marched forward to the reduction of Fort du Quesne. After much delay and many mishaps, the post was reached and occupied by Washington on the 25th of November; the French having previously evacuated the place and retired down the Ohio. Captain Crawford, after this event, remained in the service of Virginia for three years; when he returned to his home, in the valley of the Shenandoah, and resumed the labors of farmer and surveyor. Here he remained until the year 1767, an honored citizen, frequently intrusted with the direction of various local affairs by his neighbors.

While in the army of Virginia, Crawford had become familiar with the country watered by the Monongahela and its branches, many parts of which he had occasion to visit in the public service. He became enamored of the trans-Allegheny region, and resolved, at some future day, to make it his home. The time had now come for him to put his resolution to practical effect.

Early in the summer of 1767, he started for a horseback trip over the mountains, to seek a suitable local-

---

[5] *Hall's Romance of Western History.* Cincinnati: Robert Clarke & Co., 1869. Chap. vii, p. 121.

ity for his future home. Having reached the Youghiogheny river, he proceeded to give its valley a more thorough examination than he had previously done while in the army. After some time spent in an inspection of the surrounding country, he determined to locate upon the south side of that stream, at a point known at that day as "Stewart's Crossings."

The spot chosen by Crawford for his residence was on Braddock's road, near the place, on the river, where, twelve years before, Braddock had crossed on his march against Fort du Quesne. It was in Augusta county, Virginia, as claimed by that commonwealth; afterward in the district of West Augusta, and, finally, in Yohogania county until 1779, when Virginia relinquished her claim to what is now Southwestern Pennsylvania. As claimed by Pennsylvania, it was, in 1767, in Cumberland county; subsequently in Bedford; afterward in Westmoreland, and finally in Fayette county, when, on the 26th of September, 1783, the latter was formed by the legislature. It was opposite the present town of Connellsville, where the village of New Haven is now located.

When Crawford, in 1767, fixed his home upon the banks of the Youghiogheny, all around was, to a great extent, a howling wilderness. But there were many features of the country very pleasing to a new-comer. The fertility of the soil and the immense growth of the forest trees, so different from the eastern side of the mountain ranges, gave a romantic charm to this region.

In June, Crawford erected a cabin and immediately set to work clearing the forests. He also, it seems, engaged in trading with the Indians. His family, consisting of his wife, Hannah, whose maiden name was Vance, and his three children—Sarah, John, and Effie—were left behind, in the valley of the Shenandoah, at their old home.

Hugh Stephenson, Crawford's half-brother, came to the valley soon after; and the two were now living together in the log hut built by William, on the bank of the river. Hugh was also a married man, and had left his family behind him. In two years, the brothers had cleared quite an extensive tract of land, brought it under cultivation, and erected suitable buildings for their families, which were removed to the Youghiogheny, in 1769. From this time forward, to the events which led to his death, Crawford lived at the same place; always taking an active, and frequently a leading part in public affairs, and making his home—"Crawford's Place," as it was known far and wide—a famous resort for pioneers, and a tarrying-place for new-comers to the valley.[6]

Crawford's homestead contained three hundred and

---

[6] "He was a man of good judgment, singular good nature, and great humanity; and remarkable for his hospitality—few strangers coming to the western country and not spending some days at the crossing of the Youghiogheny, where he lived."—*Brackenridge*, in the Knight and Slover pamphlet, 1783, p. 16.

seventy-six acres of land. Under the laws of the State of Pennsylvania, he had, on the 3d day of April, 1769, in the name of his son John, made an application to the proper office, for an order to have this tract surveyed. The order was issued, the survey made and returned to the land-office, wherein it was described as "A certain tract of land called 'Stewart's Crossings,' situate on the south side of the Youghiogheny river;" following which was a description by metes and bounds. The spot was known as "Stewart's Crossings" from the circumstance of one William Stewart having lived near the place in the year 1753 and a part of 1754, he having been obliged finally to leave the country on account of the French taking possession of it. This home tract of Crawford's included nearly all of what subsequently became the village of New Haven, and a considerable quantity of land outside the borough.

The intimate relations between Washington and Crawford were not broken off by the removal of the latter west of the mountains. They frequently corresponded. One of the first letters of the former requested Crawford to select lands for him in the vicinity—such as he could recommend—and to send him a description of them. "If you will be at the trouble of seeking out the lands," wrote Washington, from Mount Vernon, on the 21st of September, 1769, "I will take upon me the part of securing them, as soon as there is a possibility of doing it, and will moreover be at all the cost and charges of surveying and patenting the same. You shall then have such a reasonable proportion of the whole as we may fix upon at our first meeting."[7]

Crawford did not fail to attend to the wishes of his friend. Several tracts were sought out by him, not only for Washington, but also for the brothers of the latter—Samuel and John Augustine, and his relative, Lund Washington. They are in what is now Perry township, Fayette county, on the southern side of, and near the Youghiogheny river, about sixteen miles below Connellsville. These lands, as well as tracts for other parties, were surveyed by Crawford even before they were bought of the Indians—the object being to acquire Virginia rights.[8] Crawford also took up for himself several valuable tracts in the vicinity of his home, and afterward purchased other lands from original settlers.

---

[7] *Sparks' Writings of Washington*, ii, 348. "The date is incorrectly given—21st September, 1767. It should be 1769."—*James Veech: notes to the author.*

[8] Most of the lands belonging to Washington in the West were located by Crawford. "We have frequently heard the old surveyors along the Ohio, say that they often met with his 'corners.'"—*De Hass' His. Ind. Wars W. Va.*, p. 373. "Some of the earliest surveys," continues the writer, "within the present limits of Brooke, Ohio, and Marshall counties, Virginia, were made by him. The fees in those days rendered the business of surveying rather desirable." The surveyor, according to De Hass, sometimes got one-fourth of the land for surveying it!

Early in 1770, an occurrence took place at the home of Crawford, which created considerable excitement in Western Pennsylvania. A young man in his employ, John Ingham, who had been indentured to him to learn the art of surveying, brutally murdered, while intoxicated, an Indian—a warm friend of the Crawford family. After committing the deed, the young apprentice fled to Virginia, pursued, however, by Crawford and a few neighbors, who succeeded in capturing him. He was then turned over to the authorities of the State for punishment.

Lord Botetourt, the governor of Virginia, after a conference with Crawford, sent Ingham under guard to Governor Penn, of Pennsylvania; at the same time explaining to the latter, by a letter written at Williamsburg, on the 20th of March, 1770, that he had sent "the body of John Ingham, he having confessed himself concerned in the murder of Indian Stephen,"' which, from the best information the governor could obtain, was committed on a spot of ground claimed by Pennsylvania.[9] "You will find by the paper I have inclosed," adds Botetourt, "that there never was an act of villainy more unprovoked, or more deliberately undertaken." Crawford took every pains to bring for-

---

[9] The return of this prisoner by Lord Botetourt to Pennsylvania for trial, was, in the after-controversy between the two provinces as to whom the territory belonged, wielded with great force by Governor Penn against the claim of Virginia.

ward the proper evidence against the prisoner, but the latter escaped from custody, and was never heard of afterward.

During the year 1770, Crawford was appointed one of the justices of the peace for his county—Cumberland.[10] In the autumn, he received a visit, at his home on the Youghiogheny, from George Washington. The latter was then on a tour down the Ohio, with a view to select and mark out lands for himself and others, entitled thereto as officers and soldiers in the French and Indian war, under a resolution of the council, and proclamation of Governor Dinwiddie, of Virginia.

Washington reached the hospitable cabin of his friend Crawford in the afternoon of the 13th of October, receiving a most cordial welcome. On the next day, Crawford took his guest to a coal-mine not far away. The two visited, on the day following, the lands selected for Washington. These were near the Youghiogheny, about twelve miles by land from "Stewart's Crossings." On the 16th, Washington started for Pittsburg, distant forty-three and a half measured miles, taking Crawford, William Harrison, and other friends with him. The party arrived at Fort Pitt the day following. They found the post garrisoned by two

---

[10] Bedford county was formed from a part of Cumberland, March 9, 1771. Westmoreland was formed from the former county, February 26, 1773.

companies of royal Irish, commanded by Captain Edmondson. A hamlet of about twenty houses built of logs, inhabited by Indian traders, had sprung up within three hundred yards of the fort. This was the embryo city of Pittsburg.

The party remained here until the 20th, when they embarked in a large canoe upon the Ohio, destined for the Great Kenhawa. They arrived at Mingo Bottom on the 22d. There was, at the time of Washington's visit, a village of Mingoes at this point, of about twenty cabins and seventy occupants.

At two o'clock the next day, the party left Mingo Bottom, ariving at the mouth of the Great Kenhawa on the last day of the month. All the way down, frequent stops were made, the country examined, and important points noted by Washington, who kept a daily journal during the entire tour. On the 4th of November, the tourists started on their return up the Ohio. On this day, Washington records the fact that they "met a canoe going to Illinois with sheep"—a primitive mode surely, and a very precarious one, for the transportation of live stock from Pittsburg to the vicinity of St. Louis! This was nearly a half century before the placid Ohio was first vexed with the paddles of steamboats.

On the 5th of November the party came to a great bend in the river, which forms a portion of what is now the southern boundary of Meigs county, Ohio.

On that day Washington wrote: "Walked across the neck on foot, with Captain Crawford—the distance, according to our walking, about eight miles."

The voyagers reached Mingo Bottom, on their return, on the 17th, where they were detained until the 20th of the month. At two o'clock on this last day, horses having been, in the meantime, brought down for them from Crawford's home, they set out, by land, for Pittsburg, where they arrived in the afternoon of the 21st. Leaving Fort Pitt on the 23d, the party arrived next day upon the bank of the Youghiogheny, opposite the home of Crawford. "When we came to 'Stewart's Crossings,' at Crawford's," wrote Washington in his diary, "the river was too high to ford, and his canoe gone adrift. However, after waiting there two or three hours, a canoe was got, in which we passed, and swam our horses. The remainder of this day I spent at Captain Crawford's, it either raining or snowing hard all day."

On the 25th of November, Crawford went with Washington to see the tract of land taken up for Lund Washington. It was here the two parted. Washington pursued his journey leisurely homeward, arriving at Mount Vernon on the first day of December—absent nine weeks and one day." Crawford returned to his humble cabin upon the Youghiogheny. Both these men were, at that date, in the prime of life; both had

---

[11] *Sparks' Writings of Washington*, vol. ii, pp. 516, 534.

uncommonly vigorous constitutions; both had the world before them; but alas! how different was its ending with them! By one, at least, it was well that nothing was known of the inscrutable future!

On the 11th of March, 1771, Crawford was appointed by Governor Penn to be a justice of the peace for Bedford county, along with Arthur St. Clair, Dorsey Pentecost, Robert Hanna, and other men of note, who, by virtue of their offices, were the judges of the courts of the county. Upon the erection of Westmoreland, in 1773, his commission was renewed for that county, and he was made presiding justice for the courts.

During this year he came near being again visited by Washington. The latter was to have been accompanied by Lord Dunmore, then the governor of Virginia; but his designs were frustrated by the death, on the 19th of June, of his step-daughter, Miss Custis. The two had contemplated a western tour together. On the 13th of April, 1773, Washington wrote to Dunmore from Mount Vernon, concerning the contemplated journey: "I beg the favor of your lordship to inform me, as nearly as you can, of the precise time you will do me the honor of calling here, that I may get ready accordingly, and give notice of it to Mr. Crawford (if your lordship purposes to take the route of Pittsburg), whom I took the liberty of recommending as a good woodsman, and well acquainted with the lands in that quarter, that he may be disengaged when we get to his house, which is directly on the communication. I am persuaded that such a person will be found very necessary in an excursion of this sort, from his superior knowledge of the country and of the inhabitants who are thinly scattered over it."[12]

On the 25th of September, 1773, Washington wrote to Crawford from Mount Vernon, asking him to select lands for him down the Ohio, below the mouth of the Scioto—in the event of the latter contemplating a location for himself in that locality, which he was entitled to, under a proclamation of the year 1763: "By Mr. Leet I informed you of the unhappy cause which prevented my going out this fall. But I hope nothing will prevent my seeing you in that country in the spring. The precise time, as yet, it is not in my power to fix; but I should be glad if you would let me know how soon it may be attended with safety, ease, and comfort, after which I will fix upon a time to be at your house."[13] But Washington never again visited the Youghiogheny. Momentous events were in the not distant future. The Revolution was now at hand.

For several years the country about the head-waters of the Ohio had been a subject of dispute between Pennsylvania and Virginia. The quarrel, however, did not assume a very threatening aspect until the legislature of the former commonwealth embraced all the disputed

---

[12] *Sparks' Writings of Washington*, vol. ii, p. 373.
[13] Id. 375.

territory—the whole region west of the Laurel Hill—in the new county of Westmoreland, in 1773. Immediately, Lord Dunmore, governor of Virginia, attempted by violent measures to enforce jurisdiction over the country. Fort Pitt was seized by a band of armed partisans, and its name changed to Fort Dunmore. The Pennsylvanians, however, adhered to the old name. It was fully restored when Dunmore became odious.

Crawford, however, although a Virginian by birth, remained loyal to the government he was serving, until his native State was drawn into a war with the Western Indians, in 1774, when his ardent love of adventure got the better of his Pennsylvania loyalty; and, having received a captain's commission from the Virginia governor, he raised, without difficulty, a company of men to fight the savages, who were now in arms against the frontier settlements; and, in June, marched them to Fort Dunmore.

Crawford was not a prominent actor in "Dunmore's War." He did not participate in the famous battle of Point Pleasant; nor was he present upon the Scioto when the Shawanese made peace with the Virginia troops. He had been offered a command second in rank to Colonel Andrew Lewis, who had charge of the left wing of the Virginia army on the march against the hostile Indians; but this he had declined. "You could not do better," wrote Lord Dunmore, on the 20th of June, to the commanding officer at Fort Dunmore, "than send Captain William Crawford with what men you can spare to join him, to co-operate with Colonel Lewis, or to strike a blow himself, if he thinks he can do it with safety. I know him to be prudent, active, and resolute."

The Indian war ended in November, and Crawford, who had done efficient service at Wheeling, returned to his home upon the Youghiogheny.[14] In the meantime, Arthur St. Clair was not unmindful of the fact that his associate, a sworn officer of Pennsylvania, had accepted a commission from Virginia, and was in direct conflict with the peace policy of Penn. So he wrote to the latter, on the 22d of July: "Captain Crawford, the president of our court, seems to be the most active Virginia officer in their service. He is now down the river, at the head of a number of men, which is his second expedition."—"How is it possible," reasoned the chivalric gentleman, "for a man to serve two colonies, in direct antagonism to each other, at the same time?" The keen-edged sword of Virginia could not be belted to the judicial robe of Pennsylvania. "William Crawford," reiterated this high-toned partisan, "hath joined with the government of Virginia in opposing the jurisdiction of Pennsylvania." Of course this would not

---

[14] "During Dunmore's campaign, Captain William Crawford was sent with a detachment to destroy a Mingo town. He did so, taking the prisoners afterward to Pittsburg."—*American Archives*, Vol. I, 4th Series, p. 707.

do; he must be superseded. A supersedeas was ordered; and, on the 25th of January, 1775, Crawford was removed from all positions held by him in Westmoreland county. He never again held office under Pennsylvania.

Crawford's allegiance was now fully transferred to his native State. In the spring of 1775, he took an active part in the boundary troubles, on the side of Virginia. He opened a land-office, and, as deputy surveyor, made surveys, overriding Pennsylvania claims. Entries were made, citizens dispossessed, and, in some instances where the legality of his proceedings was denied, imprisonments followed. These acts, however, though incited by Lord Dunmore and his partisans, were not, in the end, confirmed by Virginia, and the new purchasers lost their titles. Much discontent among the settlers was manifest, and Crawford became, for a time, very unpopular with those of his old friends who now suffered in the loss of money, or who adhered in their allegiance to Pennsylvania. "A set of people who call themselves Virginians," wrote Devereaux Smith from Hanna's-town, to Penn, on the 14th of February, "have taken possession of most of the land here, and say they have rights from the Virginia offices, two of which are held here—one by Captain William Crawford, and the other by Dorsey Pentecost."

After the erection of Yohogania county by Virginia, in November, 1776, Crawford was appointed deputy surveyor and one of the justices for that county, which were thenceforward the only civil offices held by him. He was surveyor of the county so long as it had an existence; sat as justice of its court, at intervals, in 1777, and the year following; and, in the latter part of 1779, and the beginning of the next year, finished his duties as land-officer.[15] During all this time, however, Crawford was an actor in other scenes, at home or abroad, which reconciled his old friends, endeared him to the West, and added much to his fame. As the day of the Revolution began to dawn, he immediately sank his partisan feelings in the nobler impulses of the patriot. He struck hands with his Pennsylvania enemies in the cause of liberty!

On the 16th day of May, 1775, the inhabitants of Western Pennsylvania, calling themselves citizens of West Augusta, met in convention at Pittsburg, to give expression to their views and sentiments regarding the troubles with the mother country. Crawford acted a prominent part at this meeting. He was bold in advocating the rights and liberties of America. A committee of defense was appointed to concert measures for the protection of the inhabitants against the aggressions of Great Britain. Crawford was placed upon this committee.

When the news of the battle of Lexington reached Pittsburg, Crawford lost no time in offering his serv-

---

[15] Communicated by James Veech, on authority of the minutes of the Yohogania County Court, in his possession.

ices to the Council of Safety, then sitting in Philadelphia; but, in view of his recent conduct in setting at defiance the laws of Pennsylvania, and the bitter feeling engendered on account of the transactions of other Virginians with whom he had associated, his patriotic offer was rejected.[16]

During the fall, Crawford made a tender to his native State of his services to raise a regiment for the defense of the colonies; his offer was at once accepted. He immediately began recruiting, and, by his own exertions, raised the full complement of a regiment. Congress, however, determined to receive only six Virginia regiments into pay on the Continental establishment. As the forces raised by this commonwealth exceeded her quota, compromises were necessary in obtaining positions of command. The consequence was that Crawford failed in obtaining a colonelcy which he had earned and well deserved. However, on the 12th of January, 1776, he entered the Revoluntionary service as lieutenant-colonel of the Fifth Virginia regiment. On the 11th of October, he was appointed colonel of the Seventh regiment of the Virginia battal-

---

[16] At least, such is a tradition. It must be admitted, however, that it is not free from a suspicion of inaccuracy. The minutes of the Council of Safety, beginning 30th June, 1775, have no notice of such an offer; and, at that time, there was, in Pennsylvania, no official or quasi-official body competent to receive such a proposal—as the governor (Penn) and council were anti-revolutionary.

ions, by Congress, his commission to be dated the 14th of August. During the year, he was with his command—first, in the campaign on Long Island, engaging in the battles and skirmishes which there took place, and, later in the season, sharing in the famous retreat through New Jersey. He was one of the heroic band which crossed the Delaware with Washington on Christmas day; participating in the victory at Trenton on the next day, and at Princeton on the 3d of January, 1777.

Crawford, it seems, was with Washington in August, gallantly aiding in the abortive attempt to keep the British out of Philadelphia. When the latter had reached the head of Elk, in Maryland, Washington posted a body of militia at Iron Hill, a few miles from the British outposts. There were also at Christiana creek, about eight miles from Wilmington, Delaware, three brigades of Virginia troops, with six field-pieces. From each of these brigades, Washington detached a body of one hundred light-armed men, to act as scouts, the command of which was given to Crawford. The latter, while in command of this detachment, rendered the commander-in-chief important services; keeping him daily posted as to the most minute movements of the enemy. While thus engaged, Crawford had a brisk skirmish with a small party of Howe's advance, but was compelled to retreat.

Crawford had early apprehensions of Indian troubles

in the country about Fort Pitt, and had expressed his fears to Washington. On account of these representations, two regiments were ordered to be raised on the frontiers of Pennsylvania and Virginia, for their defense; the latter State responding with a full regiment; the former, with several companies: all arriving at Fort Pitt in the spring of 1778. In November previous, Congress " Resolved, That General Washington be requested to send Colonel William Crawford to Pittsburg to take the command, under Brigadier-General Hand, of the Continental troops and militia in the Western Department;" whereupon, Crawford repaired to York, Pennsylvania, where Congress was then in session; received his instructions, and soon after departed for the scene of his command, having gained largely the esteem of the officers and men of his regiment,[17] and

---

[17] ADDRESS OF THE OFFICERS OF THE SEVENTH VIRGINIA REGIMENT TO COLONEL WILLIAM CRAWFORD.

We beg leave to take this method of expressing our sense of the warmest attachment to you, and at the same time our sorrow in the loss of a commander who has always been influenced by motives that deservedly gain the unfeigned esteem and respect of all those who have the honor of serving under him. Both officers and soldiers retain the strongest remembrance of the regard and affection you have ever discovered toward them; but as we are well assured that you have the best interest of your country in view, we should not regret, however sensibly we may feel the loss of you, that you have chosen another field for the display of your military talents. Permit us, therefore, to express our most cordial wish, that you may find a regi-

the confidence of Washington as "a brave and active officer." In May, 1778, he took command of the Virginia regiment, under Brigadier-General Lachlin McIntosh, who had succeeded Hand in command of the Western Department.

Crawford was fitted by nature to be a soldier and leader. He was ambitious, cool and brave. He possessed, in a high degree, that peculiar courage and skill which is adapted to Indian or border warfare. Henceforth his services were given to the protection of the frontier. He was at home in the backwoods. As an officer, fighting against the disciplined troops of Great Britain, he approved himself meritorious, judicious,

---

ment no less attached to you than the Seventh, and that your services may ever be productive of benefit to your country and honor to yourself.

COLONEL CRAWFORD'S ANSWER.

GENTLEMEN: Your very affectionate and polite address demands my warmest acknowledgments, which I beg leave to return to you in the strongest terms of gratitude and affection. Be assured the officers of the Seventh regiment will ever share my tender regard; and I have great hopes that they will continue to merit the brightest esteem of their insulted and injured country.

My kind wishes will ever attend the lowest soldier in the regiment.

My own abilities are small, but I have this serious satisfaction—that they have been, and shall continue to be, exerted to the utmost in defense of *American* liberty, justice, and the rights of humanity.

I have the honor to be, gentlemen,

Your most humble servant,

W. CRAWFORD.

and intrepid. It was in the western wilds, however, that he displayed the highest qualities of his genius. He had clearly foreseen the coming of the storm that was now raging along the border. It was his earnest desire—one which he had not been loth to communicate to his commander-in-chief—to be sent west of the mountains for active service against the marauding savages.

It has already been shown how the border settlements of Pennsylvania were overrun by scalping parties in the autumn of 1777. As many of the war-parties were known to cross the Allegheny river, it was proposed as an obstacle to their ingress in that direction, to erect a fort at a suitable distance up that stream, to serve as a rallying point for scouts, as well as afford protection for troops. In the spring of 1778, as the inroads of the savages seemed on the increase, one of the first duties assigned to Crawford was the building of this fort. Taking with him a small party of men, he went up the river to determine upon the most eligible site for the post, and to put it under way of erection. About sixteen miles above Fort Pitt, there was a shallow place in the stream used as a ford by the savages in crossing into the settlements. Here, on the south side of the river, a short distance above the mouth of Puckety creek, a stockade fort was built, which, by direction of Brigadier-General McIntosh, was called Fort Crawford. At intervals during the year 1778, and the two following ones, Crawford commanded at that post.

Early in 1778, Colonel George Rogers Clark planned a secret expedition against the British posts between the Ohio and Mississippi rivers. Clark commanded a company in Dunmore's War—he and Crawford becoming warm friends, ardently attached to each other from their association during that campaign. Clark invited his friend to join him in the proposed— and, as it afterward proved, successful—expedition to the Mississippi; but Crawford was obliged to decline the service, however pleasing it would have been to engage in the enterprise, on account of the exposed condition of the frontiers, which required his constant attention. Clark obtained many of his recruits in Yohogania county and other parts of Western Virginia. All of the British posts in the Illinois were captured. " But for this conquest made by Colonel Clark, for the United States—and particularly for Virginia—in the midst of the terrible struggle with England, the boundary of our land, conquered in the Revolution from Great Britain, would, in all probability, have been the eastern bank of the Ohio, or the Allegheny Mountains, instead of the eastern shore of the Mississippi."[18]

---

[18]*Clark's Campaign.* Cincinnati: *Robert Clarke & Co.*, 1869, p. 1. The quotation is from the *Introduction*, by Judge Pirtle, of Louisville. In using it, I do not wish to be understood as assenting to the

In the autumn of 1778, Crawford took an active part, under McIntosh, in the expedition against Detroit, which only resulted, as has already been related, in the building of Forts McIntosh and Laurens. In September, he was appointed commander of the troops from Yohogania, Monongalia, and Ohio counties, Virginia, then at Fort Pitt. On the 8th of October, he was ordered to form the militia into a brigade. On the 27th, being now at Fort McIntosh, he was required to join the Berkeley and Augusta troops into one corps, and the Hampshire and Rockingham troops into another, to be called the Third and Fourth regiments of his brigade, from which he was to select a company of officers and men for light infantry.

In building Fort Laurens there was considerable trouble with the western troops. On the 3d of December, Crawford was permitted to discharge such of the mutineers of Ohio county as he might think proper, retaining such only as could be depended upon. Crawford afterward returned with McIntosh to Fort Pitt.[19]

During the occupation of Fort Laurens, it was frequently visited by Crawford on official business. The usual route was by way of Fort McIntosh, Yellow creek, and Big Sandy; thence down the Muskingum, as it was then called. There was also another route, by

---

assertion that the conquest was made for Virginia. It necessarily inured to all the States, though undertaken by Virginia authority.

[19] MS. Order Book of General McIntosh: Irvine Collection.

an Indian trail from Fort McIntosh, by way of the Moravian missionary establishments upon that river. It was always a perilous undertaking to reach that post; for, as long as it was garrisoned, the vicinity was infested by Indians who seldom spared a captive.

On one of his journeys from the fort homeward, Crawford had a narrow escape from capture. He and a solitary companion had left the fort about eight miles behind them, when a large party of savages was descried about a mile in advance, directly in their path. The two immediately crawled into a thick clump of bushes and noiselessly awaited the passing of the warriors. As the latter approached the hiding-place of the former, an Indian dog got scent of their trail, barking furiously along almost to the spot where they were secreted, when he was called back by his master. When the savages, who were on horseback, had passed them some distance, Crawford carefully made his way out of the thicket to watch them. The actions of the dog, which was continually turning back on the trail, caused one of the Indians to dismount and examine the path closely. He soon remounted, however, and the whole band were quickly lost to view. Crawford then returned to his terror-stricken companion, and the two resumed their journey, but with greater caution. It was considered by both as a narrow escape from death—"perhaps," as Crawford afterward frequently remarked, "by the most cruel torture!"

The evacuation of Fort Laurens, in August, 1779, and soon after of Fort McIntosh, brought the Indians, without interruption, to the very door of the settlements, greatly increasing, as previously mentioned, the dismay of the borderers. Before the close of the year, Crawford had led several small parties into the wilderness in pursuit of savage depredators. In these expeditions he was usually successful. His services in protecting the exposed settlers were highly appreciated. It was not in the pursuit and destruction of the enemy alone that Crawford rendered efficient aid; but also in advice—meeting with prominent citizens and consulting upon various methods and plans of defense.

The year 1780 was one of great activity for Crawford. He visited Congress in person to urge a more effectual and energetic defense of the frontiers. What was most wanted was the necessary funds for properly arming and equipping the western volunteers and militia. He seems to have been in a measure successful; as a considerable amount of war material was soon afterward forwarded to Fort Pitt and other western posts. Upon his return he again led small parties several times in pursuit of the marauding Indians before the close of the year. He had often expressed himself in favor of an expedition against Sandusky; and had already tried to raise a force for its destruction, failing, however, for the want of supplies.

Crawford powerfully aided Colonel Lochry in the

following year in raising volunteers for Clark's expedition against Detroit. On the 18th of June, 1781, a meeting of the inhabitants of Westmoreland county was held, to devise means for the better protection and defense of the border. It was resolved to give efficient aid to Clark. Crawford took a prominent part in the proceedings. He had intended to accompany Lochry down the Ohio, but was prevented by important matters requiring his attention on the border.

Crawford energetically seconded the attempt made by Colonel Gibson, commanding at Fort Pitt, to organize an expedition against Sandusky. Had it succeeded he would have been one of the leading officers. This was his last effort as an officer on the Continental establishment.[20] After six years of but little interruption of duty as a soldier and officer of the Revolutionary army, he was not sorry to be placed upon the retired list. He did not, however, throw up his commission—resolved, nevertheless, not to again enter the service, unless there was a great necessity for it.

That the contest with Great Britain was drawing to a close, it needed no prophet to foretell. The capture of Lord Cornwallis, on the 19th of October, was, to the mind of Crawford, an assurance that peace could not

---

[20] According to *Safford's Records of the Revolutionary War*, Crawford resigned his position in the army, February 10, 1781. But the weight of authority places the time in the autumn of that year, as stated in the text.

be far distant to the country at large, and, as he believed, to the weary border. Under the circumstances, therefore, he gladly accepted the opportunity of returning to his home, desiring, henceforth, to lead a private life, and to enjoy an undisturbed retirement from all public affairs. Having, as he believed, done his whole duty to his country, he now thought only of spending the remainder of his days in quietude and peace.

Crawford's children were all married and living in the neighborhood of his home. Sarah, the eldest, was the wife of William Harrison, a man of great spirit and distinction. They had six children—Sally, Nancy, Harriet, Battell, John, and Polly. Sarah Harrison, the mother, when young was a girl of great beauty. Traditions of her splendid features still linger by the rippling waters of the Youghiogheny. "It has often been said," writes a former resident of Fayette county, "and never contradicted, that Sally Crawford, when she married William Harrison, was the most beautiful young lady in all that part of the country."[21]

John, the only son, was the idol of his father; "a young man," wrote Hugh Brackenridge, in 1782, "greatly and deservedly esteemed as a soldier and citizen."[22] Effie, the second daughter, was married to William McCormick: they had one daughter—Anne.

---
[21] Robert A. Sherrard. Notes to the author: 1872.
[22] *Slover's Narrative* (ed. of 1783), p. 23, *note*.

As the year 1782 dawned upon the still healthy and vigorous Crawford—the fiftieth of his age—there was no greater pleasure for him than to sit in his log cabin, by the river's bank, and recount to interested listeners the incidents of his eventful life. He often expressed his happiness in contemplating the now almost assured victory of his country over despotism and oppression—anxious to see her take her stand among the nations of the earth—free, happy, independent! There was but one cloud in the otherwise bright sky above him: the victories in the east brought no cessation of hostilities in the west. The savages still glutted their vengeance upon the unwary borderers. The tomahawk and scalping-knife still brought death in all the brutality with which the Indian was capable, to young and old—to either sex. Crawford could not remain an indifferent spectator of the terrible scenes still enacting in the exposed settlements. His advice was frequently and freely given; and, although resolved to draw the sword no more, yet his martial spirit was fully aroused as reports came in from the frontiers of the early appearance of the Indians, and their audacity and horrible barbarity. He could hardly restrain himself from hurrying away, with his neighbors, in pursuit of the merciless foe.

When, therefore, a project began to be agitated in the settlements against Sandusky, it is not at all surprising that we find Crawford taking a deep interest in the scheme. He was early consulted with in regard to the matter. He favored the enterprise; but thought not less than four hundred men would be necessary. Success, in his judgment, would not be assured with a less number. To venture so great a distance into the enemy's country, with a small force, would, in his view, be very hazardous.

Many eyes were turned upon Crawford as the proper person to lead the expedition; but he refused. His patriotism, however, pleaded powerfully against his settled determination, as he saw a probability of a volunteer force, respectable in numbers, being raised for the enterprise. To add to the plea, his son John, and his son-in-law William Harrison, determined to volunteer for the campaign. Pentecost was urgent that he should once more take a command. Irvine himself thought it would be expedient for him to accept.

Crawford could no longer refuse. He still held his commission as colonel in the regular army; and the commanding officer of the Western Department desired him to lead the expedition; "hence," he reasoned, "it is now my duty to go. I will volunteer with the rest; and, if elected to command, shall do all in my power for the success of the expedition." It is the testimony of a grandson of Crawford,[23] that he had often heard his grandmother say, it was against the will of his

---

[23] Uriah Springer, now living (1872), in Dunbar township, Fayette county, Pennsylvania. Communicated by R. A. Sherrard.

grandfather to go out in the Sandusky expedition; but, as he held a commission under the government, he yielded to the wishes of the volunteers.

Immediately following his determination to volunteer for the Sandusky expedition, Crawford began to set his house in order. No one knew better than he the perils of Indian warfare. His long residence west of the mountains had, in times past, brought him in contact with many of the western Indians, before the breaking out of the Revolution. He had become acquainted with the Delawares, Shawanese, Wyandots, and Mingoes. He was familiar with localities beyond the Ohio, although he had never been further west than the Muskingum. He did not expect to traverse the Indian country as far as Sandusky without encountering many obstacles, and, perhaps, fighting hard battles; so, calculating all the chances, he thought fit to prepare for the worst—not, however, from any presentiment of disaster, as has so often been alleged, but simply from the dictates of prudence.

On the 14th of May, Crawford and his wife, in consideration of love and affection and five shillings, conveyed to his son-in-law William Harrison, sixty-eight acres of land on the Youghiogheny river, adjoining where the latter then lived. The deed was acknowledged the same day, before Providence Mountz, Esq. Appended to it was a curious memorandum, in imitation of the old English feudal feoffment, "that, on the day of the date thereof, full and peaceable possession of said land being taken and had by said Crawford, the same was by him, then and there, in due form by turf and twig, delivered to said Harrison, and the five shillings thereupon paid."[24]

Two days afterward, Crawford made his will. It was witnessed by Thomas Gist, John Euler, Mary Wright, and Nancy McKee. In it were several bequests. To his wife, he gave the land whereon they then lived, during her natural life. He also gave her "one negro man, named Dick, and one mulatto man, Daniel,"—the two to be hers during her natural life; after her decease, to descend to his son John. All his personal property was bequeathed to his wife for life. To his son, he gave five hundred acres of land down the Ohio. He also bequeathed him the reversion of his home estate, to descend to his grandson William. He made bequests of four hundred acres of land, down the Ohio, to each of his other grandsons, Moses and Richard, children of John Crawford.

To his granddaughter Anne, daughter of Effie and William McCormick, he bequeathed a like amount of land. After making bequests to Anne Connell and to her four children—William, James, Nancy, and Polly—he concluded his gifts in this language: "And my will is, that after my accounts are adjusted and settled, and

---

[24] From the printed sheets of a work entitled, "*The Monongahela of Old.* By *James Veech.* The book has not been published.

all my just debts and legacies and bequests paid, that all and singular my estate, real and personal, of every kind whatsoever,—except a mulatto boy named Martin, which I give to my son, John Crawford, and a mulatto girl, named Betty, which is to continue with my wife Hanna,—be equally divided between my three children, viz: John Crawford, Effie McCormick, and Sarah Harrison."[25]

On Saturday morning, the 18th day of May, 1782, Crawford, having completed all his arrangements, prepared to take leave of his relatives and friends, who gathered around him. His son John, his son-in-law William Harrison, and his nephew William Crawford—a son of Valentine Crawford—had already gone on with the volunteers, who had assembled in the neighborhood. Bidding adieu to his near and dear ones, he mounted his horse for the journey,—intending to go by the way of Pittsburg. His wife accompanied him to the other side of the river, parting with her husband in tears and with gloomy forebodings.

Crawford had a long interview with General Irvine at Fort Pitt. The latter gave his opinions and advice freely. The particulars concerning the order of marching were discussed and agreed upon. Crawford pressed the commander for some officers to accompany him. Two only, Knight and Rose, were spared, as already

---

[25] Crawford's will is of record in Westmoreland county. It was proved September 10, 1782, and recorded December 29, 1819.

mentioned. On the 21st, Irvine wrote Washington: "I have taken some pains to get Colonel Crawford appointed to command, and hope he will be."[26] He left me yesterday, on his way down to the place of rendezvous. He does not wish to go with a smaller number than four hundred; whether this number will assemble I can not say."[27] Crawford, upon his arrival at Mingo Bottom, aided the troops in crossing the river, and in getting ready for the march—when, as before narrated, on the afternoon of Friday, the 24th of May, he was chosen by the volunteers their commander-in-chief.

"Of his election," afterward wrote Irvine, "I was informed by the county lieutenants west of the Allegheny mountains, both of Virginia and Pennsylvania, not only by verbal communication of some of them, but by written report of all."

NOTE.—In the preparation of this chapter, I have had occasion to consult a memoir of Crawford, written by Alfred T. Goodman, late secretary of the Western Reserve Historical Society, and published, in 1871, in the *Crawford County* (O.) *Forum*. I had previously been aided by the writer, in my investigations. It is a gratification to make

---

[26] Irvine had the best of reasons for desiring the election of Crawford. He was a regular army officer—on the Continental establishment of the Virginia line, and well versed in Indian modes of warfare,—as we have already seen. Besides, at this time, no man in the Western Department was more popular than he.

[27] *Sparks' Corr. Amer. Rev.*, vol. iii, p. 509.

public acknowledgment of his advice and assistance; but he who proffered them, is now

———" In the cold ground,
Where his pale form was laid, with many tears!"

The earliest published memoir of Crawford is to be found in the Knight and Slover pamphlet. It was written by Hugh H. Brackenridge, in July, 1782. It is exceedingly brief. Up to the time of his taking command of the expedition against Sandusky, all the events of his life, as given, are in these words:

"Colonel Crawford was about fifty years of age, and had been an old warrior against the savages. He distinguished himself early as a volunteer in the last war, and was taken notice of by Colonel (now General) Washington, who procured for him the commission of ensign. As a partisan, he showed himself very active, and was greatly successful. He took several Indian towns, and did great service in scouting, patrolling, and defending the frontiers. At the commencement of this war, he raised a regiment in the back country by his own exertions. He had the commission of colonel in the Continental army, and acted bravely, on several occasions, in the years 1776, 1777, and at other times. He held his commission at the time he took command in the aforesaid expedition against the Indians."

CHAPTER VI.

SKETCHES OF THE OFFICERS UNDER CRAWFORD.

DAVID WILLIAMSON was a patriot—in one thing at least: he loved his country more than office. He was willing to make every sacrifice for the public good. However mortifying his defeat for the chief command of the expedition must have been to his feelings, he cheerfully submitted. "I can not but give Col: Williamson the utmost credit," said John Rose, in his letter to Irvine, written immediately after the election at Mingo Bottom, "for his exhorting the whole to be unanimous after the election had been made known, and cheerfully submitting to be the second in command. I think, if it had been otherwise, Crawford would have pushed home, and very likely we should have dispersed; which would have been likewise the case if Williamson had not behaved with so much prudence."[1]

---

[1] It has been extensively circulated that Crawford accepted the office of commander of the expedition with apparent reluctance (*Doddridge*, 269; *De Hass*, 279, etc.); but Rose settles that question. His reluctance was not in taking command of the troops after the election, but, as we have already seen, in joining the expedition. He left his home with the full understanding that he was to lead the volunteers. Irvine, it is true, allowed the troops to choose their own commander; but he was not backward in letting it be known that *he* desired the election of Crawford. Irvine to Washington, May 21, 1782 (*Sparks' Corr. Amer. Rev.*, vol. iii, p. 509); same to Lyon, November 10, 1799—MS. letter.

How much Williamson's complicity in the affair at the Muskingum had to do with his defeat, is not now known. That he would be a candidate for the leadership, was evident to Irvine; for, in the letter of Marshal to the latter, of the 4th of April, the writer, it will be remembered, said that Williamson proposed "to carry an expedition against Sandusky." The peculiar language of Pentecost to Moore, on the 8th, while at Fort Pitt investigating the slaughter at Gnadenhütten, and the exertions of Irvine in favor of Crawford, who was not in the Muskingum expedition, and who earnestly denounced the affair, clearly indicate that he was, to a certain extent, under the ban of public opinion in the Western Department, on account of the deplorable transactions of his men at the Moravian Indian villages.

In speaking of Williamson, in connection with the lamentable occurrences just referred to, Doddridge (*Notes*, 262, 263) says: "In justice to the memory of Col. Williamson, I have to say that, although at that time very young, I was personally acquainted with him, and from my recollection of his conversation, I say, with confidence, that he was a brave man, but not cruel. He would meet an enemy in battle, and fight like a soldier, but not murder a prisoner." Certain it is, no one seemed more ready to make personal sacrifices for the protection of the country than he. As one of the field majors to rank second in command of the expedition, he received the entire vote of the volunteers.

THOMAS GADDIS, elected a field major, and third in command of the expedition, was a resident of Westmoreland county, his home being in that part which, in 1783, became Fayette—about three miles south of Uniontown. His competitor was James Marshal, lieutenant of Washington county, "who was," wrote Rose to Irvine, "within three or four votes of being the third commander." "I am very sorry," says the writer, "Col. Marshal does not march with us." He adds: "I think him very popular; as much so as Col. Williamson." Gaddis was well known to many of the volunteers as a good citizen and brave soldier. He was a field officer of the militia of Westmoreland county, at the time of his volunteering for the campaign against Sandusky. In his after-life he maintained his prominence in county affairs, filling honorable offices, civil and military; and was not undistinguished in the "Whisky Insurrection."

JOHN MCCLELLAND, elected field major and fourth in rank in the campaign, was also a resident of Westmoreland county, and of that part which soon became Fayette. He was not a novice in military affairs, having been a lieutenant-colonel of the Fourth battalion of militia of his county, to which office he was elected on 3d of January, 1778. He was a brave and efficient officer, and much respected as a citizen. His election as one of the general officers of the expedition, at Mingo Bottom, was an evidence of the confidence reposed in him by the volunteers, with many of whom he was personally acquainted.

MAJOR BRINTON, a field major elect, and fifth in command of the expedition, was a man of much spirit— a soldier, brave and active. Judging of his merits by his subsequent conduct, he unquestionably commanded the esteem as well as the confidence of the volunteers. His coolness and bravery in the face of imminent danger, were long after alluded to by his surviving comrades, in terms of the highest commendation.

DANIEL LEET, elected brigade-major, was a resident of Washington county. He was personally known to most of the volunteers as a brave soldier and accomplished gentleman. He was an old resident of the West—a surveyor; having been employed by Washington to survey and locate lands for him, at an early day, in Virginia and Kentucky. In 1776 he was surveyor of the county of Augusta, Virginia—his commission having been granted by the College of William and Mary. In 1778 he was doing military duty as a militia officer—adjutant—under General McIntosh, at Fort Laurens. On the 2d of April, 1781, he was appointed sub-lieutenant of Washington county, under James Marshal, by the Supreme Executive Council of Pennsylvania. In the original act establishing Washington county, passed the 28th of March, 1781, Leet was named one of the commissioners to purchase grounds for a court-house. On the 23d of August of the same year, he was appointed and commissioned one of the justices of the peace for his county. On the 30th of March, 1782, he resigned the office of sub-lieutenant.

DR. JOHN KNIGHT, an officer in the army under Irvine, and spared by the latter to the expedition, was, as previously mentioned, appointed its surgeon. He was a resident of Westmoreland county—of that part which became Fayette, north of the Youghiogheny. He enlisted in 1776, as a private in the Thirteenth Virginia regiment—afterward known as the Ninth, and before the close of the war, as the Seventh. He was soon after appointed sergeant, Colonel Crawford being at that time in command of the regiment. On the 9th of August, 1778, he was appointed surgeon's mate by Dr. McKenzie, the principal surgeon at Pittsburg for the West. The Virginia regiment to which he belonged was then known as the Ninth. At the time of the organization of the expedition against Sandusky, the regiment was known as the Seventh Virginia, and was commanded by Colonel Gibson. As there had been no surgeon named for the Sandusky expedition, Colonel Crawford, while at Fort Pitt, on his way to Mingo Bottom, solicited Dr. Knight to accompany him—with whom he was well acquainted. The latter expressed a willingness to go; and General Irvine finally consented to his going, provided Colonel Gibson did not object.

The permission of the latter having been obtained,[2] the doctor left Pittsburg on Tuesday, the 21st, and arrived at Mingo Bottom the next day, about one in the afternoon.

John Slover, one of the guides to the expedition, was also a resident of Westmoreland county. He was a Virginian by birth, and peculiarly fitted for the position. He had been taken captive by the Miami Indians when only eight years of age, spending the next six years of his life with that tribe, in what is now Southwestern Ohio. The circumstances attending his capture were barbarous and cruel. His father's residence was then on New river, Virginia. The Indians came to his father's house during his absence, while the children, consisting of John, his brother Abraham, and two sisters, were a short distance away, playing. On discovering the savages, John and the two sisters ran to the house; but Abraham made his escape, although pursued some distance by two Indians. The mother and three children were taken to the woods, the house plundered, and then burned.

Taking their prisoners and all they could carry of the plunder, the savages began their march for their distant homes. They had proceeded, however, but a short distance, when the father returned home. Seeing the devastation around—his family all gone—

---

[2] No better evidence is needed that Col. Gibson approved of the expedition.

he was but too well assured it was the work of the Indians. In his great distress, he lost his presence of mind, calling loudly the names of his family. The Indians hearing him, halted, and sent back two of their number. The father was soon killed. In a short time the two savages returned to their party with the horse their victim had been riding. The mother knew her husband had been killed.

On the journey of the Indians to their towns, they gave their prisoners but little to eat. Through fatigue and want of food the two sisters died in the wilderness. Slover's mother was afterward exchanged, and returned home, where she died soon after. Slover, after he had been with the *Miamis* six years, was sold to a Delaware Indian, who put him into the hands of a white man—a trader. By the latter he was taken to the Shawanese upon the Scioto river, where he remained six years longer. He was now twenty years of age. In the autumn of 1773, he came with the Shawanese to Fort Pitt, to a treaty of that year. Meeting with some of his relatives, he was persuaded, after much reluctance, to relinquish the life of a savage—though he had scarcely known any other—for the refinements of civilization.

At the commencement of the Revolution, Slover enlisted as a soldier in the Continental army, and served fifteen months, when he was discharged. He afterward married, and settled in Westmoreland county.

His long residence with the Indians in the wilderness beyond the Ohio, gave him an excellent knowledge of the country now about to be invaded by the volunteers under Crawford. Especially was he familiar with the country around the head-waters of Sandusky river and the Miami. His Indian name was Mannucothe.

JONATHAN ZANE, the other pilot engaged for the campaign, was a resident of Wheeling. He was born in Berkeley county, Virginia. . He accompanied his brother, Ebenezer Zane, to the West in 1769, when they explored the surrounding country, and located the town of Wheeling. He also made explorations in the summer and fall of 1771, in company with Silas Zane, up and down the Ohio—soon becoming familiar not only with the region east of that river, but also the wilderness beyond. He was, perhaps, the most experienced hunter of his day, in the frontier country. It would have been difficult to find a man of greater energy of character—of more determined resolution, or restless activity. He rendered efficient service to the settlers about Wheeling, in the capacity of spy. He was a guide in the Wapatomika campaign of 1774. He was remarkable for earnestness of purpose, an energy and inflexibility of will which often manifested itself in a way truly astonishing. Few men shared more of the confidence or of the respect of his fellow-men than Jonathan Zane.

Zane was one of the best marksmen upon the border. He prided himself particularly upon his skill in shooting. He was once returning home from hunting his horses, when, passing through some high weeds near the bank of the river at a spot within the present city of Wheeling, not far from his house, he saw five Indians jump into the stream and swim for the island in the Ohio, opposite the place. Having his rifle with him, he rapidly took aim at one of the savages—fired, and the Indian sunk. Loading and firing in quick succession, three more were killed before reaching the opposite bank. The fifth and last one, seeing the fate of his companions, concealed himself behind a "sawyer," near the shore of the island, hoping thus to escape the deadly aim of the white man. After several ineffectual attempts to dislodge him, the effort was about to be given up, when Zane noticed a small portion of his body protruding below the log. Drawing a fine sight on his rifle, it was discharged, and the fifth savage floated down the river![3] Zane had piloted many expeditions against the Indians;—in the one under Colonel Daniel Brodhead, up the Allegheny, in 1779, he was severely wounded.[4]

JOHN ROSE, an officer of the regular army, serving under General Irvine at Fort Pitt, as before related, and who, with Dr. Knight, had joined the expedition,

---

[3] *De Hass' His. Ind. Wars W. Va.*, pp. 324, 337.

[4] Dunlevy's Declaration for a Pension, 3d October, 1832.

was, at the time of obtaining from the commandant of that post leave of absence, aid-de-camp to the latter, with the rank of lieutenant. He volunteered for the purpose of acting as aid to whoever should be elected to command the expedition.

Some time in the early part of the struggle of the Colonies for independence, a fine-looking young man, speaking the French language, of prepossessing appearance, pleasing in manners, and, apparently, highly gifted, made his appearance in the cantonments of the American army, soliciting a Continental commission. But, as there was already an undue number of foreign officers, many of them inefficient, his pretensions had to be postponed. He gave his name as John Rose.

The story of Rose was, that, sympathizing with the colonists in their struggle with the mother country, he had left his home in the Old World, against the urgent entreaties of his friends, made his way to Baltimore, where he had arrived destitute of money, and where he had taken a brief course of surgery under Dr. Wisendorf, a German physician, whose language he spoke.

The general opinion was, that he was as certainly *a man of rank* as that he was possessed of high attainments and a finished education. But, on this point, the stranger maintained the most profound silence. His exemplary conduct and pleasing carriage soon won the esteem of the army, and he finally received an appointment as surgeon in Colonel William Irvine's regiment — the Seventh Pennsylvania — then commanded by Lieutenant-Colonel Hartley, having previously, it seems, done duty as a surgeon's mate in one of the hospitals.

Rose became the warm personal friend of Irvine, who had again joined the army at the expiration of his parole, and had been placed in command of the Second Pennsylvania brigade, and, subsequently, as has already been stated, made a brigadier-general. At length, a feeling of jealously toward the young foreigner, arose on the part of some of the American officers—a feeling that had come to be very common toward most of those not "to the manor born." He, therefore, left his regiment, in 1780, and volunteered as a surgeon in the navy of the United States, only to be taken prisoner by the British, and carried, the same year, to New York.[5]

---

[5] From New York, Rose addressed a letter to Irvine, which is here given entire. The original, which is before me, is in a beautiful flowing hand; the punctuation and spelling are strictly preserved. It shows the mastery he had acquired over the English language:

"NEW YORK, *Nov. 6th*, 1780.

"SIR: Since my last Letter to you from Philadelphia, the scene is wonderfully changed. My greatest Expectations are annilated, and I am inclosed by the impenetrable Walls of a Prevost. If I do but continue in health, I shall merrily dance through the various scenes of this *Tragie comedie,* in hopes to accomplish my latest engagements which shall always remain sacred on my Side. I am told, a General exchange

Upon being exchanged, the following year, he returned to Irvine's command, and was, it seems, made ensign of a company in one of the regiments of the Second Pennsylvania brigade. On the 8th of July, 1781, Irvine appointed him his aid, with the rank of lieutenant.[6] He was received into the family of his commander, where he was a great favorite. As he was a young man of polished manners, he made himself exceedingly agreeable to the household. It is surmised that Irvine had, all the time, a suspicion that he was entertaining "an angel in disguise." His name—John Rose—was certainly a strange one for a foreigner. The family were outwardly convinced that his story was a true one; inwardly, they were skeptical!

Rose came with Irvine to Pittsburg, upon the latter assuming command, at Fort Pitt, of the Western Department, where he soon made himself very popular

---

is to take place immediately; but should this not be the case, the thoughts of an approaching Winter, being destitute of every necessary to render Life tolerable, make me wish for a change in my present situation. Assisted by Your influence in Philadelphia, as I was taken as surgeon in the ship Revenge, I make no doubt to see my expectations shortly realized.

"I am your most obedient, humble servant,
"JOHN ROSE."

[6] "Ensign John Rose, entitled to a lieutenancy, is appointed aid-de-camp to Brigadier-General Irvine, and to be respected as such."—*Irvine's Order-Book*, July 8. 1781: MS.

with the country people. In consenting to spare his favorite aid-de-camp to the expedition against Sandusky, General Irvine showed clearly the interest he had in the success of the enterprise. "Crawford pressed me for some officers," wrote Irvine to Washington, in his letter of the 21st of May; "I have sent with him Lieutenant Rose, my aid-de-camp, a very vigilant, active, brave young gentleman, well acquainted with service; and a surgeon. These two are all I could venture to spare."[7]

The arrival of Rose at Mingo Bottom was at six o'clock in the afternoon of Wednesday the 22d of May. "The Mingo Bottom," wrote the gallant soldier to his commander, at Fort Pitt, two days after, "is not a very long day's journey from Pittsburg; notwithstanding I did not arrive here until the next day, late in the afternoon. I found every body crossing the Ohio with the utmost expedition; and I myself pushed over immediately after my arrival." "My fears," continued Rose, "that the present expedition would miscarry, have been dispelled this very moment only."[8] He also added: "Major Pollock has furnished Dr. Knight and myself forty-five pounds of bacon. I can not persuade him to take any pay for it but a mere

---

[7] *Sparks' Corr. Amer. Rev.*, iii, 509.
[8] Rose to Irvine, 24th May, 1782.

receipt. I do not understand upon what principles they furnish these articles."

The presence of Rose at Mingo Bottom gave much satisfaction to such of the volunteers as had previously made his acquaintance at Fort Pitt; yet most of the army knew as little of his splendid genius as of his real history. In his letter to Irvine, just mentioned, he wrote: "My presence caused, seemingly, uneasiness. It was surmised I had been sent to take command. An open declaration of mine, at a meeting of the officers, that I did not intend to take upon myself any command of any kind whatsoever, but to act as an aid-de-camp to the commanding officer, seemed to satisfy every one, and all goes on charmingly." "I must beg the favor of you," said Rose, in conclusion, "to receive my half-boots from Patrick Leonard, and one pair of shoes, as I am already almost barefooted."

The volunteers were captivated by the fine appearance of Rose—by his urbanity and warm-heartedness. "Mr. Rose, your aid-de-camp," wrote Marshal[9] to Irvine, on the 29th, "was very hearty when I left him at Mingo Bottom. His services, on this occasion, have endeared

---

[9] An article in *The Galaxy*, for February, 1867, written by William L. Stone, giving a sketch of Rose, assigns the writing of this letter to "Lieutenant Washington Custis!" and says it was written to Irvine "at the close of the expedition." These blunders are unaccountable, as the original letter was then in the possession of Mr. Stone.

you much to the people of this county, and given general satisfaction to the men on the expedition."[10]

NOTE.—It had been my intention to devote a portion of this chapter to sketches of the different captains elected; but, after research, I have only obtained the names of eleven, which have already been given. No account of these, worthy of being recorded, has come into my possession, except a brief mention of *Craig Ritche*, who was born in Glasgow, December 29, 1758. He came to America in 1772. At the age of thirty he married Miss Mary Price. He early evinced extraordinary talents for business—becoming a successful merchant in Canonsburg, Washington county. His energy of character, business habits, integrity of principle, and general intelligence, secured to him a widely extended reputation. He served several years in the legislature. During the "Whisky Insurrection" he was on the side of law and order. He enjoyed the confidence and friendship of George Washington, acting as the agent of the latter, so far as Washington county was concerned, in the management of his landed interest. For honesty, goodness, and charity, Mr. Ritchie had no superior in the western country. He died June 13, 1833.

---

[10] This letter concludes as follows: "A report prevails in the country that Britain has acknowledged our independence. I could wish to be informed of the truth of this report. I have been asked, by a Presbyterian minister and some of his people, to request you to spare one gallon of wine, for the use of a sacrament. If it is in your power to supply them with this article, I make no doubt you will do it, as it can not be obtained in any other place in this country."

CHAPTER VII.

MARCH OF THE ARMY FROM MINGO BOTTOM TO SANDUSKY. 25TH MAY—4TH JUNE, 1782.

EARLY on the morning of Saturday, the 25th of May, 1782, the army under Crawford, in four columns, began its march from Mingo Bottom, in the straightest direction, through the woods, for Sandusky, distant one hundred and fifty miles. "A perfect harmony existed among officers and men, and all were in high spirits."[1] The route lay through what is now the counties of Jefferson, Harrison, Tuscarawas, Holmes, Ashland, Richland, and Crawford—nearly to the center of Wyandot county, Ohio. A direct course would have led near the present towns of New Philadelphia, Millersburg, Loudonville, and Galion; but, as will hereafter be seen, this straight line was not followed. The whole distance, except about thirty miles at the end of the route, was through an unbroken forest.

The only indication of civilization—and that a very sad one—in all the region to be traversed, was the wasted missionary establishments in the valley of the Muskingum. Except in the open country just before

---

[1] Marshal to Irvine, 29th May, 1782 : Original letter.

reaching Sandusky, and along the immediate margins of the streams, the surface is hilly. The principal impediments to a rapid march were the hills, swamps, and tangled growth of the forests. The Muskingum, Killbuck, forks of Mohican, and Sandusky were the streams to be crossed; all of which, at this season of the year, and especially in the spring of 1782, were fordable without difficulty. It had been estimated by Irvine that the distance could be made in seven days, and that one hundred and seventy-five miles would have to be traveled.

As the cavalcade moved up over the bluff, an almost due west course was taken, striking at once into the wilderness, now deepening and darkening around it. The army progressed rapidly at first, moving along the north side of Cross creek, which had already received the name it still bears. After leaving what is now Steubenville township, it passed through the present townships of Cross Creek and Wayne, to the western boundary of Jefferson county, as at present defined; crossing thence into what is now Harrison county, in German township; thence across the summit to the spot where the town of Jefferson now stands.

From this point, a straight course would have led them at no great distance into what is now Carroll county. But their horses had tired under their heavy loads in the hills and swamps. This obliged them to incline to the southward toward the wasted Moravian towns, into a more level country, though more frequented by hunters and warriors.[2] This alternative was accepted by Crawford with great reluctance, as his policy was to avoid Indian trails and the region infested by the enemy, relying for success, as already stated, upon effecting a surprise. Otherwise, he would have followed "Williamson's trail" from Mingo Bottom to the Muskingum, which led along a considerable distance south, near where Smithfield, in Jefferson, and Cadiz, in Harrison county, now stand,—through a region not so difficult to be traversed, but on the line of Indian traces between that river and the Ohio.

From the moment of starting, every precaution was taken against surprises or ambuscades, and this, too, although, as yet, not an Indian had been seen. The wily nature of the savage was too well understood by the commander of the expedition, to allow of any confidence of security, because no foe had been discovered. Unceasing vigilance was the watchword. Captain John Biggs' company, its lieutenant being young William Crawford, nephew of the commander, took the advance, on the march, led by the two pilots, Slover and Zane. "John Rodgers stated to me," writes Robert A. Sherrard, "that the company he belonged to, in which were

---

[2] Rose to Irvine, 13th June, 1782. The original letter is on file in the State Department, Washington. I am indebted to the courtesy of Hon. John Sherman for a copy of it, and for other valuable MS. documents.

James Paull, Daniel Canon, Alexander Carson, my father (John Sherrard), and others, marched all the way as the first company."[3]

Nothing worthy of note transpired until Monday night, the 27th, while at their third encampment. Here a few of the men lost their horses, which were hunted for the next morning, without success. It was thought best by Crawford that these men should return home, as their continuing with the army, unable, as they would be, to carry little besides their arms, would only prove a source of embarrassment. Reluctantly, therefore, they retraced their steps to Mingo Bottom.

On Tuesday, the fourth day of the march, the army reached the Muskingum, some distance below the upper Moravian village, known as New Schönbrunn, located on the west bank of the river, one and a quarter miles south of the site of the present town of New Philadelphia, about a quarter of a mile from Lockport, in Goshen township, Tuscarawas county. Gnadenhütten, the middle village, was situated on the east side of the Muskingum, further down the river, in what is now Clay township, lying in the outskirts of the present town of Gnadenhütten. Salem, the lower village, was located on the western bank of the stream,

---

[3] Notes to the author, 1872. Several of the incidents of the campaign communicated by Mr. Sherrard, given hereafter, have already been published.

one and a half miles southwest of the present town of Port Washington, in Salem township.

Crossing the Muskingum in the afternoon, and marching up the western side of the stream until they reached the upper village of the Christian Indians, they made their fourth encampment among its ruins. Only sixty miles had been made in the four days' travel—an average of but fifteen miles a day. This was a discouraging prospect to Crawford; however, it was believed that better time could be made on the balance of the route, as the country would be less hilly and the loads upon the horses less burdensome.

The charred remains of New Schönbrunn, where the army was encamped, presented a sad spectacle. All around was silence and desolation. The village had been built during the summer of 1779, on a broad and fruitful bottom of the river, skirted by a plateau that extended to the hills. It was occupied by the Christian Indians, for the first time, in December of that year. The town was sacked, and its inhabitants carried off by the British and their allies, as before related, in September, 1781, to the banks of the Sandusky. The houses were burned, as were those of the other villages, by Williamson's men on their last visit to the valley.[4]

---

[4] On the 11th of November, 1798, David Zeisberger, one of the missionaries, returned to New Schönbrunn, and found nothing to indicate the site of the once happy village, save here and there a post of what had been the garden fences of the inhabitants. A great many

The killing of the men, women, and children, as already mentioned, occurred at the middle village—Gnadenhütten.

While the army lay encamped at this point, the horses were plentifully fed in the fields upon corn from the stalks, which was found still ungathered and in abundance—the unharvested crop of the previous year! During the evening, Major Brinton and Captain Bean went some distance from camp to reconnoiter. When but a quarter of a mile away they espied two savages, upon whom they immediately fired, but without effect.[5] These were the first hostile shots fired at the foe. It was supposed, by Crawford, that the army had not be-

---

Indian implements and vessels lay scattered on the ground. The place was then called *Tuppakin*, or, by some, *Opakin*, or the *Upper Moravian Town*. The whole region was overgrown with bushes and rank weeds.—*Schweinitz's Zeisberger*, p. 655, note.

[5] *Knight's Narr.*, p. 5. Concerning this affair, Doddridge, in his *Notes*, p. 270, says: "As soon as the news of the discovery of Indians had reached the camp, more than one-half the men rushed out without command, and in the most tumultuous manner, to see what happened." Upon what authority this statement is made does not appear. It certainly is wholly unworthy of credit. "From that time," adds Doddridge, "Colonel Crawford felt a presentiment of the defeat which followed." This adds much to its improbability; for, surely, had he such a presentiment it would have been kept in his own breast. Schweinitz (*Zeisberger*, p. 565), in copying this account from Doddridge, makes it still more absurd: "A glimpse of two Indian scouts, watching their movements, threw them into such confusion that dark forebodings filled the mind of their leader!"

fore been discovered by the enemy. Fallacious belief! Secrecy being now out of the question—as the two Indians had made their escape—it only remained for Crawford to press forward, with all practicable dispatch, to afford the enemy as little time as possible for defensive preparations. The march was continued, therefore, on the morning of the 29th, rapidly, but with greater precaution than had previously been observed. The guides, taking a northwest course through the wilderness from the Muskingum, brought the army to the Killbuck, some distance above the present town of Millersburg, county-seat of Holmes county. "Thence," says Dunlevy, "we marched up the Killbuck."[6] At not a great distance the army reached a large spring, known at the present time as Butler's or Jones' Spring, near the line of Wayne county, ten miles south of Wooster, where, on the evening of Thursday, May 30th, the volunteers encamped.

At this spring one of the men died and was buried. His name was cut on the bark of a tree close by his grave.

From this point, the army moved westward, along the north side of what is known as Odell's lake—passing "between two small lakes, where they found the heads of two large fish, freshly caught, lying on the ground, which awakened a suspicion that Indians were

---

[6] Dunlevy's application for a pension.

near."[7] Thence they passed near the spot where was afterward the Indian village of Greentown,[8] in what is now Ashland county. From this point they struck across to the Rocky Fork of the Mohican, up which stream they traveled until a spring was reached, near where the city of Mansfield now stands, in Richland county; thence a little north of west, to a fine spring five miles farther on, in what is now Springfield township—a place now known as Spring Mills, on the line of the Pittsburg, Fort Wayne and Chicago Railroad, eight miles east of the town of Crestline, in Crawford county—where, on the evening of the 1st day of June, the army halted and encamped for the night.

The army had now reached, as was supposed, the heads of streams flowing north into Lake Erie.[9] This, however, was an error; these, in reality, flowed into the Mohican. A short distance traveled on the 2d of June, brought the cavalcade to other small streams having a northern trend, which were, in fact, affluents of the Sandusky. The army crossed into what is

[7] *Philip Smith's Recollections of Crawford's Expedition.* Smith describes this incident with particularity.

[8] Greentown was situated on section 18, township 20 north, of range 16 west, in the present township of Green.—*Hough and Bourne's Map of Ohio*, 1815. It seems that a tradition has long prevailed in this region, that the route taken by Crawford was through Ashland county, but nothing definite could be traced from it.—*Knapp's Hist. Ashland County*, p. 14.

[9] Declaration for a pension: Dunlevy. The same is mentioned in his MS. notes of the campaign.

now Crawford county,[10] at one o'clock in the afternoon, and about an hour after reached the Sandusky river at a point immediately east of what is now the village of Leesville, at the mouth of a small creek called Allen's run, when a halt was called, and the volunteers took a half-hour's rest on the banks of the stream for which they had been, for some time, very anxiously looking.

The Sandusky river, upon the banks of which Crawford was now resting his army, rises in what is known

---

[10] On the 20th day of February, 1820, the General Assembly of Ohio passed an act for the "erection of certain counties" in the northwestern portion of the State, out of a vast tract of several millions of acres which had before been acquired by treaty from the Indians. This extensive area was known as the *New Purchase*. Its western and northern boundaries were the same as that of the State. It was bounded on the east by a line drawn from a point a little east of the site of the present town of Cardington, Morrow county, north to Lake Erie. Its southern boundary, beginning at the same point, stretched away, in a southwesterly direction, to the western limits of the State. Fourteen counties were constituted by *name* and *boundary*, out of most of this extensive territory, by the act of 1820, each containing a certain number of townships (and, in some cases, parts of townships), as surveyed and platted by the United States. One of these counties, to contain townships 1, 2, and 3 south, in ranges 13, 14, 15, 16, and 17 east, and all the land east of these townships, up to what was then the western limits of Richland county, was very appropriately—as we shall hereafter see—named CRAWFORD. Crawford county, Pennsylvania, also named in honor of the commander of the Sandusky expedition, was taken from Allegheny county, by act of the legislature of that State, of the 12th of March, 1800.

as the "Palmer Spring," in Springfield township, Richland county. Several small creeks flow into the main stream before the latter reaches Leesville, in Crawford county: these are what may be termed the heads of the Sandusky. The general course of the river in Crawford county is southwest. It passes into Wyandot county a little over two miles north of the southeast corner, sweeping round to the northward soon after, and following generally a northerly direction through that county. It pursues thence the same general course through Seneca and Sandusky counties, falling into the head of Sandusky Bay about eighty miles, by the course of the stream, from its source.

The Sandusky is a rapid and shallow river, having an average descent of about six feet to the mile throughout its course. Its waters are usually low in the summer, with an occasional flood to fill its banks. During the rest of the year a considerable addition is seen in its size. In 1821, according to the observations of William Spicer, a white man captured when young by the Indians, and who then had lived forty years upon its banks, the water rose higher than at any previous time within his recollection. In January, 1847, it rose considerably above the mark of 1821. Since then the waters have been still higher; the sudden overflows being the result of the clearing up of the country watered by the stream. In descending the river, the principal tributaries upon the right hand, in Crawford and Wyandot counties, are the Broken Sword and Sycamore; upon the left, the Little Sandusky and the Tymochtee.

Long before a white man lived upon the soil of Ohio, the Sandusky was a water-route of travel, from Canada to the Mississippi, of the early French travelers. These ascended the stream to the mouth of the Little Sandusky; thence up that creek four or five miles to a portage; thence across the portage—a fine road of about a quarter of a league—to the Little Scioto; thence down that stream to the Scioto proper, a tributary of the Ohio. "Ascending the Sandusky," writes William Walker,[11] "to the mouth of the west branch known as the Little Sandusky, with a bark or light wooden canoe, you could, in a good stage of water, ascend that tributary four or five miles further. Thence east, across to the Little Sciota, is a distance of about four miles. This was the portage." "This place," writes Col. James Smith, who was here in 1757, "is in the plains between a creek that empties into Sandusky and one that runs into Sciota; and at the time of high water, or in the spring season, there is but about one-half mile of portage, and that very level, and clear of rocks, timber, or stones."[12] Even before the French

---

[11] Communicated to the author, 1872.

[12] *An Account of the Remarkable Occurrences in the Life and Travels of Col. James Smith.* Lexington (Ky.): 1799, p. 86. There is an excellent reprint of this work by Robert Clarke & Co., Cincinnati, 1870; with an Appendix by William M. Darlington, of Pittsburgh, contain-

had any settlements in the valley of the St. Lawrence or the Mississippi; or before that most indomitable adventurer and explorer, La Salle—the first of Europeans to set foot upon any portion of the territory now constituting the State of Ohio, and the first of civilized men to discover the river, which washes its southern boundary—spread the first sail upon Lake Erie; the northern Indians made the Sandusky and Scioto their route of travel in their predatory wars upon southern tribes.

The name *Sandusky* is the *Sandusquet* of the old French traders and voyagers; the *Sah-un-dus-kee*, "clear water," or *San-doos-tee*, "at the cold water," of the Wyandots; from the *clear, cold water* of the springs near the south shore of Sandusky Bay; or, it may have been derived from *Sa-undustee*—"water within water-pools," also a Wyandot word. "The latter signification is peculiarly applicable to Sandusky Bay and the extensive marshes on its borders, which are intersected, in many directions, by pools and channels of open water."

We left Crawford and his army enjoying a short rest just at the spot where they first came upon the Sandusky, in what is now Jefferson township, three miles west of the present village of Crestline, Crawford

---

ing much valuable information. I have been aided frequently by Mr. Darlington in my investigations.

county. Nothing material had transpired during the march from the Muskingum. Not an Indian had been seen. The army had traveled in the last five days about eighty-five miles. They were now fairly in the enemy's country, distant due east from the point of destination only twenty-five miles. They had, however, reached the river a little too far south to strike the Wyandot trace, which led on directly west to their town. Slover announced to the commander that the open country—the Sandusky Plains—was but a few miles away, in a southwest direction. Following along the southern margin of the stream until it suddenly swept around to the north, the army then struck off from it through a somewhat broken country for two miles, and encamped a short distance beyond, where the surface was quite level. They were still in what is now Jefferson township, but very near the eastern edge of the Plains.

Early in the morning of the 3d of June, the army emerged from the dark woods, which had so long enshrouded them, into the sunlight of the open country.[13] It was at a point not very far west of a

---

[13] "A trivial incident occurred during the march, which made an unfavorable impression upon the minds of those superstitiously inclined. A fox, by some means, got into the lines, was surrounded by the men, but managed to escape unhurt. 'This,' reasoned the credulous in signs and omens, 'portends a failure; for, if the whole army is unable to kill a fox under such circumstances, what success can be expected against Indians."—*Recollections of Philip Smith.*

small creek flowing south—a tributary of the west branch of the Olentangy, or Whetstone, one of the affluents of the Scioto—in what is now Whetstone township; a memorable spot, as we shall hereafter see.

To most of the volunteers the sight of the Plains was a novel one. The high, coarse grass, the islands of timber, the gradually undulating surface, were all objects of surprise. Birds of a strange plumage flew over them; prairie hens rose before them, sailing away and slowly dropping into the grass, on either hand. Sand-hill cranes blew their shrill pipes, startled by the sudden apparition. Prairie owls, on cumbrous wings, fluttered away in the distance; and the noisy bittern was heard along the streamlets. Wild geese were frightened from their nests; and occasionally a bald or gray eagle soared far above them. Many fox-squirrels were seen; and rattlesnakes also were found to be very numerous.

The Sandusky Plains lie within the counties of Crawford, Marion, and Wyandot, south and west of the Sandusky river, seldom reaching to the bank of the stream, however; although the latter may be said to bound them on the north in Crawford, and on the east in Wyandot county. In the former county their eastern boundary is the Olentangy; in Wyandot, their western boundary is the Tymochtee.[14] On the south

---

[14] *Tymochtee* is a Wyandot word, signifying "*around the plains.*" Skirting *around the Plains*, as does this stream on the west, no name could be more appropriate. The Plains may be bounded, in general

they make a deep curve into Marion county, including a large portion of the northern half of its territory. Their extreme length, east and west, from Whetstone township, in Crawford county, to Tymochtee township, in Wyandot county, is something over forty miles; their greatest breadth, north and south, nearly twenty miles. They have an average elevation above Lake Erie of about three hundred feet.

Although cultivation is rapidly obliterating all traces of the boundary of these natural meadows, so far as indicated by the growth of the forest trees, yet they will ever be traceable by the change in the quality of the soil, which is very marked. Opinions as to the origin of these fertile prairies are speculative. The cause of the absence of forest trees is due, perhaps, to surface peculiarities, the nature of the soil, and the action of fire and water.

These Plains were always a favorite hunting-ground for the Indians. A ring-hunt, in these glades, was rare sport for the savages. "We waited," writes Smith, who participated in one as early as 1757, "until we expected rain was near falling to extinguish the fire, and then we kindled a large circle in the prairie. At this time, or before the bucks began to run, a great number of ·deer lay concealed in the grass, in the day, and moved about in the night; but as the fire burned in

---

terms, on the north by the Sandusky, on the east by the Olentangy, on the south by the Scioto, on the west by the Tymochtee.

toward the center of the circle, the deer fled before the fire: the Indians were scattered also at some distance before the fire, and shot them down every opportunity, which was very frequent, especially as the circle became small. When we came to divide the deer, there were above ten to each hunter, which were all killed in a few hours. The rain did not come on that night to put out the outside circle of the fire, and as the wind arose, it extended through the whole prairie."[15]

The route of the army was through the present townships of Bucyrus and Dallas, in Crawford county—passing a little over three miles south of what is now the town of Bucyrus—county-seat of the county—thence into what is now Antrim township, in Wyandot county. Here the army encamped near the site of the present village of Wyandot, within ten miles of their point of destination.

The next morning—the 4th of June—at seven o'clock, after careful preparations for any emergency, the army began its march, in nearly a northwest direction. After about six miles' travel, the mouth of the Little Sandusky was reached. The spot was a familiar one to Slover. Three Indian trails led off from this point: one southeast, through the Plains, to Owl creek—now the Vernon river— leading thence down the

---

[15] *Smith's Narrative*, p. 85.

Walhonding;[16] one south, up the east side of the Little Sandusky, to the portage; the other southwest, to the Shawanese towns upon the Mad river and the Miami. There was, also, a trace leading north along the east side of the river, in the woods, which was the main trail down the Sandusky.[17]

Crossing the river, Crawford's course was along the east bank of the stream, following the Indian trace in a direction a little west of north, in what is now Pitt township. The army moved with great caution. Not an Indian, however, was seen. Crawford was assured by Slover that the Wyandot town was close at hand. As yet there had not been discovered any indications of an Indian settlement, except a sugar-camp, where maple sugar had evidently been made the previous spring. Passing a bluff bank, the river made a sudden turn, flowing almost directly west. The movement of the army was now rapid. A little farther on, just where the river enters what is now Crane township, suddenly an opening in the woods before them was discernible—and the Wyandot town was reached. To the utter

---

[16] It was along this trail, from the Vernon river to the mouth of the Little Sandusky creek, that the Christian Indians and the Moravian missionaries, were marched by their captors, in September, 1781, to the banks of the Sandusky. This route from the Moravian villages down the Muskingum to the Walhonding, thence up that stream, and the Vernon river, many have heretofore supposed was the one taken by Crawford.

[17] Communicated by William Walker, 1872.

astonishment of the whole army, it was found uninhabited! All was a solitude. The log huts had, apparently, been deserted for some time. Here was a dilemma!

No one in the army had known of the removal of the Wyandots from their town. It was their principal village when Slover was a captive among the Miamis, and had been often visited by him. The volunteers began to suspect there had been a great mistake made; that there was no settlement of the Indians nearer than Lower Sandusky—over forty miles below. Crawford ordered a halt. It was now one o'clock in the afternoon; and the commander desired a brief time for a consideration of the strange aspect of affairs, and for a consultation with his officers.

The volunteers dismounted, and many slaked their thirst from a fine spring not far from the margin of the stream. Their horses were refreshed upon the wild grass growing luxuriantly upon the river bottom. The site of the deserted village was a beautiful one. There was a considerable belt of timber to the westward, skirting the Plains, which were distant nearly a mile. It was, therefore, well protected from the bleak winds of winter and from the autumnal fires which swept the open country. Its location was three miles, in a southeasterly direction, from the site of the present town of Upper Sandusky, county-seat of Wyandot county, on the opposite or east side of the river, and upon its immediate bank.[18]

NOTE 1.—In the preparation of this chapter and some of the following ones, I have had occasion frequently to rely upon the recollection of William Walker, as to the location of many places of note. In speaking of the Wyandot town in a communication before me, he says: "The village was on the east bank of the Sandusky, opposite the upper south rim of what is known as 'Armstrong's Bottom,' where Silas Armstrong, in 1840, built a brick house. When I came to the Sandusky country, in the fall of 1813, this bottom was a fine blue-grass pasture, interspersed with plum thickets; conclusive evidence that it had once been under cultivation." This is a very intelligible direction to the site of the old town, to any one acquainted with the topography of Wyandot county.

Several localities of historic interest were visited by Walker in his younger days, in company with aged and very intelligent Wyandots, who pointed out these (to them very familiar) places. His recollection of the different points, as shown him, is remarkably distinct: a most fortunate circumstance; as, perhaps, no other person now living (1872) would be competent to supply the information so necessary to

---

[18]The exact locality of this, the objective point of the expedition—the earliest Upper Sandusky known to history—"the old Upper Sandusky town" of the Moravian Heckewelder (*Narr. Morav. Miss.* 281)—was upon what is now the east half of the southeast quarter of section nine, in township three south, of range fourteen east, of the government survey. The larger part of this tract is marked on the map of Wyandot county of 1870—"Wm. Dry, 66;" indicating the owner's name and the number of acres it contains. Just where the village stood, is still to be seen (1872) an old Indian orchard. A fine spring, also, is near by.

our narrative, and concerning which all published accounts of the campaign are mostly silent.

NOTE 2.—In Moravian history, Upper Sandusky Old Town—*the* Sandusky of the borderers, but found deserted by Crawford—is a point of interest; as just below it, on the bluff bank of the river, in the woods, the remnant of the Christian Indians, with their teachers, passed the gloomy winter of 1781-2, in some miserable huts, suffering terribly from cold and hunger. The spot was abandoned some time in April, before the arrival of Crawford at the Wyandot Old Town. Now, the specific charge of the Moravian writers is, that it was to destroy the Moravians, who were supposed by Crawford to be still at the spot where they had passed the winter, that brought him and his army to the Sandusky: and that he marched to what had been their winter-quarters, where he found nothing but empty huts. The fiction of the bloody design has already been mentioned. It may now be stated, as will be presently shown, that the army did not pass within half a mile of the deserted huts of the Moravians.

The following is the language of the Moravian Loskiel: "The same gang of murderers who had committed the massacre on the Muskingum, did not give up their bloody design upon the remnant of the Indian congregation, though it was delayed for a season. They marched in May, 1782, to Sandusky, where they found nothing but empty huts."—*His. Miss.*, P. iii, p. 188. (Written in 1784.)

This, from Heckewelder: "I am sorry to be so often obliged to revert to the circumstance of the cruel murder of the Christian Indians on the Muskingum river in 1782, by a gang of banditti, under the command of one Williamson. Not satisfied with this horrid outrage, the same band, not long afterward, marched to Sandusky, where, it seems, they had been informed that the remainder of that unfortunate congregation had fled, in order to perpetrate upon them the same indiscriminate murder. But Providence had so ordered it, that they had before left that place, where they had found that they could not remain in safety, their ministers having been taken from them and carried to Detroit by order of the British government, so that they had been left entirely unprotected. The murderers, on their arrival, were much disappointed in finding nothing but empty huts."—*His. Ind. Nations* (1818), p. 281.

This, again, from the same writer: "The murdering party—for their famous commander, Williamson, was with them again—had taken a straight direction to the Christian Indian village, at Upper Sandusky, but found no 'Moravian' Indians there."—*Narr. Miss.* (1820), p. 337.

This, from Doddridge (*Notes*, 270), who wrote under the shadow of Heckewelder: "Nothing material happened during their [the volunteers'] march until the sixth of June, when their guides conducted them to the site of the Moravian villages, on one of the upper branches of the Sandusky river; but here instead of meeting with Indians and plunder, they met with nothing but vestiges of desolation. The place was covered with high grass, and the remains of a few huts alone announced that the place had been the residence of the people [the Christian Indians] whom they intended to destroy; but who had moved off to Scioto some time before."

This from Schweinitz (*Zeisberger*, p. 565), who follows and intensifies Doddridge: "On the 6th of June, they [Crawford and his army] reached Sandusky, and prepared to surprise the Christian Indians as they had done at Gnadenhütten. But Captives' Town [the winter-quarters of the missionaries and their converts] was deserted, its huts lay in ruins, its gardens and fields were covered with rank grass. The Half King's brutal expulsion of the converts had saved them from a second massacre." As the spot where the Moravians passed the winter was in the woods, and had only been occupied from October, 1781, to April, 1782, it is suggested that "its gardens and fields" could only have existed in the imagination of the writer.

CHAPTER VIII.

PREPARATIONS BY THE ENEMY TO REPEL THE AMERICANS.

EVER since the disaffection of the Delawares, the Sandusky and Scioto rivers had constituted the eastern boundary of the territory inhabited by British Indians. That portion of the western boundary of the country dotted by the settlements of the Americans, extending from Pittsburg down the Ohio to the mouth of Grave creek, a short distance below Wheeling, was under the immediate supervision of the commandant of the Western Department. Between these eastern and western boundaries was a derelict region—the ranging-ground of the belligerents.

The success of Brodhead's expedition against the Delawares upon the Muskingum, followed by the two expeditions under Williamson to the Moravian towns, aroused the British Indians to the utmost activity and watchfulness. They kept their spies all along the Ohio, at all the most public places. Lurking savages carefully watched the movements of the borderers, so that, in the event of the fitting out of another expedition to march into the Indian country, early intelligence of it might be conveyed to the Sandusky and Miami towns. When, therefore, early in May, a general stir was observed in the settlements, and the borderers were seen in agitation, as if preparing for some enterprise, the news was soon carried by swift-footed braves to the Miami and the Sandusky. From day to day, the progress of the movement was observed. From day to day, Indian runners struck swiftly into the wilderness, to carry the tidings to their towns. No sooner had the volunteers began to cross the Ohio and rendezvous at Mingo Bottom, than all doubts vanished in the minds of the savages of a contemplated invasion of their towns and settlements upon one or the other of these rivers. Their villages were soon in a wild state of excitement—from the lower Wyandot town, the present site of Fremont, county-seat of Sandusky county, to the lower Shawanese village, upon the spot where the town of Piqua, in Miami county, is now located. As yet, however, there was an uncertainty as to the particular point aimed at by the Americans.

Skulking savages cautiously, and undiscovered by the volunteers, reconnoitered the camp at Mingo Bottom;[1] but the enemy gained no intelligence of the real

---

[1] The story that no quarter was to be given the Indians was set afloat in this wise: The Moravian Heckewelder, who, when the campaign was undertaken, was at or near Detroit, was afterward *told by Indians* that *it was reported* that the Indian spies who were sent to watch the movements of the Americans, before and after their rendezvous at Mingo Bottom, had, in examining their camp on the west side of the Ohio, after it had been left by the volunteers, found on trees peeled for that purpose, these words, written with coal and other mineral substances: " No quarter to be given an Indian, whether man,

intention of the frontier-men from their spies lurking nightly upon the distant bluffs. Judging from the point chosen for rendezvous, the army undoubtedly would march westward to the burnt Moravian villages; but not until the Muskingum was crossed, could the savages determine where the blow was to fall. The mystery would be solved by observing the course then taken. However, one thing was clearly evident: the Americans were gathering in such numbers as to require a concentration of all the forces the Indians could possibly muster to repel them. Runners, therefore, were immediately dispatched from Sandusky to Detroit. These couriers took boat at Lower Sandusky, sailing down the river into Sandusky Bay, thence into the open waters of Lake Erie. Leaving a group of islands on the right hand, said to have been, at that day, greatly infested with rattlesnakes, they coursed along to the west, crossing Maumee Bay, thence onward to Detroit, with the startling intelligence to De Peyster, the commandant of that post, of the gathering of the

---

woman, or child;" and that papers, with these words written on them, were picked up in their camp.—*Heckewelder's Narr.*, pp. 341, 342. This second-hand Indian report was set down, in 1824, by Rev. Dr. Jos. Doddridge (*Notes*, p. 270) as *an historical fact;* and, as such, has been extensively copied into the current histories of the day! It has thrown wide open the flood-gates for the outpouring of fierce declamation and indignation against the patriotic borderers who marched into the Indian country to insure a better protection of their own.

Americans at Mingo Bottom. They also brought the earnest entreaty of the Wyandots for immediate help.

In the meantime the Americans began their march from the Ohio river in a direction at once disclosing to the enemy the point aimed at. Had the usual route to the Moravian villages—the one taken by Williamson,[2] which followed along near the site of the present town of Cadiz, county-seat of Harrison county—been followed, the mystery, for the reason already explained, would not have been so readily solved. Now, however, there was no longer a question that the army was directing its course for Sandusky—made doubly certain when the troops were observed to cross the Muskingum and march *up* the stream to the site of the upper Moravian town.

The dusky allies of Great Britain, now making such desperate exertions to prepare themselves for the conflict with the Americans, were principally Wyandots, Delawares, and Shawanese. The country inhabited by these Indians had been, at a period not very remote, entirely uninhabited. To the east of it, the region,

---

[2] It is asserted by Doddridge that Williamson's trail *was* the one along which the volunteers marched until their arrival at the upper Moravian village (*Notes*, 269); but, in addition to the testimony of Knight and Rose to the contrary, is the positive assertion of James Paull made to Robert A. Sherrard, in January, 1826, upon his attention being called to the subject. In that conversation, he gave the route indicated by Knight and Rose. Of this fact, I am informed by Mr. Sherrard.

when first discovered, was a desolation. The ill-fated Eries, dwelling upon the southern and eastern borders of the lake which still bears their name, were exterminated, in 1655, by the ferocious Iroquois.

In 1672, the Shawanese had to flee the valley of the Ohio, to escape the fury of the same all-conquering foe; returning again, in 1728, and locating in the unoccupied valley of the Scioto; but after the seven years' war between France and England, ending in 1763, withdrawing, most of them, to the upper waters of the two Miami rivers, where, in towns upon the Mad river, known as the Mac-a-chack, and, upon the parent streams, as Chillicothe and Upper and Lower Piqua, they now resided.

The Wyandots, driven from their ancient seat upon Lake Simcoe, Canada, by their rapacious kindred—the Iroquois—finally, after many wanderings in the Far West, located upon the Detroit and Sandusky rivers, where they arrived about the year 1690, in a country uninhabited; and here they had ever since made their homes.

The Delawares were living upon the river which bears their name when the country first became known to the Europeans; from which they were driven west to the Allegheny; thence, in 1724, to the valley of the Muskingum (an unoccupied region previously), where they resided until 1780; when, upon their disaffection to the Americans, the war faction drew back to the

Scioto and the Sandusky. Here, in 1782, they were in close alliance with the Wyandots and Shawanese.

The Wyandots who settled upon the Sandusky had several out-lying villages, although their favorite abode was upon this river. Their towns were changed from time to time, both in location and name; some of the earliest known having been located upon the shore of Sandusky Bay, which, in reality, is but an enlargement of the Sandusky river. The name Sandusky, as applicable to their principal town upon the river, seems to have come into use after the occupation of the western posts, by the English, in 1760.

Sandusky of 1782 was on the west side of the river, on its immediate bank, five miles below the site of the present town of Upper Sandusky, county-seat of Wyandot county. Its locality was in what is now Crane township, just where the "Kilbourne road" crosses the river.[3] The site of Upper Sandusky of the present day did not become a Wyandot village until many years after.

When the Wyandots were drawn into an alliance with the British, and began their hostile demonstrations

---

[3] The site of the town was upon what is now section three, of township two south, of range fourteen east, of the government survey;—on that part of the section marked on the map of Wyandot county of 1870— "H. H. Smith, 304.10," and "H. Klipfer, 14;" indicating the names of the owners and the number of acres belonging to each.

upon the borders, their head chief, or sachem, resided at Brownstown, a Wyandot village below Detroit, on the river, where the council-fire of the Northwestern Confederacy was kept. The name of this highest dignitary of the Wyandots was Pomoacan, usually called the Half King.

No sooner, however, had the war upon the frontier began to assume a somewhat serious aspect, than the Half King took up his temporary abode at Sandusky, with "Billy Wyandot," a relative. After this date, but how long is not known, the upper village,—the Sandusky known to Slover, Zane, and others of Crawford's army,—was deserted; its occupants gathering around the home of their great sachem, on the river, eight miles below.[4]

Of all the savage allies of Great Britain in the West,

---

[4] As the location of the Half King's town—*the* Upper Sandusky of the British and their allies—has been a source of much perplexity to those who have written of early incidents in this quarter, I add the testimony of Walker: "First find the locality of the old Wyandot mill, on the river, nearly three miles below Upper Sandusky. From this point proceed down the river to where the Kilbourne road crosses the river. Above and below the bridge, at this point, on the west side of the stream, a piece of bottom-land was pointed out to me as the residence of the Half King."

Knight, in his Narrative, speaks of the Half King's town as being *eighteen* miles below where the town of Sandusky formerly stood (p. 5). But this is a misprint; he afterward gives the distance as *eight* miles, which is the correct number (p. 9).

the Wyandots were the most powerful. This arose not so much from the number of their warriors, as from their superior intelligence. Their long association with the French at Detroit, and, after that post fell into the possession of Great Britain, with its later occupants, had advanced them in many respects over the surrounding nations. This was manifest in their comfortable cabins, erected with much skill and far superior to the rude lodges of other tribes; also, in their treatment of prisoners—seldom, if ever, since the commencement of hostilities, torturing them to death at the stake, as was common with the Delawares and Shawanese. Captives, however, they sometimes killed outright. An eye-witness, at Sandusky, bears testimony to the fact: "Whilst remaining at Sandusky," says the narrator, "a circumstance took place, which was in the utmost degree appalling to human nature; and raised such sensations of horror in my breast, as I never before experienced; and which the reader may imagine, but I can not describe.

"A prisoner was brought in by the Wyandots and Mingoes, to the store of my employer. Before the store-door were a number of Wyandots, waiting to join in the murdering of him. As he was passing the house, they knocked him down with tomahawks, cut off his head, and fixed it on a pole erected for the purpose; when commenced a scene of yelling, dancing, singing, and rioting, which, I suppose, represented something like demons from the infernal regions.

"After their fury and drunken frolic was abated, we sent to the chief of the nation, for liberty to bury the body; and his answer was, 'They do not bury our dead when they kill them, and we will not bury theirs:' on the return of which, we sent another petition, and informed him that we would remove our store out of the country, if we could not have the liberty to bury dead carcases out of our sight. He answered then, that we might do with it as we pleased: on which we took the head down, placed it to the body, as well as we could, wrapped them in a clean blanket, and buried them as decently as our situation would admit of."[5]

The traders at Sandusky came from Detroit, where they obtained a license to traffic with the Indians from the commandant, who also required them to give bond to report themselves at his post at stated periods. These traders sold large quantities of powder, lead, and flints, as well as fire-arms; silver ornaments and trinkets; paints for the warriors; blankets and other articles of clothing: taking in exchange furs, which were packed on horses to Lower Sandusky, and taken thence to Detroit in boats.

[5] *John Leith's Narrative*, p. 14. The copy in my possession is believed to be the only one extant. It was published at Lancaster, Ohio, by Ewell Jeffers. Leith was a captive among the Indians.

Some of these traders were men of influence with the Wyandots; one, in particular, seems to have enjoyed their confidence to a good degree. His name was Alexander McCormick. These men were doing a thriving business at the Half King's town, when the expedition was undertaken by the Americans against Sandusky.

The Wyandots, in this region, numbered, in 1782, not far from seven hundred. It was afterward estimated by intelligent Wyandots, that Zhaus-sho-toh, their war-chief, was able to muster four hundred warriors of that nation, to oppose the army of Crawford.[6] It is probable that this estimate was a liberal one. Great exertions were put forth to prepare to meet the enemy, by calling in all their braves to the rendezvous near Sandusky; and the wise policy was adopted of not attempting to impede the progress of the Americans, by moving forward with their own forces; but to wait for reinforcements from the Miami towns and from Detroit; and, in the meantime, should Crawford reach the Plains, and threaten the Half King's town before help had arrived, then, with the aid of the Delawares, to retard his progress, to the best of their ability, until the arrival of their allies.

The last encampment of the army under Crawford, on the evening of the 3d of June, nearly eighteen miles up the river from the Half King's town, was carefully

---

[6] Communicated by William Walker, 1872.

reconnoitered by the Indians; as there was a possibility that the Americans might bear away to the Miami towns, by a forced march that night, after this feint against Sandusky. But the dawn of the day—the 4th of June—found them still in their camp, and the Wyandots prepared to contest, inch by inch, their near approach to their town.

The Delawares, who were preparing to make common cause with the Wyandots against the invaders, had, upon their disaffection with the Americans two years before, drawn back from the Muskingum, and located themselves near the home of the Half King. Their village was upon both sides of the Tymochtee creek, the principal western branch of the Sandusky. It was in what is now Crawford township, about one mile and a half northeast of the present village of Crawfordsville, Wyandot county, eight miles from Upper Sandusky of the present day, and nearly eleven from the old village of the Wyandots, where we left the American army.[7]

---

[7] There can be no doubt about the location of the Delaware village. All accounts agree as to the Wyandot traditions concerning its locality. "It was pointed out to me," writes Jonathan Kear (*Notes to the author*, 1872), "by several Indians, when I first came to the vicinity." It corresponds also with Knight's account (*Narr.*, p. 12). William Walker, than whom no better authority is needed, informs me that it was certainly in this immediate vicinity, but is unable to determine its *exact* locality. The village is known in most historical accounts as "Pipe's town." It should not be confounded, however, with a town of the

There was also a camp of Delawares about two miles in a northwest direction from the present village of Crestline, in Crawford county. Crawford and his men passed to the south of, but very near, this camp, on the 2d of June, without discovering it. It was the temporary abode of a war-chief, Wingenund,[8] and a small number of his tribe; and was located upon a trace leading eastward from the old Wyandot town upon the Sandusky, along near the site of the present town of Bucyrus, to Jeromeville, in what is now Ashland county. It was distant a little over twenty-five miles, due east, from Upper Sandusky Old Town, and about thirty-four, by way of the Indian trail, from the Half King's town.

At the Delaware village, upon the Tymochtee, lived

---

same name seen on early maps of Ohio, located upon a small Delaware reservation in the south part of what was formerly the western part of Crawford county. This was a more modern village. Consult *His. Wyandot Mission*. By Rev. James B. Finley. Cincinnati, 1840, p. 77.

[8] The camp of Wingenund (pronounced Win-*gay*-noon'd) was located upon what is now the southeast quarter of section five, and the northeast quarter of section eight, of township twenty north, of range twenty west—of the government survey—in Jefferson township, Crawford county: marked on the map of the county published by M. H. and J. V. B. Watson—"Jos. Brown, 160," and "John Newman, 160;" indicating the owners' names of the tracts and the number of acres in each. The site is about three-fourths a mile northeast of the present town of Leesville. Upon the map it is marked in Jackson township. It is in that part which has since been erected into Jefferson township.

THE PIPE—Captain Pipe, as known to history—another and much more famous war-chief of the Delawares. His town was entirely unknown to the army of Crawford. His village and the Half King's home were the only Indian towns upon the waters of the Sandusky above Lower Sandusky (Fremont), in 1782. Upper Sandusky, the site of the present county-seat of Wyandot county, and Big Spring, the site of a town of the same name in Seneca county, were Wyandot villages of more modern times.

Of all the savage enemies of the Americans, in the western wilderness during the Revolution, Captain Pipe was the most implacable! He appears upon the historic page, for the first time, in the year 1764. It was upon the occasion of the march of Colonel Henry Bouquet against the Ohio Indians, in what is known as "Pontiac's War." This officer led an army, consisting of regulars, provincials, and backwoodsmen, from Carlisle, Pennsylvania, against the Delawares and Shawanese upon the Muskingum and Scioto, arriving at Fort Pitt on the 17th September, 1764.

While at this post, ten Indians appeared upon the north bank of the Ohio, desiring a conference. Three of the party consented to come over to the fort. As they could give no satisfactory account of themselves, or reasons for their visit, they were detained as spies. Their associates fled to the wilderness. One of the three thus captured was Captain Pipe. He was kept at

Fort Pitt until Bouquet had dictated to the Delawares and Shawanese, upon the banks of the Muskingum, his own terms of peace, after which he was set at liberty.

The Pipe, whose Indian name was Kogieschquanoheel, was the principal captain of the Wolf tribe of the Delawares, becoming afterward its tribal chief. His nation was at peace with the colonies, after Pontiac's war, until 1780, a period of nearly sixteen years, although they came near being drawn into hostilities against the Americans in 1774, in Dunmore's war. Nothing is known of his history during this time. However, no sooner had the war of the Revolution begun than he became a prominent actor, always hostile to the Americans at heart, although sometimes making treaties with them. At this period he had his home upon the Walhonding, about fifteen miles above the present site of Coshocton—which is at the junction of that stream with the Tuscarawas—in Coshocton county, Ohio, where he continued to reside until the disaffection of his nation in 1780, when he removed, with others of the hostile Delawares, to the Tymochte creek, forming a close league with the Half King against the Americans.

Captain Pipe was, in many respects, a remarkable savage. The Moravian missionaries, who knew him well, say that he was cunning, artful, and ambitious. He seems always to have been their bitter enemy, so long as they remained upon the Muskingum—a period, beginning in 1772, and ending with their being forced to remove to the Sandusky, in 1781.

His enmity, however, was not so much against these Christian teachers, personally, as against all attempts, come from what source they might, having a tendency to make the Delawares a civilized and an agricultural people. That a large majority of this nation, in 1780, took up the hatchet against the Americans, forming a close alliance with the British Indians, was almost wholly due to his machinations. As the army of Crawford approached the Sandusky, nowhere upon that stream was to be found an enemy more determined than he.

At the close of the Revolutionary war, a complete change came over the feelings of this noted Indian warrior. He steadfastly advocated peace with the Americans in the councils of his nation, which had now drawn back to the Maumee river; and, although fighting, with his people, in the campaign against Harmer, in the autumn of 1790, yet he still urged for a cessation of hostilities. His advice was unheeded. At St. Clair's defeat, in 1791, he distinguished himself, slaughtering white men until his arm was weary with the dreadful work.

A grand council of nearly all the Northwestern tribes assembled in the autumn of 1792, at the confluence of the Auglaize and the Maumee rivers, where the town of Defiance now stands, to take into consideration the condition of affairs with the United States.

The result was that the Indians agreed to hold a treaty with commissioners of the new government the next summer. The warriors again gathered upon the Maumee; and The Pipe was among the foremost advocates for peace. But the nations declared for war; and the United States sent against them an army, under the command of the heroic Anthony Wayne, by whom they were reduced to entire submission. Captain Pipe did not live to witness the total defeat of the confederate tribes, on the 20th of August, 1794, upon the banks of the Maumee, by that victorious general. He died a few days previous.

Upon the morning of the 4th, while Crawford was preparing to move northward from his camp, distant about twenty miles from the village of The Pipe, the Delaware war-chief began his march from the latter place with his braves, numbering about two hundred. With him were a few of the Christian Indians who had relapsed into heathenism.[9] A short march through the Plains brought them to the place appointed for the assembling of the allied forces—a spot nearly two miles southwest of the Half King's town—where they met the Wyandot braves, under their war-chief, Zhaus-sho-toh.[10] Their combined forces considerably outnumbered the American army.

---

[9] Irvine to Moore, 5th July, 1782. This letter should have been dated the day previous.

[10] The spot where the Wyandots and Delawares assembled was on

That very morning, two hundred Shawanese started from the Indian towns (in what is now Logan county), distant about forty miles, to the aid of the Delawares and Wyandots. They were not expected to arrive until the next day. Singularly enough, at the same time succor from the north, of a very different character, however, was, at about the same distance away, also moving to their relief. Upon the Wyandots and Delawares, therefore, rested the responsibility of baffling, impeding, or, if necessary, fighting the Americans, until assistance, now coming both from the north and south, should arrive.

Arentz Schuyler de Peyster, commandant at Detroit, lost no time, after receiving intelligence of the probable invasion of the Sandusky country, in dispatching a considerable force, consisting of Butler's Rangers, to the help of his Indian allies.[11] These troops were all mounted. They took with them two field-pieces and a mortar. Their horses were sent around the lake,

---

what is now section 9, of township 2 south, of range 14 east, of the government survey, in Crane township, Wyandot county. The locality is given upon the authority of current Indian traditions, and corresponds, in distance, from the deserted village of the Wyandots, with the estimate made by Knight.—*Narrative*, p. 6.

[11] In the spring of 1777, there were two companies of Butler's Rangers at Detroit, commanded by Captain Caldwell.—*Address of Hon. Charles I. Walker, before the State Hist. Soc. of Wis., Jan.* 31, 1871, p. 20. As to the presence of British Rangers at Sandusky, consult *Loskiel's Hist. Miss.*, P. iii, p. 189; *Heckewelder's Narr.*, p. 337.

while the Rangers themselves took boats for Lower Sandusky—shipping their cannon, trappings, arms, and ammunition, and all their baggage and supplies. They arrived in the Sandusky waters without accident, where they had not long to wait for their horses. They began their march early on the morning of the 4th, from Lower Sandusky, making all possible haste up the valley, to succor their allies.[12]

Great was the excitement in Sandusky, on Tuesday morning, the 4th of June, 1782. In a deep ravine, on the south side of Tymochtee creek, about a mile from its mouth, in what is now Tymochtee township, a point almost equally distant from Pipe's town and the Half King's village, were hidden away the squaws and children of the Delawares and Wyandots. With them was Samuel Wells, a negro boy of fourteen years, captured by the Indians some years previous.[13]

---

[12] These particulars rest mostly upon tradition. But see also *Heckewelder's Narr.*, p. 337, as to the Rangers crossing the lake.

[13] The spot is on what is now the southwest quarter of section 17, in township 1 south, of range 14 east, of the government survey, marked on the Wyandot county map of 1870, " D. Straw." The locality is given upon the authority of Jonathan Kear, an old-time resident of Wyandot county, who, in a communication before me, says: " Wells, who spoke good English, frequently assured me that the squaws and children were hidden away in a deep ravine, on the south side of Tymochtee creek, about one mile from its mouth." Walker, however, is of opinion that the hiding place of the Wyandot families was farther north—in what is now Seneca county. " The Wyandots certainly re-

The British traders, who had kept their spies out for several days reporting the direction taken, and progress made, by the Americans, were now hastening with their goods out of the town, packing them to Lower Sandusky.

Leith was employed in Sandusky, at this time, by some of these men. The English would not suffer him to trade on his own account. Five of them, having placed their funds into one general stock, employed him to attend to their business for them. He affirms that he was closely watched by the Indians as Crawford's army approached, and had to make his movements with particular regularity; yet he had spies going to and fro, by whom he could hear every evening where the American army was encamped, for several days previous.

He was informed, on the evening of the 3d, that the Americans were only about fifteen miles away. He immediately set his hands at work gathering in his horses and cattle, intending to pack his goods upon the former and drive the latter to Lower Sandusky. He had under his care a large stock of silver trinkets, furs, powder, lead, and clothing, worth nearly seven thousand dollars. He started down the river the next

---

moved their women and children into what is now Seneca county," is his emphatic language. The two statements, however, are reconcilable if it be assumed that only the Delawares removed their families to the spot pointed out by Wells.

morning at daylight, but was so incumbered as to make very slow progress. He met, during the early part of the forenoon, MATTHEW ELLIOT, a British captain, hurrying forward with all possible speed. He afterward "met the whole British army, composed of Colonel Butler's Rangers." They took from him his cattle and let him pass. That night Leith encamped in what is now Seneca county, about fourteen miles above Lower Sandusky.[14]

Captain Elliot was an Irishman. At the commencement of the Revolution, he lived in Path Valley, Pennsylvania. A number of tories resided in his township, among whom Elliot was a leader. But, as hostilities increased, the place became too warm for them, as a large portion of the population was whigs. Elliot fled to the West, where he was well known as an Indian trader.

On the 12th of November, 1776, he made his appearance in one of the missionary establishments of the Moravians, upon the Muskingum, with a number of horse-loads of merchandise, a female Indian companion, and a hired man, on his way to the Shawanese towns upon the Scioto. Elliot left the next day, but was followed by a party of six warriors from Sandusky, and made prisoner, his goods being distributed among the Indians. He would have been murdered but for

---

[14] *Leith's Narr.*, p. 15.

the interposition of some Christian Indians who had followed the warriors, purposely to intercede for him.

Elliot was taken to Detroit, where he soon succeeded in convincing the commandant of his tory proclivities, who gave him a commission as captain, and sent him back to Pittsburg as a spy. Here he remained some time, and finally, in company with Alexander McKee, who had formerly been a British agent among the Indians, but who was now suffered by the Americans to go at large on parole, and other disaffected persons and deserters from Fort Pitt, again appeared upon the Muskingum early in 1778, to stir up the Delawares to hostility against the United States. As an officer of the Indian department at Detroit, he served during the Revolution, vibrating between that post and the country of the Ohio Indians, as his services seemed to be needed.

At the close of the war we find him at Detroit; and on the 9th of November, 1785, Hamilton, who was that year governor of Canada, issued an order that no one should disturb him in possession of a lot near the dock-yard by the water side, without producing titles. When the Indian war of the Northwest was renewed in 1790, Elliot, who was married to a squaw, took sides with the savages. He was present at St. Clair's defeat, but kept himself at a respectable distance from danger. He was the owner at this time, in conjunction with McKee, of a considerable tract of land, cleared ready for cultivation, on which were several houses, on the east, or Canada side, of the Detroit river, just above its mouth.

He took part in the last war with Great Britain on the side of the English, holding a colonel's commission. He was then an old man; and his hair was very white. He had much of the savage look notwithstanding his age. He probably died soon after in Canada, holding at the time the position of agent of Indian affairs by appointment from the British government. Elliot was an uncle, by his father's side, to Commodore Elliot, of the United States navy, and had a son killed on the Maumee, in the war of 1812.

The arrival of Elliot at the rendezvous of the savages, in the full uniform of a British captain, was lustily greeted by the assembled Delawares and Wyandots. He immediately assumed command of the Indians—a position he was eminently qualified to fill, owing to his intimate acquaintance with their language and customs, and to his knowledge of the surrounding country.[15]

NOTE 1.—JOHN LEITH, whose narrative has been consulted in the preparation of this chapter, was born in Leith, Scotland. His father emigrated, when John was young, to the Pedee river, South Carolina,

---

[15] "Dr. Knight was informed by an Indian that a British captain commands at Sandusky."—*Irvine to Washington*, 11th *June*, 1782. Further knowledge upon this point is derived from tradition alone. Strongly corroborative however is the positive assertion of Leith with regard to meeting Elliot *so far in advance* of his army, on the morning of the 4th of June.

where he soon afterward died. The boy then journeyed northward, spending some time at Little York, Pennsylvania. At the age of fifteen, he was at Fort Pitt, where he hired himself to an Indian trader, and with the latter started for the wilderness beyond the Ohio.

Hostilities having been brought on between the Indians and the Americans, and an Indian chief having taking a fancy to Leith, he was adopted into the tribe of the former. His employer was fortunately at Fort Pitt at this time, and of course lost all his Indian goods, but saved himself. The Indians soon after moved farther west, taking John along, to the waters of the Miami. The Indian life of Leith was full of trials and romantic incidents. He finally married a white woman, whose name was Sally Lowry, who had been captured by the Indians when twenty months old, at Big Cove, above Pittsburg, and had ever since remained a prisoner in the wilderness. At the time of her marriage, she was about eighteen years of age; Leith was in his twenty-fourth year.

Leith had two children, and was living with his family at one of the Moravian towns in 1781; but was taken to the Sandusky when the missionary establishments upon that river were broken up. He was employed as agent, as before stated, for some British traders at the Half King's town when Crawford's army approached.

For the next eight years, Leith resided in the Indian country, three of which were passed at Sandusky. He and his family during this period passed through many vicissitudes of fortune, and suffered many hardships.

In 1790, Leith, with his family, returned to Fort Pitt, where he arrived on the 2d of November; thence he went to Bud's Ferry, where he found some of his wife's relations, who received them with a cordial welcome. There they settled and set up farming. Leith afterward moved to the State of Ohio, and died about the year 1832. George W. Leith, a grandson, is now (1873) living at Nevada, Ohio. His father, Samuel, a son of John Leith, was, so far as is known, the *first* white child born in the valley of the Sandusky.

Note 2.—The fact of the sending of British troops from Detroit to the Sandusky, by De Peyster, seems heretofore to have been overlooked by most writers who have related the story of the campaign. Not so, however, by western archæologists. Lyman C. Draper, Esq., corresponding secretary of the State Historical Society of Wisconsin, in a communication before me, says, in speaking of the authorities upon this point, cited in this and subsequent chapters: "I had long since noticed all these authorities, concerning a white party aiding the Indians at Sandusky, except the statement of Leith; that narrative, except some traditions of it derived from three grandchildren of his in Illinois a few years since, I never have had. The evidence of the presence of the British is sufficiently conclusive."

Note 3.—Fixing the objective point of the expedition—Upper Sandusky Old Town, the deserted village of the Wyandots—three miles up the Sandusky river from the present town of Upper Sandusky, county-seat of Wyandot county; and assuming (what is acknowledged on all hands) that the winter-quarters of the Moravian missionaries and their converts during the winter of 1781-2 were in its immediate vicinity, and the distances to the Half King's town and the Delaware village (Pipe's town) are correctly pointed out by the Moravian writers.—*See Heckewelder's Narr.* 281, 285, 305; *Schweinitz' Zeis.* 516, 518.

The following memoranda are from the manuscript journal of Zeisberger, preserved in the archives of the Moravian Church: "Christian Indians came to Sandusky river, October 1, 1781." "Wyandots there left them and went to their capital [Half King's town] about ten miles off." "October 4th, moved several miles down the river." "Camped on a bluff in a small wood, not far from a Wyandot village [Upper Sandusky Old Town] on the Sandusky, October 25th." "Same day, missionaries left their encampment and went to Pipe's town, which was reached in the afternoon." These distances agree with those given by Heckewelder (*Narr.* 281, etc.), with those furnished me by William Walker, and with those mentioned by

Knight (*Narr.* pp. 9, 10). Schweinitz, in his *Life of Zeisberger*, has, however, confused them, by placing the winter-quarters of the Christian Indians too far up the river—" one mile above the junction of the Broken Sword" with the Sandusky,—and by making the site of the Half King's town identical with that of Upper Sandusky of the present day.

CHAPTER IX.

SKETCH OF SIMON GIRTY, THE WHITE SAVAGE.

ON the forenoon of the 4th day of June, there were but few white men in the wild assemblage of whooping and stamping Delawares and Wyandots at their rendezvous.[1] But of these few there was one deserving particular notice. He was dressed as an Indian, but without ornaments. He seemed, as he really was, the very incarnation of fierceness and cruelty. His name was SIMON GIRTY. His voice rose high above the din and tumult around. He spoke the Delaware and Wyandot languages fluently. As he rode furiously back and forth, he volleyed forth fearful oaths in his native tongue!

Girty was born in Northwestern Pennsylvania. His father was an Irishman. "The old man was beastly intemperate. A jug of whisky was the extent of his ambition. 'Grog was his song, and grog would he have.' His sottishness turned his wife's affection. Ready for seduction, she yielded her heart to a neighboring rustic, who, to remove all obstacles to their wishes, knocked Girty on the head, and bore off the trophy of

---

[1] "A few scattering Canadians and renegades—one by the name of Hazle."—*William Walker: Notes to the author.*

his prowess."² There were four children at the time of the father's death: Thomas, Simon, George, and James. During the Old French War the three last were taken prisoners by the Indians. Simon was adopted by the Senecas, and became an expert hunter. His Indian name was Katepacomen. It must be passed to his credit that his early training as a savage was compulsory, not voluntary, as has generally been supposed. His tribe roamed the wilderness northwest of the Ohio; and when the expedition under Colonel Henry Bouquet, at the close of Pontiac's war in 1764, marched into the western wilderness to punish the Ohio Indians, one of the hostages delivered to that commander by the latter was Girty. He escaped, however, soon after, and returned to his savage life. But, as one of the conditions of peace was the yielding up by the Senecas of all their captives willing or unwilling, Girty was compelled to return to the settlements, making his home in the vicinity of Pittsburg.³

Girty took part in Dunmore's war in 1774, on the side of Virginia, during which time he was the bosom friend and companion of Simon Kenton. He was intimately acquainted with Colonel Crawford, taking sides

---

² Biographical Sketches: With other Literary Remains of the Late John W. Campbell, Judge of the United States Court for the District of Ohio. Compiled by his Widow. Columbus, Ohio, 1838, p. 147.

³ A stream of water called Girty's Run, an affluent of the Allegheny (north side), about three miles above the point—Pittsburg—commemorates the residence of the Girty family.

with the latter in opposition to Pennsylvania rule, in the boundary controversy. He was frequently a guest at Crawford's hospitable cabin, on the banks of the Youghiogheny.[4] On the 22d of February, 1775, he was commissioned an officer of the militia at Pittsburg, taking the test and other necessary oaths upon that occasion. He aspired to a captaincy in the regular army; but in this was disappointed; which, it seems, was the reason of his deserting to the enemy, early in the year 1778. It is probable, however, that his early education among the Senecas had much to do with his desire and resolution again to return to the wilderness. Much of his time previous to this had been employed in interpreting, as he was well skilled in Indian lore.

General Hand was commandant at Fort Pitt when Girty deserted to the enemy. The greatest consternation was produced at Pittsburg when the event became known, as with him went a squad of twelve soldiers and the notorious Elliott and McKee. From this defection the worst might reasonably be expected, as they would certainly have great power for mischief in persuading and assisting the Indians to murder and pillage. The now assured hostility of this ignoble trio of desperadoes to the government of the United States—Girty, Elliott, and McKee—made at this time a dark outlook from the border across the Ohio. Their evil

---

[4] "It is a tradition that Girty aspired to the hand of one of Crawford's daughters, but was denied."—*James Veech: MS. letter.*

designs might be calculated on with certainty. And, as was feared, they went directly to the principal town of the now vacillating Delawares, situated upon what is the present site of Coshocton, Ohio, where they came very near changing the neutral policy of that tribe, as has already been observed, into one of open hostility against the Americans.

They represented that the white people were embodying themselves for the purpose of killing every Indian they should meet, be he friend or foe; that the American armies were all cut to pieces by the British; that General Washington was killed; that there was no more Congress; that the English had hung some of the members, and taken the rest to England; that the whole country beyond the mountains was in possession of their armies; and that a few thousand Americans on this side were all that were left in arms; and that these, as just stated, were determined to kill all the Indians in the western country—men, women, and children. Thus did Simon Girty signalize his return to the savages; but the Delawares still remained firm; and he and his two noted associates moved on to the westward— among the Shawanese upon the Scioto. However, the principal chief of the Delawares sent word to that tribe not to put confidence in their representations: "Grandchildren!" (for so ran the message) "ye Shawanese! Some days ago, a flock of birds, that had come on from the east, lit at our village, imposing a song of theirs upon us, which song had nigh proved our ruin! If these birds, which, on leaving us took their flight toward Scioto, endeavor to impose a song on you likewise, do not listen to them, for they lie!"

Girty now started for Detroit. On his way thither he was captured by the Wyandots. Recognized, however, by some Senecas, the latter demanded him as their prisoner; stating at the same 'time the nature of their claim; that he had been adopted by them; and had afterward joined their white enemies and taken up arms against them. But Leatherlips, a distinguished Wyandot chief, ignored their claim to the prisoner. "By your own showing," said he, "he only returned to his own country and people. Ever after then you can have no claim upon him as one of your own. He is now found in our country bearing arms. He was captured by our warriors. He is our prisoner." This argument was unanswerable; and the Senecas yielded the point. But Girty stated to his captors, in the Seneca language, that he had been badly treated at Fort Pitt, by his own people, on account of being true to the king and his cause, and was therefore forced to leave the country; and that he was on his way now to Detroit to take up arms against the Americans. He was thereupon set at liberty.

Arriving at Detroit, Girty was welcomed by Hamilton, the commandant of the post, very cordially, and immediately employed in the Indian department, at sixteen York shillings a day,[5] and sent back to the Sandusky, to assist the savages in their warfare upon the border. He took up his residence with the Wyandots. His influence soon began to be felt in the Indian Confederacy—sometimes with the Shawanese, and again with the Wyandots, on their murderous forays into the border settlements; he was always a leader with them. His name became a household word of terror all along the border, from Pittsburg to the Falls of the Ohio. With it was associated everything cruel and fiend-like. To the women and children in particular, nothing was more terrifying than the name of Simon Girty. Although he called himself "Captain Girty," yet whether he ever received a commission from the British government, as did his associate, Elliott, is a mooted question. His lack of education was probably the cause, if he was not commissioned; he could not write his name. It is certain, however, that he was in the regular pay of Great Britain.

Strangely enough, one of Girty's first exploits, after becoming fairly domiciled among the Indians, was highly creditable to him. Mention has been made of his intimacy, during Dunmore's war, with Simon Kenton. The latter was brought a captive to the Mac-a-chack towns, in September, 1778, at which time Girty also happened to be in the Shawanese villages. Kenton

---

[5] C. I. Walker's Address before the Wis. Hist. Soc., pp. 15, 41.

was under sentence of death, and was to be burned at Wapatomika, just below the site of the present village of Zanesfield, Logan county, Ohio, where he was now awaiting his doom. Girty came to see the prisoner, and, as the latter had been painted black, a custom among the Indians when captives are to be burned, did not recognize his old associate. A few words between them, however, was enough for a recognition; whereupon Girty threw himself into Kenton's arms, calling him his dear and esteemed friend. "Well," said he to Kenton, "you are condemned to die; but I will do all I can—use every means in my power to save your life." Girty immediately had a council convened, and made a long speech to the Indians, in their own language, to save the life of their prisoner. This they consented to, and Kenton was placed under the care and protection of his benefactor, by whom he was well cared for. The Indians, however, again condemned him to death, but Girty induced them to take him to Sandusky; when, at the interposition of a captain in the British service, he was sent to Detroit, and finally effected his escape.[6]

Girty now began his wild career against the border settlements. General McIntosh wrote from Fort Pitt, under date of 29th January following, that Captain

---

[6] *Biographical Sketches.* By *John McDonald.* Cincinnati, 1838, p. 227–231.

Clark, of the Eighth Pennsylvania regiment, while returning from Fort Laurens with a sergeant and fourteen men, was attacked three miles from that post, by Simon Girty and a party of Mingoes, who killed two of his men, wounded four, and took one prisoner. From this time onward, to the approach of Crawford and his army against Sandusky, his career is mostly known by his cruel visitations of the frontier. His headquarters were at Sandusky, where he exercised great influence over the Half King, head chief of the Wyandots. He was frequently at Detroit; and De Peyster, the commandant, who had succeeded Hamilton upon the capture of the latter at Vincennes, on the 25th of February, 1779, by George Rogers Clark, found him ready for any undertaking, either against the Americans or the missionaries and their converts upon the Muskingum, as his hostility to the latter seemed as unbounded as to the former. Sharing with him in his hate were his associates, Elliott and McKee.

In the early part of July, 1779, a party of Indians, led by Girty, attempted to kill or capture David Zeisberger, one of the missionaries, who was then at Lichtenau, a Christian Indian village on the east bank of the Muskingum, two and a half miles below the site of the present town of Coshocton, Ohio, but which was deserted soon after. The missionaries, having received timely information of the design by the arrival of Alexander McCormick, the trader living at Sandusky, were on the alert; and, although the Moravian teacher came near being captured or killed, yet the assailants were so warmly received by the Delawares, who showed a determination, upon this occasion, to protect Zeisberger by all the means in their power, that Girty was forced to retreat, "gnashing his teeth in impotent rage."

Upon the arrival of the Christian Indians and their teachers in the Sandusky country, in October, 1781, they were brought almost face to face with their archenemy, at the Half King's residence. Girty was one of the plotters of the scheme which resulted in the breaking up of the missionary establishments upon the Muskingum. He seemed to take delight in rudely treating the missionaries while in their winter-quarters near Sandusky. The Moravian Heckewelder says: "At one time, just as my wife had set down to what was intended for our dinner, the Half King, Simon Girty, and another Wyandot entered my cabin, and seeing the victuals ready, without ceremony began eating."[7] In the final removal of the missionaries from the Indian country to Detroit, resulting in the entire disbanding of the Christian Indians, Girty was one of the chief instruments—a willing tool in the hands of the Half King—the power behind the throne.

Pomoacan was determined to drive the Moravians

---

[7] *Heckewelder's Narr.*, p. 300.

from the Sandusky. In April, just previous to the advent of Crawford's army, Girty tried to induce McCormick, who was still a resident of the Half King's town, to write a letter to De Peyster, at Detroit, for the Wyandot chief, implicating the missionaries as his enemies. But the trader refused. However, some one was found to write for him as he and Girty desired; and a response was soon received, ordering the Moravians to leave the country, and asking the Half King to give Girty assistance in bringing them and their families to Detroit.

On the 1st day of March, a messenger, sent by the Half King and Girty, arrived at the rude cabins of the missionaries, ordering them to appear before them the next morning to hear the letter read. Accordingly, two of them, Zeisberger and Heckewelder, although the order was for all to go, started for the residence of the chief, nearly eight miles down the river, where they finally arrived after a toilsome walk through the deep snow, and found Girty and the Half King already waiting for them at the house of McCormick. At the meeting Girty insulted the Moravians, giving them the letter to read, with a string of black wampum to intimidate them. He extorted a written pledge from these teachers to meet him at Lower Sandusky in two weeks, with all the missionaries and their families, to be conducted by him to Detroit.

On the morning of the 13th of March, a Frenchman named Francis Levallie, from Lower Sandusky, informed the missionaries that Girty had gone, with a war-party of Wyandots, against the border settlements upon the Ohio, and that he had been deputed to take his place. He told them, also, that Girty had ordered him to drive them before him to Detroit the same as if they were cattle, and not make a halt for the purpose of the women giving suck to their children; and that he should take them around the head of Lake Erie and make them foot every step of the way. The humane Frenchman saw fit, however, to disobey orders. He treated them kindly; and in four days' journey brought them to Lower Sandusky, where they were hospitably received by Arundle and Robbins, traders from Detroit, while Levallie wrote to De Peyster to send boats for their transportation thence to their place of destination.

Awaiting the arrival of the boats from Detroit, the missionaries became uneasy lest Girty should return from his murderous foray against the Americans and find his orders disobeyed; in which event they would have the worst to fear. "He *did* return," is the testimony of Heckewelder, "and behaved like a madman, on hearing that we were here, and that our conductor had disobeyed his orders, and had sent a letter to the commandant at Detroit respecting us. He flew at the Frenchman, who was in the room adjoining ours, most furiously, striking at him, and threatening to split his head in two for disobeying the orders he had given him. He swore the most horrid oaths respecting us, and continued in that way until after midnight. His oaths were all to the purport that he never would leave the house until he split our heads in two with his tomahawk, and made our brains stick to the walls of the room in which we were! I omit the names he called us by, and the words he made use of while swearing, as also the place he would go to if he did not fulfill all which he had sworn he would do to us. He had somewhere procured liquor, and would, as we were told by those who were near him, at every drink renew his oaths, which he repeated until he fell asleep.

"Never before did any of us hear the like oaths, or know any one to rave like him. He appeared like an host of evil spirits. He would sometimes come up to the bolted door between us and him, threatening to chop it in pieces to get at us. No Indian we ever saw drunk would have been a match for him. How we should escape the clutches of this white beast in human form no one could foresee. Yet at the proper time relief was at hand; for, in the morning, at break of day, and while he was still sleeping, two large flat-bottomed boats arrived from Detroit, for the purpose of taking us to that place. This was joyful news! And seeing the letter written by the commandant to Mr. Arundle respecting us, we were satisfied we would be relieved from the hands of this wicked white savage, whose equal, we were led to believe, was perhaps not to be found among mankind." [8]

Girty afterward returned to Sandusky and plotted against the Christian Indians, who, after their teachers were gone, disbanded, most of them proceeding to the Scioto, while others, as before mentioned, stopped for a while in the neighborhood, at Pipe's town—all intending to meet together, after some time, on the Maumee and there establish themselves—when, Crawford's army approaching, a few, as already intimated, took up arms and joined the Delawares, under Captain Pipe. Shortly after the Christian Indians were thus scattered, news arrived of the probable invasion of the Sandusky country by the Americans, and Girty now busied himself in assisting the gathering together of the Indians to repel the invaders. His influence was as great with the war-chief of the Delawares as with Zhaus-sho-toh or the Half King.[9] Elliott, therefore, upon his arrival at Sandusky, as before stated, found Girty full of excitement and ferocious zeal.

Passing over the events of the few days following the advent of Elliott to the Indian lines, wherein

---

[8] *Heckewelder's Narr.*, p. 332–334.

[9] In after years the Wyandots became the firm friends of the Americans; and then, jealous of the fair fame of their nation, they vehemently disclaimed against the idea of Girty's ever having any influence in their councils; nevertheless, the testimony to the contrary is so overwhelming as not for a moment to be doubted.

Girty, as we shall hereafter see, played a notable part, we loose trace of him to August following, when, on the 16th of that month, we find him the leader of a large Indian force against Bryant's Station, five miles from Lexington, Kentucky. The Kentuckians made such a gallant resistance that the Indians become disheartened and were about abandoning the siege, when Girty, thinking he might frighten the garrison into a surrender, mounted a stump within speaking distance and commenced a parley. He told them who he was; that he looked hourly for reinforcements with cannon, and that they had better surrender at once; if they did so, no one should be hurt; otherwise he feared they would all be killed. The garrison were intimidated; but one young man named Reynolds, seeing the effect of this harangue, and believing his story, as it was, to be false, of his own accord answered him: "You need not be so particular to tell us your name; we know your name and you too. I've had a villainous, untrustworthy cur-dog this long while, named *Simon Girty*, in compliment to you; he's so like you—just as ugly and just as wicked. As to the cannon, let them come on; the country's roused, and the scalps of your red cut-throats, and your own too, will be drying on our cabins in twenty-four hours."[10] This spirited reply produced good results. Girty in turn was disheartened,

---

[10] *Howe's Hist. Coll. of Ohio*, p. 247.

and, with his Indians, soon withdrew. The country was indeed aroused. The enemy were pursued to the Blue Licks, where, lying in ambuscade, the Kentuckians, three days after, suffered a cruel defeat. This, it is believed, was the last battle Girty was in during the Revolution; as peace was soon after declared, and comparative tranquillity was restored along the western border.

During the next seven years but little is recorded of the noted desperado. He, however, remained in the Indian country, employed, it is believed, most of the time, in trading with the savages. Certain it is that he lost meanwhile none of their confidence or esteem; for, when war again broke out between the United States and the Indians of the Northwest in 1790, rendered famous by the campaign of Harmer of that year; of St. Clair, in 1791; and of Wayne, in 1794; — Girty again became a famous character. After St. Clair's defeat, a grand council was held at the confluence of the Maumee and the Auglaize, by nearly all the Northwestern tribes, to take into consideration the situation of affairs. Simon Girty was the only white man permitted to be present. His voice was for a continuance of the war. Another conference was held in 1793, and it was determined, mainly through the exertions of Girty, to continue hostilities. But the decisive victories of the next year, gained by Wayne, forever destroyed the power of the Indians of the Northwest; and the famous treaty of Greenville brought about an enduring peace, in 1795.

In this second war against his countrymen, Girty made his first appearance in the attack on Dunlap's Station early in 1791—a point on the east side of the Great Miami river, eight miles from the spot where the town of Hamilton now is, in Butler county, Ohio, and seventeen miles from Cincinnati. The station was most gallantly defended; and Girty was compelled to retire without effecting its capture. The last battle in which he was known to be actively engaged, was at St. Clair's defeat, on the 4th of November, 1791, twenty-three miles north of the present town of Greenville, county-seat of Darke county, Ohio. Among the dead, he found and recognized the body of General Richard Butler, second in command of the American army. On the retreat and general rout of our army, Girty captured a white woman. A Wyandot squaw who accompanied the warriors of her nation, perceiving this, demanded the prisoner, on the ground that usage gave all female captives to the women accompanying the braves. Girty refused and became furious; when some warriors came up and enforced a compliance with this rule of the Indians—to the great relief of the prisoner. The woman was afterward sold to a respectable French family in Detroit.

After this, Girty was engaged in the Indian trade at Lower Sandusky; going thence to " Girty's town," on the St. Mary's, where he established a trading-house on the site of the present town of St. Mary's, in Mercer county, Ohio, which he must have abandoned while General Wayne was marching his army to the victory of the "Fallen Timbers," on the 20th of August, 1794; for he was present upon that occasion with his old associates, Elliott and McKee, though they kept at a respectable distance from the contest, near the river. After the treaty of Greenville, Girty sold his trading establishment at Girty's town to an Irishman named Charles Murray, and removed to Canada, where he settled on a farm just below Malden, on the Detroit river.

Girty married in the neighborhood and raised a family. In vain he tried to become a decent citizen, and command some degree of respect. The depravity of his untamed and undisciplined nature was too apparent. He was abhorred by all his neighbors. In the war of 1812, Girty, being then nearly blind, was incapable of active service. After the capture of the British fleet on Lake Erie, in 1813, and upon the invasion of Canada immediately after, he followed the British army on their retreat, leaving his family at home. He fixed his residence at a Mohawk village on Grand river, Canada, until the proclamation of peace, when he returned to his farm below Malden, where he died in 1818, aged over seventy years.

"The last time I saw Girty," writes William

Walker, "was in the summer of 1813. From my recollection of his person, he was in height five feet six or seven inches; broad across the chest; strong, round, compact limbs; and of fair complexion. To any one scrutinizing him, the conclusion would forcibly impress the observer, that Girty was endowed by nature with great powers of endurance."[11] Spencer, a prisoner among the Indians, who saw Girty before he left the Indian country, was not favorably impressed with his visage: "His dark shaggy hair; his low forehead; his brows contracted, and meeting above his short, flat nose; his gray sunken eyes, averting the ingenuous gaze; his lips thin and compressed; and the dark and sinister expression of his countenance;—to me seemed the very picture of a villain."[12]

No other country or age ever produced, perhaps, so brutal, depraved, and wicked a wretch as Simon Girty. He was sagacious and brave; but his sagacity and bravery only made him a greater monster of cruelty. All of the vices of civilization seemed to center in him, and by him were ingrafted upon those of the savage state, without the usual redeeming qualities of either. He moved about through the Indian country during the war of the Revolution and the Indian war which followed, a dark whirlwind of fury, desperation, and barbarity. In the refinements of torture inflicted

---

[11] Notes to A. H. Dunlevy: 1872. These have been published.
[12] *Howe's His. Coll. of Ohio*, p. 248.

on helpless prisoners, as compared with the Indians, he "out-heroded Herod." In treachery, he stood unrivaled.

There ever rankled in his bosom a most deadly hatred of his country. He seemed to revel in the very excess of malignity toward his old associates. So horrid was his wild ferocity and savageness, that the least relenting seemed to be acts of positive goodness—luminous sparks in the very blackness of darkness! "I have fully glutted my vengeance," said the Mingo Logan, when he had taken a scalp for each of his relations murdered; but the revenge of Simon Girty was gorged with numberless victims, of all ages and of either sex! It seemed as insatiable as the grave itself. And what is the more astonishing, is, that such insatiety could arise in any human breast upon a mere fancied neglect!—for it will be remembered that he deserted to the enemy because of not being promoted to the command of a company!

Of Girty's fool-hardiness, there is ample testimony. He got into a quarrel at one time with a Shawanese, caused by some misunderstanding in a trade. While bandying hard words to each other, the Indian, by innuendo, questioned his opponent's courage. Girty instantly produced a half-keg of powder, and snatching a fire-brand, called upon the savage to stand by him. The latter, not deeming this a legitimate mode of settling disputes, hastily evacuated the premises!

Upon one subject, however, Girty seemed to be ill at ease. He was curious to know of prisoners what was in store for him should he be captured by the Americans. The idea of falling into the hands of his outraged countrymen, was, in short, a terror to him. In the summer of 1796, when the British surrendered the posts of the Northwest to the United States, Girty was at Detroit. When the boats laden with our troops came in sight, he became so much alarmed that he could not wait for the return of the ferry-boat, but plunged his horse into the river, at the risk of drowning, and made for the Canada shore, which he reached in safety; pouring out a volley of maledictions, as he rode up the opposite bank, upon the United States government and troops, mingled with all the diabolical oaths his imagination could coin.[13]

---

[13] Communicated by William Walker to A. H. Dunlevy. See *The Wyandotte* (Kan.) *Gazette*, of April 18, 1872. Girty, it seems, " once resided five miles above Napoleon, Ohio, at a place called ' Girty's Point.' "—*His. Coll. of Ohio*, p. 246. Near this is *Girty's Island*, in the Maumee river, also called after the famous renegade. The date of his residence in this vicinity, I have not been able to determine with any degree of certainty.

CHAPTER X.

BATTLE OF SANDUSKY—JUNE 4, 1782.

A BRIEF hour terminated the halt of the American army on the site of the deserted Wyandot town, where, at one o'clock on the 4th of June, we left Crawford,—in doubt as to what ought to be done, owing to the strange state of affairs. Of the location of an Indian village eight miles below, on the west side of the Sandusky, Crawford was pretty well assured; but would not that one, also, be found without inhabitants? Slover was of opinion that the Indians of the upper town had moved to the lower one. Settlements, he thought, would soon be reached. He remembered their proximity in former years. Crawford, therefore, determined to move forward in search of them.

The army crossed the river just below the site of the old town, at a point half a mile from the deserted Moravian huts, following the Indian trace, which led across a broad, level bottom, in a northerly direction, to the bluffs, or high ground, beyond. Three miles from the starting point brought them to the springs, where Upper Sandusky is now located;[1] when, after

---

[1] Walker, in a communication before me, gives the direction of the old trace with great minuteness: "From the upper village, it crossed the river from east to west about midway between the upper and lower south rims of Armstrong's Bottom; thence to Half King's vil-

marching a mile further, some of the men, for the first time, expressed a desire to return home—alleging they had but five days' provisions in reserve. Crawford, stopping the march, immediately called a council of war, consisting of the captains and field officers. Knight and Rose were also invited, as were Slover and Zane. The opinion of the latter had great weight with Crawford, who knew Zane to be exceedingly well versed in Indian strategy.

Zane advised an immediate return. He was of opinion that the Indians would, in the end, bring an overwhelming force against them. A further march into their country, he reasoned, even though the army had supplies in abundance, would only be giving more time to the enemy to gather reinforcements. That none of the Indians had, as yet, been discovered in the Plains was a sure evidence, in his judgment, that they were concentrating at some point not far away for a determined resistance. The views of Crawford coincided with those of Zane. It was finally determined by the council that the army should continue its march that afternoon, but no longer.[2]

---

lage, eight miles below, by way of what is now the town of Upper Sandusky." The springs mentioned in the text are within the present corporate limits of Upper Sandusky, and are now (1873) owned by Hon. Curtis Berry, Jr.

[2] *Knight's Narr.*, p. 5. Doddridge speaks of the officers holding a council, but is in error as to the time and place; also, as to its determination. (*Notes*, 270.) Rose is silent upon the subject.

Crawford had previously formed a company of light-horse to act as scouts in advance of the army.[3] These could now move a considerable distance in front of the main body with comparatively little risk—the woods having, to a great extent, disappeared, and there being no bushes or undergrowth in the groves for ambuscades by the enemy. From this company Crawford had detached a small party for observation, soon after leaving the old village. They followed along the Indian trail, and were now reconnoitering the open country to the northeast of the spot where the council of war was deliberating. To the left of the trace they saw a beautiful island, or grove, which seemed to beckon them from the fierce heat of the sun. They drew up for a moment to enjoy the cool shade of its clustering oaks.

The spot where the party halted was slightly elevated above the surrounding country, and, notwithstanding the overshadowing branches of the thickly-growing trees, was covered with a luxuriant growth of the tall, wild grass of the Plains. To the north and west the prairie spread out before them—a broad champaign of exceeding beauty, with here and there, in the distance, small island-groves, to break the otherwise uninterrupted view. Eastward, at not more than a mile away, a long line of forest trees of the usual variety of the country, decked the margin of the Sandusky. Midway, and

---

[3] Affidavit of Hugh Workman, appended to the declaration of James Workman for a pension, dated March 29, 1833.

near the edge of the Plains, the Indian trace led onward in a direction nearly northeast to the Wyandot town— the Half King's residence—only a little over two miles distant. Not very far off, in a southwest direction, there was a large swamp, impassable to horsemen.[4] The scouts had passed to the right of this swamp without discovering it.

They now struck out into the open prairie to the north, moving leisurely on, when, at a distance of a mile from the grove they had just left, they suddenly came in full view of the enemy, having unsuspectingly reconnoitered, very near the rendezvous of the latter. When first seen, the Indians were running directly toward them. The scouts immediately drew together, and dispatched one of their number, riding their fleetest horse, as an express, to inform Crawford of the discovery of the savages; and then wheeling about, retired slowly as the foe advanced.

The Indians had chosen a favorable point for the assembling of their forces.[5] It was not far distant

---

[4] This swamp (or " cranberry marsh," as it is usually called,) is mostly on section nineteen of township two south, of range fourteen east, of the government survey, in the present township of Crane—extending, a small portion of it, into section twenty of the same township and range. (*See William Brown's Map of the Wyandot Reservation.*) It lies about a mile and a half north of the present town of Upper Sandusky.

[5] The place of rendezvous of the Delawares and Wyandots was four miles east of north of the present town of Upper Sandusky, and to the right of what was afterward the old Lower Sandusky (Fremont) road.

from the two traces—the one leading northeast to the Half King's town; the other, northwest to Pipe's town,—branching off from the springs, the spot where Upper Sandusky now stands. The warriors in advance were the Delawares under The Pipe, their famous war-chief. With him were Wingenund and Girty. Their object in moving south was to secure the grove before the arrival of the Americans. The Wyandots under Zhaus-sho-toh were held back by Elliott for the present.

Just as the officers of the American army had ended their council of war, the scout from the north came riding up at full speed, announcing the discovery and advance of the savages. The news was received with evident satisfaction by the whole army. Rapidly the volunteers mounted and fell into line. Crawford immediately prepared to meet the enemy he had been so anxiously looking for. An advance was ordered, which was obeyed with alacrity. The army was now joined by the retiring scouts, who reported the Indians just ahead in considerable force, evidently prepared to offer them battle.

The resplendent genius of Rose, the aid of Colonel Crawford, began now to exhibit itself. As the belligerents rapidly approached each other he aroused himself. Although his keen, dark eyes flashed with excitement, yet his voice exhibited no trepidation. In all his movements he was cool and collected. The genial, complaisant, and retiring gentleman was now the bold, dauntless, and spirited soldier. He rode the best horse in the army; and as he galloped up and down the lines carrying the orders of his commander, his gallantry and martial bearing attracted general attention. It was well, as we shall presently see, that Irvine consented to spare his aid-de-camp to Crawford.

The Americans had advanced scarcely a mile when the enemy were discovered immediately in front, taking possession of the grove the light-horse had so recently abandoned. Crawford, instantly detecting the advantage this would give the foe, ordered his men to dismount; and a quick, forward movement, with brisk firing by the Americans, soon drove the Indians out of the wood into the open prairie to the north, the former getting full possession of the grove. The savages then attempted to gain a small skirt of woods on the right of our army, but were prevented by the bravery and vigilance of Major Leet, who had command in that quarter. Just then the Delawares, who had bravely met the first shock of the battle, were reinforced by the Wyandots under Zhaus-sho-toh.

Elliott, who was now present and in command of the entire force of the enemy, ordered The Pipe, with his Delawares, to flank to the right and attack Crawford in the rear. This was quickly accomplished, the Indians passing along just beyond the edge of the grove on the west; and the action became at once general, close, and hot. This skillful maneuver of the savages came well nigh proving fatal to the Americans; but the latter, having the advantage of position, maintained their ground, although clearly outnumbered by their assailants. The firing began at four o'clock and continued very warm on both sides. Girty was conspicuous in his excitement and endeavors.[6] The enemy were sheltered by the grass which grew high and rank upon the Plains, so that they could scarcely be seen, when on foot, at any great distance away. On the other hand, the Americans were better protected by the grove they had so bravely secured.

At times it was doubtful how the day would end, as the battle continued with varying success. After a while, however, it was evident to Crawford that the Indians were slacking their efforts. Toward sunset they became more cautious in their attacks, being evidently less inclined to expose themselves to the deadly aim of the frontiersmen; and finally, at dusk, they drew back farther into the Plains, and the firing ceased as daylight disappeared.

The afternoon had been unusually hot. Little or

---

[6] Dunlevy, several times during the conflict, heard the voice of Girty. Philip Smith not only heard him, but more than once saw and recognized him—beyond gunshot, however, each time. Girty rode a white horse; appropriately—"death on a pale horse." Both Dunlevy and Smith had been previously acquainted with the renegade.

no air was stirring. The river was over a mile away from the battle-ground, and the soldiers suffered very much from thirst. No spring was near nor running stream. Many canteens were emptied long before the battle was ended. Several of the volunteers went in search of water. John Sherrard was one of the number—his gun having become useless to him from forcing a bullet into the barrel without powder. After a while, in wandering about, he came to a spot where a tree had been blown down and a considerable depression in the ground had been caused by the upheaval of the roots. Here he found some stagnant water. After quenching his thirst he filled his canteen and hat, and, thus supplied, made his way to his company—the men eagerly drinking of the water, bad as it was. The residue of the time, during the battle, Sherrard employed in traveling back and forth with canteens filled at the pool, the bullets flying thickly around him, but he escaped unhurt.

As the battle progressed, the savages, skulking in the high grass, of the prairie, would frequently get within close range of the guns of the Americans, generally to be shot before they could make good their retreat; for, in all maneuvers of that sort, the volunteers were the equals of the Indians. Some of the borderers climbed trees, and from their bushy tops took deadly aim at the heads of the enemy as they arose above the grass. Daniel Canon was conspicuous in this novel mode of warfare. He was one of the dead-shots of the army; and, from his lofty hiding-place, the reports of his unerring rifle gave unmistakable evidence of the killing of savages. "I do not know how many Indians I killed," said he, afterward, "but I never saw the same head again above the grass after I shot at it!"[7]

"About a hundred feet off," says Philip Smith, "an Indian was hid in the tall grass, firing at me. I felt the bark of a tree, where I stood, fly in my face several times. Having discovered the position of the savage I fired several shots; and, at the seventh one, catching sight of his body, I brought him down. No more balls came from that quarter. After waiting a reasonable time, I crawled along to find his body, but it had been dragged away. I could see plainly the trail of blood it made."

Another soldier, who had climbed one of the trees of the grove, witnessed, from his lookout in its scrubby top, the pursuit of the gallant Rose by a party of mounted Indians, who were so close to him, at times, as to throw their tomahawks! They were, however, finally baffled by his coolness and superior horsemanship. It was, according to the narrator's account, a most exciting race—even to a forgetfulness, by the latter, of his own dangerous position.[8]

---

[7] Communicated by Robert A. Sherrard: 1872.

[8] This was communicated by one of the officers of the expedition to Callender Irvine, father of Dr. William A. Irvine, and by the latter to the author.

Francis Dunlevy, who belonged to Captain Craig Ritchie's company, had, during the fight, been engaged with an Indian of huge proportions. The latter, as evening approached, crept carefully and cautiously toward Dunlevy, through the top of a tree lately blown down, which was full of leaves, when, getting near enough as he supposed, he threw his tomahawk, but missed his aim, and then escaped. This Indian was afterward recognized by Dunlevy, as he believed, in "Big Captain Johnny," who, in the war of 1812, was with the friendly Shawanese at Wapakoneta. "In a campaign in which I served," writes A. H. Dunlevy, "under General William Henry Harrison, in 1812–13, I frequently saw this Indian. He must have been seven feet in height! He was as frightfully ugly as he was large."[9]

At dark, the victory was clearly with the Americans.[10] The enemy drew off, "with the loss of several scalps,"

---

[9] Original communication: 1872.

[10] The following ludicrous account of the battle is from Heckewelder (*Narr. Miss.* 336): "The Americans reached a certain spot in an open prairie, where they had no hiding places; the Indians were under cover of a grove of trees. The latter *compelled* them to fight; and it is said they would have completely routed the whole of them (though by the papers they were said to have been five hundred strong), had it not been for the lateness of the day, and that the Indians were hourly in expectation of a large reinforcement from the Shawanese towns."

afterward wrote Rose to Irvine."[11] How many savages were killed must be left entirely to conjecture. The loss of the enemy was doubtless severe—much more so than with the borderers. No prisoners were captured on either side.

Although Crawford was left in full possession of the battle-field, yet the Indians were far from being dispirited. They well knew that reinforcements were hastening to their relief; that these would certainly reach them on the morrow. The American army, during the three hours and a half contest, lost five killed and nineteen wounded.[12] Of the latter were Major Brinton,[13] Captains Munn and Ross, Lieutenant Ashley, Ensign McMasters, and Philip Smith.[14] Captain Ogle was

---

[11] June 13, 1782. One of these scalps was taken by the brave, but afterward unfortunate, Captain Biggs.

[12] Rose to Irvine, 13th June, 1782. Dunlevy's estimate is in round numbers: "About twenty were killed and wounded." Knight puts the killed one less than Rose.

[13] The song—Crawford's Defeat—has these lines concerning Major Brinton:

"And as this brave hero was giving command,
The rifle-balls rattled on every hand;
He received a ball, but his life did not yield;
He remained with the wounded men out on the field."

[14] "I stood behind a small sapling to shelter myself from the bullets; but the tree was so small that I was compelled to stand with my shoulder to it. While in this position I was wounded in the elbow, which served to keep me in remembrance of the battle the rest of my life."—*Smith's Recollections of Crawford's Expedition.*

killed; also, private John Campbell, of Pigeon creek, Washington county.[15]

Both parties lay on their arms during the night, and both adopted the policy of kindling large fires along their lines and then retiring some distance in the rear of them, to prevent being surprised by a night attack. The camp of the Wyandots was in the prairie north of the grove; that of the Delawares, in the open country to the south.

The battle of Sandusky was fought in and around the grove since well known as "Battle Island," in what is now Crane township, Wyandot county, three miles north, and half a mile east, of the court-house in Upper Sandusky. This spot has always been readily identified, by reason of the scars upon the trunks of the trees, made by the hatchets of the Indians in getting out the bullets after the action. But the "Island" may now be said to have disappeared. Cultivated fields mark the site where the contest took place. Occasionally an interesting relic is turned up by the plowshare, to be preserved by the curious as a memento of the battle.[16]

---

[15] *Creigh's Hist. Wash. Co.*, App. 56.

[16] The action took place on what is now the southeast quarter of section 17, of township 2 south, of range 14 east, of the government survey, now owned (1872) by G. Nace, extending eastward into what is now the southwest quarter of section 16 of the same township and range. The spot is marked on the map of Wyandot county of 1870, "Crawford's Battle Ground." It is also correctly laid down by William Brown, on his map of the Wyandot Reservation.

CHAPTER XI.

RETREAT OF THE AMERICAN ARMY. JUNE 5-6, 1782.

AT six o'clock on the morning of the 5th, the firing was renewed between the contending parties, but in a desultory manner, and at long shot only, and so continued during the day.[1] Little damage was done on either side. The relative position of the belligerents was unchanged. The Americans still occupied the island of timber, with their outposts extending well up to the edge of the prairie surrounding them. The Wyandots on the north and the Delawares on the south were abundantly satisfied with being able to hold the foe between them until reinforcements, hourly expected, should arrive; while the Americans attributed the slackness of their fire to the chastisement of the evening previous.

Crawford would gladly have attacked the foe at early dawn, but there were obstacles in the way. Some of

---

[1] "At the distance of two or three hundred yards."—*Knight*. "The enemy had received so severe a blow the preceding evening, that he did not venture an attack; but contented himself to annoy us at a distance."—*Rose*. "Next day the Indians lay around us at long-shot distance. Skirmishing continued all day, but there was no regular battle."—*Dunlevy*. "The next day, fired on each other at the distance of three hundred yards, doing little or no execution."—*Slover*.

his men were sick from the fatigues of the march, some from the extreme heat of the weather, and others from the bad water they had been compelled to drink since leaving the river; and, as already mentioned, there were several wounded. To give all of these the proper attention and care would require the services of several of the volunteers; and it was thought best, as the savages were in such force, not to attack them until every soldier, unless sick or disabled from wounds, could take part in the engagement. It was, therefore, determined not to make a general attack upon the Indians until after nightfall. "We were so much incumbered with our wounded and sick," is the language of Rose, " that the whole day was spent in their care, and in preparing for a general attack the next night."[2]

The volunteers felt confident of an easy victory; and there was much in the conduct of the troops the previous day to inspire such a belief in the mind of the commander. Orders had been obeyed cheerfully; and the officers displayed much bravery and coolness. The firing interfered but little with the active measures being taken for the coming conflict. The loss of the Americans through the entire day was four wounded. Crawford was making every effort to be fully prepared to strike a decisive blow. Plans were discussed and fully matured for the attack in force. Suddenly, however, all wore a changed aspect!

---

[2] Rose to Irvine, June 13, 1782. Not the *whole* day however.

The afternoon was not far advanced when the quick eye of a sentinel, stationed in a small copse to the northeast of the grove, caught sight of an advancing troop, partly to the left and in the rear of the Wyandots, rapidly approaching the lines of the latter. That they were all mounted he plainly saw. The next moment disclosed to his astonished vision that they were a body of white troops. It was Butler's Rangers. They had encamped, the evening previous, six miles north, at the mouth of Tymochtee creek.[3] Crawford was soon informed of this sudden apparition of a civilized foe. That the savages would be able, in any event, to obtain aid from Detroit, had not been dreamed of by any one in the American army. It was surmised now, that they had been stationed at Lower Sandusky or upon the Miami of the Lake—the Maumee—and had thus been enabled to reach the Plains in so short a time.[4] Their appearance was certainly well calculated to strike dismay to the hearts of the whole army.

---

[3] In response to a letter written by Irvine to Marshal, on the 18th of July following, the latter speaks of information he had received from a returned soldier as to the last encampment of these Rangers. The soldier had escaped from captivity; and while a prisoner had been told that the British camp was but six miles from the battle-field. The same distance is inferable from Leith's narrative.

[4] The volunteers returned to their homes with that impression. "The Sandusky people collected light dragoons from the British posts between Sandusky and the post at Detroit."—*Pentecost to Moore*, June 17, 1782.

Crawford saw that the contemplated attack must be abandoned, and that a defensive policy would have to be adopted. He immediately called a council of war of the field officers, to take into consideration the changed aspect of affairs. While they were deliberating, a large reinforcement—apparently two hundred strong—of Shawanese was discovered advancing from the south. They moved along in full view, and took up a position to the west of the Delawares; so that the trail from the south, which had been followed by the Americans, ran along between the two camps of the savages. At a distance, in the prairie, parties of the enemy were seen to pass to and fro, and small squads were discovered constantly arriving as reinforcements. "They kept pouring in hourly from all quarters," are the words of Rose.[5]

The council of war unanimously resolved upon a retreat that night, as the succors of the enemy rendered their entire force so much superior in numbers, that to risk an engagement would be, in the judgment of all, hazardous in the extreme.[6] Besides, it was now fairly to be presumed that the enemy would continue to be reinforced. "Prudence, therefore, dictated a retreat," wrote Rose to the commandant at Fort Pitt. Orders

---

[5] Rose to Irvine, June 13, 1782.

[6] "The field officers then assembled, and agreed, as the enemy were every moment increasing, and as we had already a number of wounded, to retreat that night."—*Knight*. Doddridge, in his *Notes*, p. 272, mentions (upon what authority does not appear), a proposition as

were given, and preparations at once begun, for a retrograde movement, to commence at nine o'clock. There was, it was evident, no other course to be pursued.

The volunteers killed were now buried, and fires burned over their graves to prevent discovery. Of the twenty-three wounded, seven were in a dangerous condition. Biers were prepared for these. The wounds of the others were mostly slight; none so bad but they could ride on horseback. The whole body was to form in four lines, or divisions, keeping the wounded in the center. By sundown the arrangements were all complete.

During the afternoon, as in the early part of the day, occasional shots were interchanged between the outposts of the contending parties, but usually at a distance of from two to three hundred yards. Dunlevy, who was engaged in the edge of the prairie watching the enemy, frequently heard, as during the battle the day before, the voice of Simon Girty. He was very well acquainted with the renegade, and thought there could be no doubt of his identity, and so expressed himself to his comrades at the time. It was generally believed among the volunteers—though in this they were mistaken—that Girty had the chief

---

having been made at the council, by Williamson, to take one hundred and fifty volunteers and march "directly to Upper Sanduskey," to destroy the village. That such a proposition was made at the council held the day previous, is not beyond the bounds of probability: it would hardly have been made at the last council.

command of the enemy; and many afterward so reported.[7]

The day had been as hot as the one previous; and, as then, there had been much suffering for the want of water. John Sherrard sought the pool from which he had supplied his comrades during the battle; but, to his surprise, found it entirely dry. His narrative of what followed is interesting: "After searching the grove around, I was fortunate enough to find another supply, and again busied myself relieving the men of my company. At length, overcome with heat and fatigue, I sat down at the foot of a large oak tree, and in a short time fell asleep. How long I slept I can not say. I was aroused by some bark falling upon my head from above, which had been knocked off the tree by the balls of the enemy. I then resumed my task of carrying water."[8]

It was no sooner dark than the officers went on the outposts and brought in the men as expeditiously and quietly as possible. The whole body was then formed to begin the march, with Crawford at the head. Each of the four divisions was commanded by the same field officer as on the outward march, except that of Major Brinton. This officer being wounded, Major Leet had

---

[7] Although, as already mentioned, it is not settled as to whether Girty held a commission from the British government or not, yet it is a significant fact that the Moravian missionaries considered him an English officer.

[8] Communicated by Robert A. Sherrard: 1872.

already taken command of his division. Just at this time the enemy discovered the intentions of the Americans, and opened a hot fire. Some of the men became alarmed. This precipitated matters. A few in the front lines hurried off, and most of those in the rear were not slow to follow, leaving the seven dangerously wounded men; some of whom, however, got off on horseback by the help of kind comrades, who waited for and assisted them.

It was the express order of Crawford that the wounded should all be taken along; and it was only the confusion arising from the army being so unexpectedly attacked, just at the critical moment the retreat was to have commenced, that interfered with that humane command. It was, indeed, generally supposed by the officers that all the wounded had been brought off; hence Rose to Irvine:[9] "We secured all our wounded." Lieutenant Ashley was carried from the field by the brave and magnanimous Captain Biggs, unknown, however, to the army. Only two, it is believed, were left to the insatiate vengeance of the savages.

The whole army was soon in motion, with Crawford at their head; and the only wonder is, that the movement did not degenerate at once into a total rout. Such, however, was not the case, although there was considerable confusion and a great noise. Says Rose to Irvine, apologetically: "In a body trained to the

[9] June 13, 1782.

strictest discipline, some confusion would have arisen, upon such an occasion."[10] Major McClelland led the division in front, and was soon engaged with the Delawares and Shawanese. It had been determined at the council to retreat on the same route followed by the army in their march out. This led due south from the battle-field for a short distance, until the Indian trace was struck, which would then take the army in a course toward the southwest—directly between the two camps of the savages. It was at this point that McClelland's line suffered severely. That officer fell from his horse, desperately wounded. Calling to John Orr, who was near, he told him to take his horse (Orr was on foot) and "clear himself," which he did. Little did the unfortunate major imagine the awful fate that was awaiting him—or he certainly would have craved the mercy of a bullet through his heart! Orr afterward related that he heard several of the men who were in the conflict,

---

[10] The account given by Doddridge (*Notes*, 273), concerning the commencement of the retreat, is wholly fictitious: "Most unfortunately," says the writer, "when a retreat was resolved on, a difference of opinion prevailed concerning the best mode of effecting it. The greater number thought best to keep in a body and retreat as fast as possible, while a considerable number thought it safest to break off in small parties, and make their way home in different directions, avoiding the route by which they came. Accordingly, many attempted to do so, calculating that the whole body of the Indians would follow the main army." "The whole body was formed to take up their line of march," is the language of Rose. All the straggling therefore was evidently the result of subsequent events.

say that the horsemen on the retreat rode over McClelland; and it was the general belief that he was killed where he fell. Such, however, was not the fact. Frightful tortures by the merciless savages were doled out to him afterward.

Although the enemy had early discovered the movement of the Americans, and had opened fire upon them, yet they were in great confusion and apparent alarm. It was not clear to them that a retreat was really intended by Crawford. They were fearful it was only a feint— a ruse or maneuver of some kind, not a flight. It was, perhaps, this uncertainty, or the well-known aversion of the Indians to night contests, that saved the borderers. Certain it is the enemy did not make an immediate effort to pursue them.

While McClelland's party was hotly engaged with the Delawares and Shawanese in front, the other divisions, to avoid the savages, bore off in a southwest direction, leaving the combatants to the left. This brought them near the swamp before spoken of, into which, owing to the darkness, rode some of the Americans.[13] The rear division was here attacked by the

---

[13] A small swamp near the battle-field has generally been mistaken for the one in which some of Crawford's men became entangled. The fact that a human skull and Indian relics have been found there, has served to strengthen the belief; but the distance traveled by the army after leaving the grove and the direction taken, make it evident that it was the "cranberry marsh" in which several men of the three divisions got involved.

Indians, and suffered some loss. Several of the men were compelled to leave their horses hopelessly entangled among the bogs, or stuck fast in the oozy soil.

The march was continued around the western margin of the swamp with considerable confusion.[14] When it was supposed by the volunteers that they were entirely beyond the enemy's lines, they changed their course to the southeast. A little before daylight, the trail they had followed on the inward march was reached; and, at break of day, they came to the site of the deserted village of the Wyandots—Upper Sandusky, Old Town—when a halt was called.[15]

The three divisions, in their march from the battlefield, had described the half of a circle, the center of which is the site of the present town of Upper Sandusky; but McClelland's division had marched, in a greatly demoralized condition, along the trail leading by the springs, and had already arrived irregularly and in much confusion, at the Old Town. It was evident they had suffered severely in their contest with the combined forces of the enemy; luckily, however, they had not been pursued far by the savages.

Detached parties continued to arrive at the deserted village,[16] and the army, in a short time, numbered about

---

[14] That this was the course taken is a current Wyandot tradition. Besides, it is corroborated by Knight (*Narr.*, p. 7).

[15] This fact is particularly mentioned by both Dunlevy and Rose.

[16] The following, from Doddridge, is wholly unreliable (*Notes*, 273): "The only successful party who were detached from the main

three hundred.[17] It was now discovered that Colonel Crawford was missing—"whose loss," says Rose, "we all regretted."[18] No one could give any information concerning him;—whether killed, captured, or making his escape through the wilderness, was a matter of conjecture with every one. Dr. John Knight and John Slover were also missing. Major McClelland was reported killed.

The command of the army now devolved upon Williamson, who immediately exerted himself in collecting the different parties, and in bringing order out of the general confusion.[19] He was powerfully aided by the gallant Rose, and the retreat was again continued.

It will be remembered that, on the march out, as the army passed along the Indian trace in the woods before reaching the deserted village of the Wyandots, a sugar-camp had been noticed, where, apparently in the

---

army, was that of about forty men, under the command of a Captain Williamson, who, pretty late in the night of the retreat, broke through the Indian lines under a severe fire and with some loss, and overtook the main army on the morning of the second day of the retreat."

[17] "We had about three hundred men when collected."—*Dunlevy.* Rose is silent as to the number. He says: "Several were separated; but the main body was collected at daybreak, five miles from the place of action, on the ground where the town formerly stood."

[18] Rose to Irvine, June 13, 1782.

[19] The wisdom of Irvine in instructing the volunteers at Mingo Bottom to determine, before the march begun, the relative rank of the field officers, was now clearly seen.

early spring, maple sugar had been made by the savages. Isaac Vance, one of the volunteers from Washington county, as the army was passing along, espied a brass kettle that had been used by the Indians in this camp to boil sap in, and which had apparently been left in the bush through an inadvertence. This kettle, in the eyes of the backwoodsman, was a prize of too much value to be left in the enemy's country; so, dismounting, and seizing a bowlder, he soon had the utensil flattened, ready for transportation. It was then securely fastened to his saddle; and, notwithstanding the stirring scenes through which the finder soon after passed, was transported all the way to the home of the borderer.[20]

John Sherrard, whose services in supplying his company with water upon the battle-field have been noticed, overtook the army just before the latter left the woodland again to thread its way in the open country in what is now Crawford county. His story was a melancholy one. In company with Daniel Harbaugh, after having become separated from the division to which he belonged, just as the retreat commenced the evening before, he had followed, as best he could, the main body of the troops—making, however, very slow progress owing to the darkness, which rendered it exceedingly difficult to keep the trail of the retreating forces.

---

[20] Communicated by Hon. Josiah Scott, of Bucyrus, Ohio, who heard, when a boy, the particulars related by Vance, as narrated.

It was a fortunate circumstance the two followed in the rear of the divisions moving to the southwest from the field of battle; for, had they taken the track of McClelland's party, which led between the camps of the Delawares and Shawanese, both, doubtless, would have been killed or captured. Not long after sunrise the next morning, they had gained the woods, and were moving along the trace on the east side of the Sandusky, some distance south of where the Old Town formerly stood, when Sherrard, who was riding in advance of his companion, saw an Indian a short distance away on his left. He immediately dismounted and got behind a tree, calling, at the same time, to his comrade to place himself in a like posture of defense.

Harbaugh had not been quick enough in discovering the Indian; for, getting upon the exposed side of the tree, he was quickly shot by the savage; exclaiming, as he gradually sunk down in a sitting posture: "Lord, have mercy upon me! I am a dead man!" and immediately expired. As soon as the smoke of the Indian's gun had cleared away, the savage was discovered by Sherrard, running as if for life, doubtless expecting a shot from the latter. But he had already escaped beyond the reach of a bullet.

At the sight of Harbaugh's pale face, his friend was greatly moved—more unmanned than at any of the scenes he had witnessed during the battle. After a moment to collect his thoughts, Sherrard stripped the saddle and bridle from his dead companion's horse, turning the animal loose. He then relieved his own horse of a very uncomfortable pack-saddle, and put in its place the saddle of Harbaugh. Mounting and taking a parting glance at the lifeless form of his comrade, still in a sitting posture, he rode sadly onward.

Sherrard had proceeded on the trail not a very great distance, when he made the discovery that, in the excitement of the moment, he had forgotten to disengage from the pack-saddle he had left behind, his supply of provisions, which were rolled up in a blanket. He resolved to retrace his steps, and secure what had thus inadvertently been left. Upon returning to the spot where Harbaugh was shot, a shocking spectacle was presented to his view. The Indian had returned, scalped the lifeless soldier, and then made off with his horse, gun, and bridle. Sherrard's pack-saddle and blanket had, however, not been discovered by the savage. A brief examination disclosed the fact that Harbaugh had received the fatal bullet in his right breast.

Sherrard, securing his blanket and provisions, again resumed his journey, overtaking the retreating army soon after, without any further encounter with an enemy, and was cordially greeted by his companions in arms.

Not long after the army had reached the open country southeast of the mouth of the Little Sandusky creek, and was well on its way in the Plains, a large body of the enemy was discovered a considerable distance in the rear. It consisted of mounted Indians and the British light cavalry. At noon, the army had reached a point on the trail due south of the present site of Bucyrus, in Bucyrus township, Crawford county. "The enemy," says Rose, "hung on our rear through the Plains;"[21] and they now began to press the Americans.

The eastern verge of the prairie was now not very far ahead. By two o'clock, the woodland had almost been reached, when the enemy crowded hard upon their rear, and began a flank movement of the Americans both right and left. "It was evidently their design," wrote Rose to Irvine,[22] "to retard our march, until they could possess themselves of some advantageous ground in our front, and so cut off our retreat, or oblige us to fight them at a disadvantage. Though it was our business studiously to avoid engaging in the Plains, on account of the enemy's superiority in light cavalry, yet they pressed our rear so hard, that we concluded on a general and vigorous attack, whilst our light-horse secured the entrance of the woods."[23]

NOTE 1.—JOHN SHERRARD, whose name is frequently mentioned in this narrative, was born the latter part of the year 1750, near Newtown-

---

[21] Rose to Irvine, 13th June, 1782.

[22] 13th June, 1782.

[23] In speaking of the retreat, Doddridge says: "The Indians paid

Limavady, a flourishing town situated on a stream emptying into Lough Foyle, Ireland. It is located about fifteen miles from the city of Londonderry. He was the eldest son of William Sherrard and Margaret Johnson—persons of fortune and respectability. He came to America in October, 1772, staying in Philadelphia until the spring of 1773, when he crossed the Allegheny Mountains on foot, following Braddock's trail, and settled in what is now Fayette county, Pennsylvania.

In March, 1774, Sherrard, in company with about twenty others, went down the Ohio to Kentucky, landing at Limestone (Maysville), whence they journeyed to the vicinity of the present town of Lexington, where each one selected a tract of land. Sherrard cleared about thirty acres and raised a crop of corn. This entitled him to hold four hundred acres. He returned in the fall, and took up his residence in Lancaster county, Pennsylvania. In the spring of 1775, he volunteered for one year in the service of his country, joining the famous " Flying Camp of Pennsylvania." He was with this body of men in their several engagements, and returned to Lancaster at the close of his term of enlistment.

In the fall of 1778, he again removed west of the mountains, residing in Dunbar township, in what is now Fayette county. In May, 1783, he married Mary Cathcart; and, in 1805, removed to Jefferson county, Ohio, where he died in 1809. He had five sons, two of whom—David A. C. Sherrard and Robert A. Sherrard—are still (1873) living, but well advanced in years.

NOTE 2.—In 1844, Joseph McCutchen, a resident of that part of Crawford which soon after became Wyandot county, Ohio, published

but little attention to the main body of the army, but pursued the small parties with such activity, that but very few of those who composed them made their escape."—*Notes*, 273. He seems to have had no information whatever concerning the stirring incidents which transpired the day after the retreat began.

in *The American Pioneer* (vol. ii, p. 283), a fiction respecting the battle of Sandusky and commencement of the retreat. The writer says:

"As I have it, the story respecting the battle is, that if Crawford had rushed on when he first came among the Indians, they would have given way and made but little or no fight; but they had a talk with him three days previous to the fight, and asked him to give them three days to collect in their chiefs and head men of the different tribes, and they would then make a treaty of peace with him. The three days were therefore given; and during that time all their forces gathered together that could be raised as fighting men, and the next morning Crawford was attacked, some two or three miles north of the island where the main battle was fought.

" The Indians then gave back in a south direction until they got into an island of timber, which suited their purpose, which was in a large plain, now well known as Sandusky Plains. There the battle continued until night. The Indians then ceased firing; and, it is said, immediately afterward a man came near to the army with a white flag. Colonel Crawford sent an officer to him. The man said he wanted to talk with Colonel Crawford, and that he did not want Crawford to come nearer to him than twenty steps, as he (Girty) wanted to converse with Crawford, and might be of vast benefit to him.

" Crawford accordingly went out as requested. Girty then said, 'Colonel Crawford, do you know me?' The answer was, 'I seem to have some recollection of your voice, but your Indian dress deprives me of knowing you as an acquaintance.' The answer was then, 'My name is Simon Girty;' and after some more conversation between them, they knew each other well.

" Girty said, 'Crawford, my object in calling you here is to say to you, that the Indians have ceased firing until to-morrow morning, when they intend to commence the fight; and as they are three times as strong as you are, they will be able to cut you all off. To-night the Indians will surround your army, and when that arrangement is fully made, you will hear some guns fire all around the ring. But there is a large swamp or very wet piece of ground on the east side of you, where there will be a vacancy: that gap you can learn by the firing; and in the night you had better march your men through and make your escape in an east direction.

"Crawford accordingly in the night drew up his men and told them his intention. The men generally assenting, he then commenced his march east; but the men soon got into confusion and lost their course."

NOTE 3.—Equally as absurd is Heckewelder's account of the retreat. He says: "The plan now being that they [the Indians] would surround them [Crawford and his men] during the night, and at daybreak attack them from all sides, they moved on at the proper time; when, however, to their mortification, they discovered that the heroes had fled during the night; not choosing, as it appeared, to stand an engagement with the kind of 'warriors' they met here [a reference to the Americans having anticipated meeting only peaceable Moravian Indians]. Some few who were not awoke from their sleep when their comrades went off, were found yet in that condition, lying in the high grass."—*Narr. Miss.*, p. 337.

NOTE 4.—The following brief history of the expedition, up to the time of Crawford's army leaving the Sandusky battle-ground, is from the *American Pioneer*, vol. i, p. 378, communicated by John McCaddon. It is, as will be seen, singularly erroneous. The account of the escape of the valorous Longstreet is ludicrous enough! The writer says:

"The American government ordered a few hundred men to march out and chastise the Indians. These were mostly or entirely drafted. I lived then in Fayette county, Pennsylvania, and was one; but hired a substitute by the name of Aaron Longstreet, a very active young man. When they arrived at the Sandusky Plains, they were met by the Indians, with whom they skirmished and fought for several days. The Indian forces increased every day, until our men were overpowered and surrounded. There was left to them no alternative but to force their way through the enemy. They placed themselves in solid column, the horsemen foremost. Mr. Longstreet caught hold of one of the horse's tails, and scampered through the fire."

NOTE 5.—A work entitled *Sketches of Western Adventure*, is frequently cited as an authority by writers upon Crawford's expedition. In the Preface of the book (p. viii), the author, John A. McClung, says: "For the striking incidents attending the expedition of Crawford, I am indebted to the printed narratives of Knight and Slover, which were published immediately after their return to Virginia, when the affair was fresh in the recollection of hundreds, and any misstatement would instantly have been corrected." Nevertheless, a comparison of his account (Chapters V and VI) with the Knight and Slover pamphlet of 1783, discloses his work to be so defectively done that I have found it valueless as a reference. His failure is in attempting to speak *for* his captives, instead of letting them speak *for themselves*. As the writer essays only to follow the narratives of Knight and Slover, he gives, of course, no account of the retreat of the main army or the battle of June 6th.

CHAPTER XII.

BATTLE OF OLENTANGY—RETURN OF THE AMERICANS. JUNE 6-14, 1782.

IT was two o'clock in the afternoon of the 6th of June, when the retreating army was brought to a stand by the pursuing enemy. The spot was at the eastern edge of the Plains, in what is now Whetstone township, Crawford county, not far from a small branch of the Olentangy creek—a tributary of the Scioto. This creek was formerly called, and still is frequently, the Whetstone, as the Delaware Indian name was *Keen-hong-she-con-sepung*, or Whetstone creek in English. Its present name, Olentangy, was "restored," in 1833, by the Legislature of Ohio; but whether, in this restoration, the right name was substituted, is doubtful.[1]

The forenoon had been excessively hot, but clouds now began to obscure the fierce rays of the almost vertical sun. Indications rapidly multiplied of an approaching storm. Already the change in the temperature was a grateful relief to the Americans. The latter had faced about, fronting to the west—the light-horse some distance in the rear, resting in the skirt of the woods. The superiority of the enemy, in numbers and equipment, was painfully evident to the borderers. They

---

[1] See *Smith's Narr.* 87, 99; also, Robt. Clarke & Co.'s reprint, 175.

were all mounted;[2] but, fortunately, owing to the rapidity of the pursuit, the British had been compelled to leave their artillery at the Sandusky.[3]

Williamson exerted himself to the utmost to encourage his heroic little band, and was ably seconded by the indefatigable Rose, whose cheerfulness, suavity, and coolness were only equaled by his wonderful skill and intrepidity. It is not too much to say that the undaunted young foreigner was the *good angel* of the American forces now standing at bay. "Stand to your ranks, boys," were his inspiring words sounding along the lines; "stand to your ranks, and take steady aim, fire low, and do'n't throw away a single shot. Remember, everything depends upon your steadiness." In less than an hour the enemy, whose exertions had been daring and furious, and who, according to Dunlevy, "attacked on the front, left flank, and rear," gave way on all sides. "We had three killed and eight wounded in this action," is the testimony of Rose.[4] Captain

---

[2] "The Indians, in company with some red-coats, mounted horses for speed, and overhauled our people."—*Fort Pitt Correspondence of the Pennsylvania Journal and Weekly Advertiser* (Philadelphia), July 23, 1782. Dunlevy speaks of the army being pursued by mounted Indians; Rose, by the enemy's light cavalry.

[3] There lingers around the headwaters of the Sandusky a tradition to the effect that one of the cannon belonging to Crawford was buried somewhere in the Plains. It is hardly necessary to speak of the absurdity of this tradition. Crawford had no cannon; the British lost none.

[4] Rose to Irvine, June 13, 1782.

Joseph Bean was shot through the body, but recovered.[5] The loss of the enemy was never ascertained. It was probably much severer than that of the Americans.[6]

A circumstance mentioned by Leith illustrates the fatal accuracy of the shots of the backwoodsmen during the battle. It will be remembered that this man had encamped, on the night of the 4th, about fourteen miles above Lower Sandusky, on the river. Just after he had fixed his camp and put out his horses to graze, a Frenchman—an interpreter to the Indians—made his appearance from below. "Well," said he, "I believe I will stay with you to-night and take care of you." Exactly *how* he was to be protected by the doughty Frenchman was not apparent. Leith informed his vis-

---

[5] Dunlevy's application for a pension, October 3, 1832.

[6] The battle of Olentangy was fought on what is now the northwest quarter of section 22, in township 3 south, of range 17 east, of the government survey, in what is now Whetstone township, Crawford county. A Wyandot Indian trail afterward ran along to the north of the battle-field. I find in the *Pennsylvania Journal and Weekly Advertiser*, of July 23, 1782, that the battle was fought "at a certain plain, twenty-five miles from the town;"—where the old Wyandot town that was found deserted, is evidently referred to. The distance, as traveled by the army, is very accurately given. The battle-ground is five miles in a south-easterly direction from Bucyrus; about six, in a northwesterly course, from Galion; and nearly nine, a little south of west of Crestline. As the battle was fought in the Plains, there were no traces of the battle-field to be seen afterward, as at "Battle Island."

itor that he was welcome for the night; at the same time explaining to him his intentions of making a very early start on the morrow.

Next morning, after Leith had his horses loaded ready to pursue his journey to Lower Sandusky, and the Frenchman had also got in readiness for a start up the river, a report was heard, which both believed to be the firing of a cannon at Upper Sandusky. The interpreter clapped his hands in great glee. "I shall be there before the battle is begun," said he, and immediately rode off. It appears he found his friends too soon for his personal safety. Hastening onward, he came upon a party of Wyandots who were preparing for battle. The valorous Gaul was determined not to be outdone by the painted and plumed heroes around him, so far as appearances were concerned. After putting on a ruffled shirt, he completed his war-toilet by painting a large red spot upon his breast; remarking, at the same time, to his dusky and yelling associates: "Here is a mark for the Virginia riflemen." He afterward marched with the Indians to the battle of Olentangy, where he received a ball *in the very spot* he had so boastfully decorated his person with, and died immediately.[7]

Scarcely had the battle ended when the threatened rain-storm swept the Plains with great fury. The air

---

[7] *Leith's Narr.*, p. 16. Walker, in a communication before me, speaks of this Frenchman as having been "disguised as an Indian."

became chilly, and the troops were drenched to the skin. Fire-arms were rendered nearly useless. No sooner, however, had the wounded been cared for and the dead buried, than the retreat was again continued. The enemy, observing the movement, rallied their scattered forces in the Plains, and renewed the pursuit, firing occasionally, but keeping at a respectable distance. Captain Biggs' company, which led the advance on the outward march, now reduced to nine men, was in the rear covering the retreat. All its officers were missing; John Rogers was acting as lieutenant, in place of Edward Stewart.

After the Americans had procceded some distance, Rogers asked Williamson to have his company relieved from its dangerous position, as some of his men were wounded and the residue greatly exhausted. It was given a place next to the front. But the enemy's shots had now become so galling, that the sudden exposure of other men in the rear to the firing caused them to move forward in some confusion. This was immediately followed by irregularities in the advance; and a panic had well nigh been the result, but for the almost superhuman efforts of Williamson and Rose. Already several of the companies began to waver; and the regular marching order was in imminent danger of being broken, ending in a confused and hopeless rout. Williamson earnestly entreated his men to keep their ranks. "Not a man of you will ever reach home," he exclaimed, "if each one attempts to shift for himself. Your only salvation is in keeping in line. Our ranks once broken, and all is lost." These remonstrances had, at length, the desired effect. Order was restored. The company in front filed to the left, and when the others had passed, immediately wheeled into line in the rear, occupying that position for some distance, when another one from the front took its place, and so on in a continuous round; the army all the while making good progress forward, while no particular company was required, for any considerable length of time, to cover the retreat.

By night-fall the army had reached the spot on the Sandusky river first seen by the army in its outward march, in what is now Crawford county, just to the east of where Leesville is located, a distance in a northeasterly direction of nearly six miles from the battlefield, where a halt was called, with the enemy a mile in the rear. Both parties now encamped for the night. Every precaution was taken by Williamson to guard against a surprise. The soldiers slept upon their arms. They were now directly east from the old village of the Wyandots twenty-five miles, and a little over thirty from the battle-ground of the 4th; but the route as traveled by most of the soldiers, since the retreat first began, was a distance of full forty miles. Many were on foot; they were incumbered with the wounded and sick; they had fought a severe battle, as we have seen, during the day: it may be imagined, therefore, how greatly the troops enjoyed a night's repose; for the enemy did not venture to disturb them.[8]

"At day-break," says Dunlevy, "the retreat was renewed."[9] Scarcely had the Americans formed their lines when the enemy appeared in the rear and opened fire. Two of the borderers were, at this juncture, unfortunately captured, and, it is supposed, immediately tomahawked. Now, however, to the great relief of the army, the pursuit was abandoned. "The Indians," continues Dunlevy, "pursued the main body no longer." The last hostile shot was fired near where the village of Crestline now stands. Here the Americans had their last view of the foe; it was a welcome adieu. Not a single savage or British Ranger was afterward seen by the army.

---

[8] In speaking of the day following the one upon which the retreat commenced, Doddridge says: "They continued their march the whole of the next day, with a trifling annoyance from the Indians, who fired a few distant shots at the rear guard, which slightly wounded two or three men. At night they built fires, took their suppers, secured their horses, and resigned themselves to repose without placing a single sentinel or vidette for safety! In this careless situation they might have been surprised and cut off by the Indians, who, however, gave them no disturbance during the night, nor afterward during the whole of the retreat!" As this describes, pretty nearly, the events of the day after the *second* battle, it is probable that the information of the writer was derived from some straggler who did not reach the army until that day.

[9] See his declaration for a pension: 1832. The incidents occurring

When it became apparent there was no longer any danger from the enemy, the discipline of the army was, to a considerable degree, relaxed; but there was no straggling, and orders were promptly obeyed. "The unremitting activity of Col. Williamson," says Rose, "surmounted every obstacle and difficulty in getting the wounded along."[10] As the army continued its march, stragglers would occasionally come up with the main body—some having become separated from their command the night of the beginning of the retreat, and others during the battle the following day. They were received by their comrades with loud hurrahs; and as some of them were nearly famished, their wants were quickly relieved, by sharing with them a portion of their now scanty supply of food.

The homeward march was along the trail of the army when outward bound,—to the Muskingum. This stream was crossed on the 10th, between the two upper

---

after the battle are narrated by Dunlevy with clearness and circumspection. These are corroborated by Indian traditions, and the recollection of Robert A. Sherrard of the conversations of his father, John Sherrard. Nevertheless, Rose, in his letter to Irvine, of 13th June, says, in speaking of the battle on the afternoon of the 6th: "In less than an hour the enemy gave way on all sides, and never after attempted to molest us any more on the march." The gallant young aid is evidently at fault in this. However, he may have thought the desultory firing of the enemy after the battle not worthy of mention; it could hardly have escaped his recollection.

[13] Rose to Irvine, June 13, 1782.

Moravian towns. From this point to the Ohio, "Williamson's Trail" was followed—the troops reaching Mingo Bottom on the 13th; when, to their great joy, they found that several of the missing had arrived before them—some, indeed, two days previous.

On the 11th, Marshal wrote Irvine from Washington county, informing him of the failure of the campaign, and inclosing a letter from one of the soldiers who had left the army on the 6th. "This moment," says Marshal, "came to hand the inclosed letter, by which you will learn the unhappy fate of our little army. What the consequences may be, God only knows. I would fondly hope that matters are not quite so bad as they are represented." Pentecost, whose home was but twenty-five miles from Mingo Bottom, also heard, on the same day, of the result of the expedition, and made haste to inform himself of the true state of affairs. "I met the men," he wrote to the Executive of the State on the 17th, "at Mingo Bottom last Wednesday."[11] He also informed Moore that the men were much confused when he met them, and he could not get as much information as he desired. "What little I got," adds Pentecost, "was from Major Rose, aid-de-camp to General Irvine, who went as aid to Colonel Crawford. I hope the general

---

[11] Pentecost to Moore, June 17, 1782: *Penn. Arch.*, vol. ix, p. 556. Pentecost gives the wrong day of the week; the army did not reach Mingo Bottom until *Thursday*, June 13th.

will give you a particular account, as he will receive it from the major."

The army recrossed the Ohio river immediately upon reaching it, without accident. It was while the troops were thus engaged that Rose wrote to Irvine:[12] "Those volunteers who marched from here . . . under the command of Col. William Crawford, are this moment returned, and recrossing the Ohio with Col. Williamson."—"I am sorry to observe," continues the chivalric writer, "they did not meet with that success which so spirited an enterprise, and the heroic bravery of the greater part deserved."

Williamson, also, at the same time and place, wrote to the commander of the Western Department: "I take this opportunity to make you acquainted with our retreat from Sandusky Plains, June 6th. We were reduced to the necessity of making a forced march through the enemy's lines in the night, much in disorder; but the main body marched round the Shawanese camp, and were lucky enough to escape their fire. They marched the whole night, and the next morning were reinforced by some companies, of which I can not give a particular account, as they were so irregular and so confused. . . .

"I must acknowledge myself ever obliged to Major Rose for his assistance, both in the field of action and in the camp. His character in our camp is estimable,

---

[12] Dated at Mingo Bottom, June 13, 1782.

and his bravery can not be outdone. Our country must be ever obliged to General Irvine for his favor done on the late expedition. Major Rose will give you a particular account of our retreat. I hope your honor will do us the favor to call the officers together and consider the distress of our brave men in this expedition, and the distresses of our country in general. Our dependence is entirely upon you; and we are ready and willing to obey your commands, when called upon."[13]

To this noble and patriotic letter was added an ominous postscript: "Col. Crawford, our commandant, we can give no account of since the night of the retreat." Equally startling to Irvine were the last words in the letter of Rose: "Col. Crawford has not been heard of since the night of the 5th instant, and I fear is among the killed." Inquiries of those who had been separated from the main body and afterward came up with the enemy, or who had reached the Ohio in advance of the principal force, failed to throw any light upon the subject, or give the least clue to his probable fate. Most of the volunteers, however, were sanguine of his safe return. Pentecost, in his letter of the 17th, to Moore, says: "There are a good many missing; among them Col. Crawford and a number of other valuable men; but, as the scattered parties are coming in daily, I have hopes of them."

[13] Williamson to Irvine, June 13, 1782. I have a copy of this letter before me, in the handwriting of Irvine.

Opposite Mingo Bottom, on the evening of the 13th, the troops went into camp for the last time. On the 14th they were discharged; and the campaign, of only twenty days' duration, was ended.—But our narrative must be continued, until all the scenes of this wilderness tragedy—terrible as some of them were—are brought fully upon the page of history.

It will be remembered that Irvine, in his instructions to the commander of the expedition, requested to be informed, upon the return of that officer, of whatever might be the success of the campaign. As Crawford was still missing when the army recrossed the Ohio, this duty devolved upon Williamson. That the latter addressed a letter to the commander at Fort Pitt from Mingo Bottom has already been mentioned. It was the only official report of the campaign sent in by that officer. It was provokingly meager. The duty of giving particulars was turned over to Rose, who kindly consented to send in an account of the expedition,[14] along with Williamson's. These two letters formed the basis for Irvine's official account sent to Washington on the 16th, in which he says:

"The inclosed letters—one from Col. Williamson, second in command, and the other from Lieut. Rose, my aid-de-camp—contain all the particulars of this transaction which have yet come to my knowledge. I am of opinion had they reached the Plains in seven

---

[14] Rose to Irvine, June 13, 1782, already frequently cited.

days (instead of ten), which might have been done, especially as they were chiefly mounted, they would have succeeded. They should also have pushed the advantage evidently gained at the commencement of the action. They failed in another point, which they had my advice and indeed positive orders for, viz: to make the last day's march as long as possible and attack the town[15] in the night. But they halted in the evening within nine miles, fired their rifles at seven in the morning before they marched.

"These people now seem convinced that they can not perform as much by themselves as they some time since thought they could; perhaps it is right that they should put more dependence on regular troops. I am sorry I have not more to afford them assistance."[16]

---

[15] In the original letter on file in the State Department at Washington City, this word is *plan;* evidently an inadvertency.

[16] The copy of this letter, retained by Irvine, differs somewhat from the one sent to the commander-in-chief. "I am of opinion," is the reading of the copy, "the cause of their failure was owing to the slowness of the march and their not pushing the advantage they evidently gained at their first commencing the action. They were ten days on the march, when it might have been performed in seven, particularly as they were chiefly mounted. My advice was to attack the town *in the night*, but instead thereof they halted within ten miles, in the evening, and did not take up their line of march until seven in the morning." The following sentence in the copy has a line drawn over it: "Dr. Knight, mentioned in Mr. Rose's letter, is one of the regimental surgeons of this garrison, whom I spared to Col. Crawford, and is also missing."

On the 5th of July, Irvine wrote the Executive of Pennsylvania, informing him of the failure of the campaign, and mentioning several disastrous circumstances connected with it which had come to his knowledge. Six days after, he sent a second communication to Washington concerning the expedition, but confined himself wholly to the relation of particular incidents. The official correspondence relative to the subject was closed by Washington on the 6th of August, in a letter to Irvine dated at headquarters, in which he says: "I lament the failure of the expedition."[17]

The State of Pennsylvania was not slow in recognizing the legality of the campaign. The claims for losses of those who served in the expedition were adjusted by its officers from time to time and promptly paid. Horses, guns, blankets, pack-saddles, bags, and many other things, were, when proven to have been lost, paid for at a fair valuation. The volunteers who furnished their own supplies were compensated for the provisions taken with them, as were those who advanced them rations.[18] State aid did not stop there.

---

[17] The original letter is in my possession. A copy is on file in the Department of State at Washington.

[18] Extracts from the Minutes of the Supreme Executive Council of Pennsylvania, relating to the expedition against Sandusky:

"*In Council:*
"PHILADELPHIA, *January* 7, 1785.

"The comptroller-general's reports upon the following accounts against the State for losses sustained, etc., upon the Indian expedition

Under a special law, pensions were granted, based upon services rendered upon this and other occasions. Many of 1782, under the direction of Colonel William Crawford, were read and approved, viz. :

"Six pounds due to *John Crawford* (a); twelve pounds to James Alexander; four pounds three shillings and two pence to the estate of *Col. William Crawford*; two pounds nine shillings and five pence to *Moses Smith*; six pounds four shillings and five pence to Noble Graham; six pounds to Samuel Dualls; thirteen pounds to John Dean; seven shillings and six pence to Samuel Cane; seven pounds to Richard Clark; thirty-eight pounds ten shillings to the estate of *William Crawford*; twenty-four pounds ten shillings and three pence to *Zachariah Connell*; seven pounds to *Reuben Kemp*; twelve shillings to *Edward Hall*; fifty pounds two shillings and six pence to the estate of Colonel William Hall; fourteen pounds to *Michael Frank*; fifteen pounds to Louis Heming; eleven pounds to *Jeremiah Gard*; eighteen pounds ten shillings to *Colonel Thomas Gaddis* (b); and sixteen pounds to Joseph Barker."

"January 10, 1785. Eighteen pounds to Dr. *John Knight* (c); thirty-three pounds fifteen shillings to *James Paull* (d); thirteen pounds to James Woods; eight pounds ten shillings to Jacob Vankirk; thirty pounds to James Nicholl; fourteen pounds to *James McCoy*; two pounds seven shillings and six pence to *Peter Patrick* (e); four pounds nineteen shillings and six pence to Joseph Parish; fifteen pounds to *Audley Rhea* and *Zachariah Brashears*; six-

---

(a) Colonel Crawford's son. [Names in italics are those known to have been residents, at that time, of that part of Westmoreland county which is now Fayette.]

(b) Third officer in the expedition.

(c) The surgeon of the expedition.

(d) See Chapter XVII.

(e) For information concerning this man, the reader is referred to *The American Pioneer*, vol. 1, p. 57.

also died pensioners to the general government for duties performed in campaigns, of which this was one.

teen pounds to Jacob South; ten pounds to Jacob Swartz; eight pounds to *William Ross;* thirty-six pounds to the estate of *William Crawford;* eleven pounds to *John Hardin, Jr.* (*f*); five pounds sixteen shillings and three pence to John Lucas; eight pounds seven shillings and six pence to the estate of *John McClelland* (*g*); five pounds to Alexander McDonald; two pounds ten shillings to *Thomas Kendall;* four pounds ten shillings to Robert Jackson; fifteen pounds to William Case; fifteen pounds to Aaron Rollins; eleven pounds to Lewis Duvall; three pounds eight shillings to Charles Burdin; fourteen pounds to *Charles Hickman;* six pounds ten shillings to Dennis Stevens."

"March 2, 1785. Accounts approved of Craig Ritchie (*h*) and Andrew Munro (*i*) for horses lost on the Sandusky expedition.

"Of the aforesaid Captain Craig Ritchie for rations due from the 20th of May to the 20th day of June, 1782.

"Of *John Smilie,* for a horse and rifle lost on the Sandusky expedition." (*j*)

"August 30, 1785. The comptroller-general's report upon the

(*f*) Father and son—branches of the celebrated Hardin family of Kentucky, of which there were officers in the war of the Revolution, of 1812, and with Mexico.

(*g*) Fourth officer of the expedition.

(*h*) A sketch of Mr. Ritchie has already been given, page 135.

(*i*) Postmaster at Canonsburgh for many years prior to 1830.

(*j*) John Smilie was not in the expedition, but his son Robert is believed to have been one of the volunteers. They were near neighbors of Colonel Crawford. The father was a prominent man in Revolutionary movements, in Lancaster county, Pa. After moving to that part of Westmoreland, now Fayette, he became a member of the legislature, also of the Supreme Executive Council. He was a member of Congress for several years, and died in office in December, 1812.

Concerning the causes which produced the failure of the expedition against Sandusky,—it may be said there

accounts of William Shearer, of the county of Washington, for a horse lost on the Sandusky expedition, was read and approved."

"September 15, 1785. Upon the account of James Scott for a horse, blanket, etc., lost on the Sandusky expedition."

"September 21, 1785. Of Peter Peterson for rations due on the Sandusky expedition.

"Of Henry Taylor, for thirty days rations furnished John Blean upon the aforesaid expedition.

"*Note.*—All the (3) persons above named are inhabitants of Washington county."

"October 19, 1785. Of *Robert Miller*, of Fayette county, for a horse lost on the Sandusky expedition.

"Of *John Crawford*, of Fayette county, for a horse lost on the Sandusky expedition."

"December 31, 1785. Of Richard Graham, for a horse lost on the Sandusky expedition."

"April 19, 1786. Of Hugh Sprouls, of the county of Washington, for a horse lost on the Sandusky expedition.

"Of Joseph Brown, of said county, for rations furnished to the militia employed on the said expedition.

"Of Thomas Brown, of said county, for rations furnished as aforesaid."

"March 30, 1789. For nine pounds, amount of *John Custard's* account for a horse lost on the Sandusky expedition under Colonel Crawford in 1782.

"For seven pounds, amount of *Richard Hale's* account for a gun taken into actual service, and lost in 1782, in the expedition under Colonel Crawford."

"December 8, 1789. Of George Tompoh, for his provisions while employed as a militia-man on the frontiers of Washington

was a concatenation of circumstances contributing to the disaster. The expeditions of Brodhead and Williamson to the Muskingum, produced more than usual watchfulness of the border by the enemy. This led to

county, and for a blanket, a pack-saddle, and two bags lost on the (said) expedition under Colonel Crawford, in 1782, amounting to two pounds seven shillings and six pence.

"Of John Hill, for a saddle, blanket, two bags and a wallet, or knapsack, lost on the said expedition, amounting to four pounds two shillings and six pence.

"Of Robert Taylor, for thirty days' provisions due him while employed on said expedition, amounting to one pound two and six pence.

"Of Richard Hopkins, for a horse lost on the said expedition, amounting to four pounds.

"Of John Turvey, for thirty days' provisions, due to him while employed on said expedition, amounting to one pound, two shillings and six pence."

"December 17, 1789. Of Robert Walker, Jr., of Washington county, for provisions furnished by him for the Sandusky expedition, under Colonel Crawford, in the year 1782, amounting to one pound two shillings and six pence."

"February 18, 1790. Of Alexander Lashley, for a horse which was taken into public service and lost on the Sandusky expedition against the Indians under Colonel Crawford, in the year 1782, valued at twelve pounds, and allowed."

"August 28, 1790. Of Moses Cook, for a horse which was lost on the Sandusky expedition against Indians, in the year 1782, amounting to fifteen pounds."

"September 6, 1790. Of the estate of James Guffee, for a horse which was lost on the Sandusky expedition against the Indians, in 1782, amounting to fourteen pounds."

an early knowledge of the movement; whereby the savages were enabled to make preparations to meet the invaders of their territory. And to *this* is chargeable, to a great extent, the calamitous result of the enterprise. The strictures of Irvine, as given in his official account of the campaign to the commander-in-chief, were, as viewed from his stand-point, undoubtedly just. It seems that he supposed the Wyandot town was only deserted just before the arrival of the army. The opinions of the rank and file were, as hereafter mentioned, that inexperience on the part of the officers contributed greatly to the failure of the expedition; nevertheless, if this *was* the approximate cause of the failure, the remote ones were as we have stated. But great praise must be awarded the patriotic volunteers, who so bravely imperiled their lives, notwithstanding the enterprise did not prove successful. During the twenty days of the campaign, each one, with a single exception, was a day of marching. Two battles were fought in the meantime, and two victories won. The extrication of the army from the toils woven around it by a foe so much superior in numbers, may be considered remarkable.[19]

---

[19] The summing up of Doddridge of the results of the campaign is, to a great extent, unwarrantable and particularly unjust to the memory of those engaged in the expedition on the American side. His reflections, of course, are warped by the belief that one of the objects of the march into the wilderness was the destruction of the remnant of

NOTE.—FRANCIS DUNLEVY, whose declaration for a pension and MS. notes of the campaign, have been consulted in the preparation of this and other chapters of this work, was born near Winchester, Virginia, December 31, 1761. His father, Anthony Dunlevy, came from Ireland about the year 1745, and afterward married Hannah White, sister to Judge Alexander White, of Virginia. Of this marriage there were four sons and four daughters. Francis was the eldest of the sons. About the year 1772 the family removed from Winchester to

---

the Christian Indians. "Thus ended," says the writer (*Notes*, 278, 279), "this disastrous campaign. It was the last one which took place in this section of the country, during the Revolutionary contest of the Americans with the mother country. It was undertaken with the very worst of views—those of murder and plunder. It was conducted without sufficient means to encounter, with any prospect of success, the large force of Indians opposed to ours in the plains of Sandusky. It was conducted without that subordination and discipline so requisite to insure success in any hazardous enterprise, and it ended in a total discomfiture. Never did an enterprise more completely fail of attaining its object. Never, on any occasion, had the ferocious savages more ample revenge for the murder of their pacific friends, than that which they obtained on this occasion.

"Should it be asked what considerations led so great a number of people into this desperate enterprise? Why, with so small a force and such slender means, they pushed on so far as the plains of Sandusky?

"The answer is, that many believed that the Moravian Indians, taking no part in the war, and having given offense to the warriors on several occasions, their belligerent friends would not take up arms in their behalf. In this conjecture they were sadly mistaken. They did defend them with all the force at their command, and no wonder; for notwithstanding their Christian and pacific principles, the warriors still regarded the Moravians as their relations, whom it was their duty to defend."

what was supposed to be Western Virginia, on the west of the Alleghany Mountains, and settled near Catfish (Washington), in what is now Washington county, Pennsylvania.

In this frontier settlement, when the Revolutionary war broke out, there was great exposure, as we have already seen, to Indian depredations. The men of the new settlements were constantly called upon to serve in longer or shorter tours of militia duty, which were considered essential to the safety of the frontiers.

Dunlevy volunteered as a private, on the 1st of October, 1776, under Captain Isaac Cox; his lieutenant was David Steele. His company encamped in the woods, at Holliday's Cove, on the Ohio river, opposite a large island, in what is now Brooke county, West Virginia, now known as Brown's Island, above Steubenville, Ohio, but below the mouth of Yellow creek. Here the company erected a chain of log cabins—blockhouses—and scouted, in pairs, up and down the river, for the distance of twelve miles. This fort, or station, was on the line of defense from Fort Pitt to Grave creek;—erected as a protection to the border against the Indians. Dunlevy afterward remembered that he frequently saw at this post, Col. John Gibson, of the Thirteenth Virginia regiment, who supervised the several stations upon the river. His tour of duty expired on the 20th of December, and he was then discharged. During the latter part of the service of this tour, he, with others, was detached and sent down the river about twelve miles, where Decker's Fort was erected, and where a small settlement was protected while the inhabitants gathered their corn.

In July, 1777, Dunlevy served fourteen days in the militia, at Fort Pitt, as a substitute for his father, Anthony Dunlevy, who had been drafted for a month and had served the first half of it. General Hand had just arrived at the post, unaccompanied by any troops. Notwithstanding Dunlevy was a militia-man, he did duty in garrison under officers belonging to the regular army. Captain Harry Heath had command of the post upon the arrival of Hand. Colonel John Gibson and some of his regiment—Thirteenth Virginia—were in the garrison a short time. Captains Scott, Bell, and Steele, well known about Pittsburg before, during, and after the Revolutionary war, were in Fort Pitt at this time. Simon Girty was also present, then a subaltern. He seemed wholly taken up in intercourse with the Indians, a great number of whom were in and around the fort.

Dunlevy volunteered about the 1st of March, 1778, for one month's service. The rendezvous was at Cox's Station, on Peters' creek. Colonels Isaac Cox and John Canon attended to organizing the men; but in eight days the militia relinquished their arms to some recruits for the regular army, who relieved them, and they returned home to attend to putting in their crops.

On the 15th of August, 1778, Dunlevy was again drafted for one month; the place of meeting was Pittsburg. He served this tour under Lieut. John Springer, the troops being attached to the command of Captain Ferrol, lately from the seaboard, who had a company detached from the Thirteenth Virginia regiment. This body of men ranged the woods, visiting the stations on the frontier line between Pittsburg and Wheeling, and finally relieving a company of militia from Hampshire county, Virginia, at the latter place, commanded by Capt. Daniel Cressap, brother of the celebrated Mike Cressap. Dunlevy was discharged at Pittsburg at the end of the month's service.

About the 5th of October he again entered the service. He went this time as a substitute for Andrew Flood, joining the company of Capt. John Crow. His battalion commander was Col. Hugh Stephenson; regimental commander, Col. William Crawford. The army was then under the command of Brigadier-General Lachlin McIntosh. Dunlevy afterward remembered that Col. Evans was commander of one of the militia regiments, and that there were also present Col. John Gibson, of the Thirteenth Virginia, and Daniel Brodhead, colonel of the Eighth Pennsylvania regiment. It was this army that built Fort McIntosh at mouth of Beaver. The army marched into the wilderness on the 5th of November, crossing the forks of the Muskingum, and building Fort Laurens on the west bank of that river. He afterward returned to Fort McIntosh, and was discharged on the 20th of December.

Dunlevy was again drafted on the 25th of August, 1779; the rendezvous, Fort Pitt. He was in camp three days at the "King's Orchard," on the Allegheny river. He then marched up that stream under Col. Brodhead as chief officer, Col. Gibson next in command. His captain was one Ellis. In this army were Lieutenants John Hardin, of the Thirteenth Virginia, and Samuel Brady, of the Eighth Pennsylvania,—both afterward famous in Indian warfare. John Monteur, a half-blood (son of Andrew Monteur, a Frenchman), a man of information and education, but a great savage, accompanied the expedition, which consisted of about seven hundred whites, including some lighthorse, and about sixty Indians.

Proceeding up the east bank of the Allegheny, they crossed the Kiskiminitas at i's mouth, and Crooked creek, and came to Kittanning, where there was a garrison. The army lay severaldays at an old Indian town on the river, about twelve miles above the Kittanning. They then marched up the river and crossed about fifteen miles below the mouth of French creek. They then crossed the latter stream and moved toward the Monsey towns, meeting and defeating a small body of Indians—some thirty or forty in number. Four or five of the Americans were wounded; among them Jonathan Zane, who was acting as pilot to the expedition. The Monsey villages were deserted.

The army lay in the abandoned towns nearly a week, destroying several hundred acres of growing corn on the banks of the river. On their return, a young man named John Ward was badly injured by a horse falling on a rock in a creek. This accident occurred in what is now Butler county, Pennsylvania, where there is a township and post-office, called "Slipping Rock." Dunlevy was discharged September 29th.

In the spring of 1782, Dunlevy was a student in Rev. Thaddeus Dod's Latin and Mathematical "Log-cabin" School on Ten-mile, in Washington county, near Amity. He was then considered "a young man of superior talent and of amiable disposition." He did not remain long in this school, for, in April of that year, he again volunteered against hostile Indians, under a call from James Marshal, lieutenant of his county. The men rendezvoused at Decker's Station, or fort, on the east bank of the Ohio, one mile above Cross creek. After a few days the men were dismissed,—a sufficient number to have undertaken any important movement, not having assembled. He was absent from home only ten days.

No sooner was the expedition against Sandusky announced than Dunlevy once more shouldered his rifle. By the 15th of May he had returned to Decker's Station. He soon after crossed the Ohio to Mingo Bottom; and, upon the organization of the army, was made lieutenant in Capt. Craig Ritchie's company.

After the return of Dunlevy from the Sandusky campaign, and as soon as the peace of the country permitted, he was sent to Dickinson College. He was afterward a student of divinity, under Rev. James Hoge, of Winchester, Virginia, and finally taught a classical school in that State—having several pupils who subsequently were distinguished for their talents and learning. About the year 1790, he moved with his father's family to Washington, Kentucky, or to that neighborhood. In 1792 he came to Columbia, near Cincinnati, where he opened a classical school, in connection with the late John Reily, of Butler county, Ohio. This school was continued for several years. He afterward removed to Lebanon, Warren county.

Dunlevy was twice a member of the legislature of the Northwestern Territory; afterward elected to the convention which formed the first Constitution of Ohio. He was a member of the first State Legislature, and was subsequently chosen President Judge of the Court of Common Pleas of the first circuit, which office he held fourteen years. After this he practiced law ten years, retiring from business, however, some time previous to his death, which occurred November 6, 1839. In many respects he was a remarkable man. His memory was astonishing. He read and wrote the Latin language with ease. I am informed by the Commissioner of Pensions that his declaration for a pension is one of the completest on file in the Pension Office. It contains the only *positive* account of the incidents occurring immediately after the battle of Olentangy that has come under my notice. All others are traditionary, but corroborative, however, of his statement.

CHAPTER XIII.

ALARM OF THE BORDER—DETERMINED SPIRIT OF THE BORDERMEN.

GREAT was the alarm upon the frontiers, when it became known that the expedition against Sandusky had proved a failure, and that the discomfited army was nearing the Ohio. Stragglers who had reached the settlements in advance of the main body, gave greatly exaggerated accounts of the disaster. It was currently reported and generally believed, that the volunteers were being pursued even to the river. Marshal, with his usual energy and promptness, hastened to make preparations to succor the returning army. The general fear of an immediate invasion by the emboldened savages caused a wide-spread panic among the settlers, who flew with their families to the numerous forts for protection.

"I shall be as expeditious as possible," are the words of Marshal, in his letter of the 11th, to Irvine, "in raising a party of men to secure the retreat across the river, should the pursuit be continued so far." But the ever-watchful lieutenant of Washington county soon learned that no help was needed—that the army had not been pursued but a short distance beyond the Sandusky Plains. But that officer, with other prominent citizens, hastened to Mingo Bottom to learn the extent of the disaster. All were soon convinced that the loss had been overstated—that the calamity was by no means as overwhelming as reported.

It was not positively known, at the date of the recrossing of the Ohio by the Americans, that more than ten officers and men had been killed. "Our loss," said Rose in his letter to Irvine, "will not exceed thirty men, at a moderate computation, in killed and wounded."[1] But there were still a number missing.[2] "There are about twenty wounded (few dangerously), and about half that number killed," is the testimony of Pentecost also.[3] There were arrivals in the settlements, of the missing, as late as the 10th of the following month. Adding to the number of those whose deaths were reported at the time of the return of the expedition, such as died of their wounds, with those afterward known to have suffered death in the wilderness, together with a few whose fate was never known, and the result is a total loss of less than seventy.[4]

---

[1] Rose to Irvine, 13th June, 1782.

[2] "In the very neighborhood where I was then living, about two miles from Catfish (Washington), John Campbell, William Nimmons, William Huston, and William Johnson never returned, though their individual fate was, I believe, never revealed."—Wm. Darby to W. De Hass, March 30, 1850. (*Hist. Ind. Wars W. Va.*, p. 328.)

[3] *Pentecost to Moore*, 17th June, 1782. "General Lincoln sent information of the failure of the expedition against Sandusky, and the loss of about thirty men, killed and wounded, and the return of the remainder."—*Extract from the Minutes of the Supreme Executive Council, Philadelphia, Monday, July* 1, 1782.

[4] A communication from Fort Pitt, in the *Pennsylvania Journal and*

The unremitting exertions of Williamson in caring for the wounded have been referred to. Their great want, upon their arrival at Mingo Bottom, was medical attendance. "Several of them," wrote Rose to Irvine, "are in a dangerous condition, and want immediate assistance, of which they have been deprived since the loss of Dr. Knight."[5] Of those able to ride on horseback all soon reached their homes. Such as could not be moved except upon litters, were taken to the nearest settlements by their comrades, and tenderly cared for by sympathizing settlers.

The return of the visitors to their homes from Mingo Bottom tended somewhat to allay the excitement upon the frontiers. It was, nevertheless, plainly evident that the result of the expedition would be an increased boldness of the savages in depredating upon the border. The inquiry now was, how shall it be met? All eyes were naturally turned upon the commander of the Western Department for an answer. Now, more than ever, would a defensive policy be futile against the

---

Weekly Advertiser, of July 6th (after which only one more volunteer returned), estimates the missing at "from fifty to seventy." The reader will fully appreciate the absurdity of the following summary disposal of the expedition: "Soon after the disappointment which the murderers [the Americans] met with at Sandusky, they were attacked by a party of English and Indian warriors, and the greater part of them were cut to pieces."—*Loskiel's Hist. Miss.*, P. iii, p. 189.

[5] Letter of 13th June, 1782.

stealthy inroads of the exultant foe. Clearly then, to the minds of the frontiersmen, they must continue to act on the offensive. Another expedition was, therefore suggested; this time to be commanded by Irvine in person.

"The unfortunate miscarriage of the late expedition," wrote Captains Robert Beall and Thomas Moore, of the Westmoreland county militia, from near Stewart's Crossings, to Irvine, on the 23d of June, "the common interest of our country, and the loss of our friends, induce us to be thus forward in proposing another." "We do not wish to be understood," add the writers, "as giving our own private sentiments, but of those of the people generally in our quarter; for which purpose we are authorized to address you, and from accounts well authenticated, we assure you it is the wish of the people on this side the Monongahela river, without a dissenting voice."

The reply of Irvine was encouraging: "Inclination, as well as duty, is a continual spur to me, not only to acquiesce in, but to encourage every measure adopted for the public good. Your proposals, on this occasion, are so truly patriotic and spirited, that I should look on myself unpardonable were I to pass them unnoticed." On the same day, June 26th, Irvine wrote to Colonel Cook, lieutenant of Westmoreland county: "Your people seem so much in earnest, that I am led to think, if other parts of the country are so spirited and patriotic, something may probably be done; but, as it will take some time to come to a proper knowledge of this matter, and that must be accurately done, there can be no harm in making the experiment." "I have no intimation," continues the writer, "of any plan being on foot in Washington county for this purpose, though it is said the people wish another expedition."

Irvine was informed by letter from John Evans, lieutenant of Monongalia county, on the 30th of June, that the Indians were frequently in the settlements of his county. "Without your assistance," says that officer, "I much fear our settlements will break. The defeat of Colonel Crawford occasions much dread."

"The disaster," wrote the commander at Fort Pitt, to Lincoln, Secretary of War, on the 1st of July, "has not abated the ardor, or desire for revenge (as they term it), of these people. A number of the most respectable are urging me strenuously to take command of them, and add as many Continental officers and soldiers as can be spared; particularly officers, as they attribute the defeat to the want of experience in their officers. They can not, nor will not, rest under any plan on the defensive, however well executed; and think their only safety depends on the total destruction of all the Indian settlements within two hundred miles: this, it is true, they are taught by dear-bought experience.

"They propose to raise, by subscription, six or seven hundred men—provision for them for forty days, and horses to carry it, clear of expense to the public, unless government, at its own time, shall think proper to reimburse them. The 1st of August they talk of assembling, if I think proper to encourage them. I am, by no means, fond of such commands, nor am I sanguine in my expectations; but rather doubtful of the consequences;—and yet absolutely to refuse having anything to do with them, when their proposals are so generous and seemingly spirited, I conceive would not do well either; especially as people too generally, particularly in this quarter, are subject to be clamorous, and charge Continental officers with want of zeal, activity, and inclination of doing the needful for their protection.

"I have declined giving them an immediate, direct answer, and have informed them that my going depends on circumstances; and, in the meantime, I have called for returns of the men who may be depended on to go, the subscriptions of provisions and horses. The distance to headquarters is so great that it is uncertain whether an express could return in time with the commander-in-chief's instructions. As you must know whether any movements will take place in this quarter;—or if you are of the opinion it would, on any account, be improper for me to leave the post, I request you would please to write me by express. But, if no answer arrives before, or about the 1st of August, I shall take for granted you have no objections, and that I may act discretionally.

"Should it be judged expedient for me to go, the greatest number of troops fit to march will not exceed one hundred. The militia are pressing that I shall take all the Continentals along and leave the defense of the fort to them; but this I shall by no means do. If circumstances should seem to require it, I shall throw in a few militia with those regulars left,—but under Continental officers."

Irvine wrote to Washington on the same day relative to this proposed second expedition against Sandusky: "I would not presume to go on any account without your excellency's express orders, or, at least, permission, did I not conceive that, before the day appointed for rendezvousing, I will receive information if any movements are intended this way this campaign; as, by that time, it will be full late enough to undertake anything more than on a small partisan way."

"By the best information I can obtain," continues Irvine, "we may lay out our accounts to have to fight the Shawanese, Delawares, Wyandots, Mingoes, and Monseys,—in all, about five hundred. They are all settled in a line from Lower Sandusky, near Lake Erie, to the heads of Miami; not more than seventy-five miles from the two extremes: Upper Sandusky lies near the center. If all these could be beat at once, it would certainly nearly, if not entirely, put an end to the Indian war in this quarter."

The frontiersmen had the best of reasons for anticipating a visitation in force from the allied savages, now that the expedition against Sandusky had proven so signal a failure. Already they were upon the Ohio, and the most active exertions of Marshal were necessary to watch their movements and prevent their depredating into the exposed settlements. Their principal force was at Mingo Bottom; smaller parties were in the vicinity. Irvine was informed of their movements, on the 2d of July, by a letter from Marshal. "Colonel Williamson has marched to Coxe's fort," continued the writer, "about four miles below the Mingo Bottom, at which place I have directed him to stay until further orders. Colonel Crook is gone to Wheeling. I have also directed him that if he apprehend no danger in leaving that post for a few days, to form a junction with Colonel Williamson. To-morrow I intend marching whatever men may rendezvous in this quarter, to Richard Wells' fort, which is within five miles of Mingo Bottom; at which place I intend to stay, if circumstances will admit, until I hear from you; and I shall expect, if you think it necessary, that a number of your troops will march to our assistance as soon as possible."

On the 4th of July another letter, dated at Catfish, by Marshal, informed the commander of the Western Department of repeated applications by the inhabitants on the south line of the county—from Jackson's fort to Buffalo creek—for assistance. "The people declare," is the emphatic assurance of the lieutenant of Washington county, "they must abandon their habitations unless a few men are sent to them during harvest. They also declare their willingness to submit to, and supply the men on the faith of, the government."

It will be premised that the commander at Fort Pitt availed himself of whatever information was obtainable from the returned volunteers, not only as to the particulars of the campaign itself, but also concerning the intentions of the enemy in the future. One only, of all who escaped the disasters of the expedition, was competent to throw much light on the plans of the savages. This one was John Slover, whose captivity and remarkable escape will hereafter be narrated. He spoke the language of the Miamis, the Shawanese, and the Delawares with fluency; and, while detained in the wilderness, heard their deliberations and the measures they concerted in their councils. In their meetings he understood what was said, perfectly. All their designs, after his arrival, he did not fail to make known to Irvine; but the latter, not knowing how much confidence to repose in the narrator, interrogated Marshal on the 18th of July by letter, concerning him.

The response of Marshal was not calculated to increase the faith of Irvine: "I am not surprised," he wrote, "at the account you have received from Slover. The intelligence he gave me was bad, but nothing equal to what he has reported to you. He told me that the

Indians expected we would carry another expedition against them this summer, and that, at their council, they had determined upon two expeditions, one of which was designed against Wheeling; the other they were not fully determined whether this country or Kentucky should be the object; that, in the meantime, they would keep out spies on our frontier, in order to watch our motion, and take a prisoner to know our determination."

"He did not mention a word to me," continues Marshal, "either of their number or of bringing artillery. He said the Indians informed him that the night our people left the field at Sandusky, there were some British troops from Detroit within a few miles of them (I think six); that they had two field-pieces and one mortar. This, I think, is mostly what he told me on his arrival. With regard to his character, I am altogether unacquainted; but I think there is reason to suspect his veracity. I could wish he might be checked, for the reports in the country have a most evil tendency." But the testimony of other volunteers corroborated many of Slover's assertions; and subsequent events confirmed the public in its opinion of his truthfulness.

General Irvine, on the 11th of July, informed Washington by letter from Fort Pitt, that the solicitations of the people for making another excursion against Sandusky were increasing daily, and that they were actually beginning to prepare for it. The reply of Washington was dated at headquarters on the 6th of August: "I have not given you my ideas on this expedition," says the commander-in-chief, "as the plan, if adopted, must have begun its execution before my letter would have reached you. If attempted, I can only give you my good wishes for its success." A letter from Lincoln, Secretary of War, was of like tenor: "It is impossible for me at this distance," says that officer, "and with my present information, to judge of the propriety of your proceeding or not. Your own judgment must determine you, when all circumstances are combined. If you should succeed,[6] it will be a pretty stroke indeed." "I have only to add," continues the writer, "if your movements are such as can be justified on military principles (I presume you would not attempt a movement upon any other, however strongly urged by those who wish the expedition to go forward at every hazard), whether you succeed or not, you will be justified by all good men."

The frontiers were harassed during the summer months by frequent inroads of the enemy. On the 11th of July, three sons of Mr. Chambers, of Westmoreland county, were tomahawked and scalped; and on Saturday afternoon, the 13th of the month, Hanna's-town, the county-town of that county, was burned by a large party of Indians, and a number of the in-

---

[6] The word is *proceed*, in the original—doubtless an inadvertency.

habitants killed and captured.[7] This place was about thirty-five miles in the rear of Fort Pitt, on the main road leading to Philadelphia. "The express," wrote Irvine to Moore, on the 16th, "sent by Mr. Hoofnagle, through timidity and other misconduct, did not arrive here till this moment (Tuesday, 10 o'clock), though he left Hanna's-town Sunday evening; which I fear will put it out of my power to come up with the enemy, they will have got so far away. However, I have sent several reconnoitering parties to try to discover whether they have left the settlements, and what route they have taken."

The people were greatly alarmed. "I fear," continued Irvine in his letter to Moore, "this stroke will intimidate the inhabitants so much that it will not be possible to rally them or persuade them to make a stand. Nothing in my power shall be left undone to countenance and encourage them."

About the 15th of July, a party of seven Wyandots made an incursion into one of the settlements, some distance below Fort Pitt, and several miles from the Ohio river. Here, finding an old man alone in a cabin, they killed him, packed up what "plunder" they could find, and commenced their retreat.

The news of the visit of the Indians soon spread through the neighborhood, and a party of eight good

---

[7] Fort Pitt correspondence of the *Penn. Packet*, printed July 27, 1782.

riflemen was collected in a few hours for the purpose of pursuit. Among those assembled were two brothers —Andrew and Adam Poe. These were both famous for courage, size, and activity.

The party commenced the pursuit of the Indians with a determination, if possible, not to suffer them to escape, as they usually did on such occasions, by making a speedy flight to the river, crossing it, and then dividing into small parties, to meet at a distant point, in a given time. The pursuit was continued the greater part of the night. In the morning, the borderers found themselves on the trail of the savages, which led to the Ohio. When they had arrived within a little distance of the river, at a point in what is now Hancock county, West Virginia, about two miles below the mouth of Yellow creek, a western confluent of the Ohio, Andrew Poe, fearing an ambuscade, left the party who followed directly on the trail, to creep along the bank of the stream, under cover of the weeds and bushes, to fall on the rear of the Indians, should he find them lying in wait.

He had not gone far before he saw some Indian rafts at the water's edge. Not seeing any savages, he stepped softly down the bank with his rifle cocked. When about half way down, he discovered two Indians —one very large, the other small. Both were standing with their guns cocked, and looking in the direction of the party which was approaching by the trail, and was some distance down the bottom. Poe took aim at the big Indian, but his rifle missed fire. The two hearing the snap of the gun, instantly turned round and discovered their foe, who, being too near to retreat, dropped his weapon and sprang from the bank upon the savages. He seized the larger one with a powerful grip, at the same time embracing the neck of the smaller one, and threw them both upon the ground—all three falling together, but Poe uppermost.

The small Indian soon extricated himself, ran to the raft, got a tomahawk to dispatch Poe, while the big Indian held the latter with all his might, the better to enable his companion to effect his purpose. Poe, however, watched the motions of the Indian so well, that when in the act of aiming a blow at his head, by a vigorous and well-directed kick, he staggered the savage, and knocked the tomahawk out of his hand. This failure on the part of the smaller Indian was reproved by the larger one with an exclamation of contempt.

In a moment the Indian caught up his tomahawk, approached more cautiously, brandishing it, and making a number of feigned blows, in defiance and derision. Poe, however, still on his guard, averted the real blow from his head, by throwing up his arm, and receiving it on his wrist. He was severely wounded, but still able to use his hand. In this perilous moment, by a violent effort, he broke loose from the big Indian, snatched up one of the guns of the savages, and shot his assailant through the breast as he ran up the third time to tomahawk him.

Meanwhile the prostrate Indian got upon his feet, and now, seizing Poe by the shoulder and leg, threw him, in turn, upon the ground; but the latter instantly regained his standing; when the savage again grasped him, and another struggle ensued; which, owing to the slippery state of the bank, ended in both being precipitated into the river. Each now endeavored to drown the other. Their efforts were continued for some time, with alternate success—first one being under the water, then the other. Poe, at length, seized his antagonist by the tuft of hair on the scalp, and held his head down until he supposed him drowned.

Relaxing his hold too soon, Poe found his gigantic foe ready instantly for another combat. Again they grasped each other; but, in the contest, they were carried into the water beyond their depth. This compelled each to loose his hold and swim for life. Each sought the shore, to seize a gun, and end the strife. The Indian proved the best swimmer and reached the land first. Poe, seeing this, immediately turned back into the water to escape being shot, if possible, by diving. Fortunately, the savage caught up the rifle with which Poe had killed the other warrior!

At this juncture, Adam Poe, missing his brother from the party, and supposing from the report of the gun, that he was either killed or engaged in conflict with the Indians, hastened to the spot. On seeing him, Andrew called out to him from the water to "kill the big Indian." But Adam's gun, like that of the Indian's, was empty. The contest was now a question of time only—as to which would load first. The savage, in using his ramrod, was not as quick as his antagonist. This gave Adam the advantage; and, just as the Indian was raising his gun, he shot, mortally wounding him.

Adam now jumped into the river to assist his wounded brother to the shore; but Andrew, thinking more of the honor of carrying home the scalp of the big Indian as a trophy of victory, than of his own safety, urged him to go back and prevent the struggling savage from rolling himself into the stream and escaping. But Adam's solicitude for the life of his brother prevented him from complying with his request. The consequence was that the Indian, although in the agonies of death, succeeded in reaching the water and getting into the current; so that his scalp was not obtained.

During the conflict, and just as Adam had arrived at the edge of the bank for the relief of Andrew, one of the party who had followed close behind him, seeing a person in the river, and supposing him to be a wounded Indian, shot and wounded him in the shoulder. It was the struggling Andrew who thus received the second wound; but, from these injuries, he afterward recovered. In the meantime, the remaining Indians had been overtaken by the borderers, and all but one killed; with the loss, however, of three of the pursuers—one, a young man by the name of Cherry. The Indian shot by Adam Poe, was a noted chief of the Wyandots, known as Big Foot.[8]

On the 25th of July, Irvine wrote to Major-General Lincoln: "The incursions of the Indians on the frontier of this country will unavoidably prevent the militia from assembling as soon as the 1st of August. Indeed, I begin to entertain doubts of their being able to raise and equip the proposed number this season."

On the 10th of August, an address was presented to Irvine, signed by the principal inhabitants of the frontier on the waters of Buffalo and Ten-mile, asking for protection against the savages. "Though I do not think," is the language of Irvine to Marshal, on the same day, "there is as much danger as they apprehend, yet, if they run, the consequence is the same; and I

---

[8] *Doddridge, Notes,* 301–307. De Hass (*His. Ind. Wars W. Va.,* p. 365) mentions this contest as having occurred in 1781; but, as no authority is given for the statement, I have followed Doddridge. And, as corroborative, see *Smith's Hist. Jefferson College,* p. 391. As to the correction of Doddridge, by the substitution of Adam for Andrew and *vice versa,* as in the text, De Hass is in the right, as I am informed by S. R. Harris, Esq., of Bucyrus, O., who had an account of the contest from Adam Poe himself. See, also, *Howe's His. Coll. Ohio,* p. 106.

do not wish any more breaks made in the settlements." Marshal was therefore ordered to call out one officer and twenty men to range in that quarter.

The officers and principal citizens of Washington county met at Catfish Camp, on Thursday, the 22d of August, for the purpose of devising ways and means for carrying forward the second campaign against Sandusky. At this meeting it was resolved that the different battalions of the militia of the county furnish, as their quota for the expedition, six hundred and seventy-one men, two hundred and fifty-two horses, and forty thousand two hundred rations. It was also agreed that any person furnishing two hundred rations —to consist of one and one-fourth pounds of flour and the same quantity of beef, each—and delivering them at the time and place appointed by the commanding officers of each battalion, should be exempted a two months' tour of duty under the law; or, in lieu thereof, he might, if he choose, deliver a good pack-horse fit for the service, properly equipped with a halter, pack-saddle, lashing-rope, and two kegs, or one good bag, and be entitled to a like exemption.

Arrangements were made at the meeting for the proper assessment of every delinquent citizen in the county, in proportion to the value of his estate,—such an amount as might be necessary to cover his share of the expense of furnishing provisions and pack-horses; and it was agreed that all horses lost on the expedition, unless paid for by the government in one year, be compensated for by each member of the company to which it belonged, in proportion to the value of his estate. It was also resolved that each battalion should deposit at one or more mills in its district, its quota of wheat, on or before the ensuing 6th day of September.[9]

General Irvine was informed by Marshal, on the 26th, of the proceedings of the meeting: "I have no doubt of raising and equipping of the proposed number, about five hundred men, perhaps more; and that we shall be able to rendezvous at such place as you may appoint, by the 15th of September, which will be as soon as the people of the county can possibly be in readiness." Irvine immediately replied, approving the resolutions—"their execution," he suggested wisely, "is another thing." "However," he added, "I trust you will not be mistaken notwithstanding." He thought the 15th of September would be full late enough for the general meeting.

Ever since the return of Slover, Irvine had kept constantly in mind the warnings he brought from the wilderness, and had ever a watchful eye in the direction of Wheeling. On the evening of the 11th of September, this post was attacked by two hundred and thirty-eight Indians, under George Girty, and a company of forty Rangers from Detroit, commanded by Captain

---

[9] I have the original account of the proceedings of this meeting. It is signed by Marshal, and attested by the clerk, William Pollock.

Pratt. An attempt was made to storm the fort; but, by the aid of a small cannon, it was repulsed. On the second day of the siege three more attempts were made, but with no better success. "The enemy continued around the garrison till the morning of the 13th," wrote Ebenezer Zane to Irvine, from the fort, on the next day, "when they disappeared."[10]

Before recrossing the Ohio, the enemy attacked

---

[10] This I find corroborated in a letter from Marshal to Irvine, in my possession, dated the 15th. Zane's letter is as follows:

"WELING, 14th September, 1782.

"SIR: on the Evening of the 11th Instant a Body of the Enemy appeared in Sight of our garrison the immediately formed thire Lines Round the garrison paraded British Cullars and demand the fort to Be Surrenderred which was Refused about twelve o clock att Night they Rushed hard on the pickets In order to Storm But was repulsed they made two other attemts to Storm Before Day to No purpos.

"about eight o clock Next morning thare come a Negro from them to us and informed us that thire forse Consisted of a British Captain and forty Regular Soldiers and two hundred and Sixty Indians they Enemy kept a continual fire they whold Day a Bout ten o clock att Night they made a forth attempt to Storm to no better purpos then the former the Enemy Continued Round the garrison till the morning of the thirteenth Instant when they Disappeared Our loss is none Daniel Sullivan who arrived here in the first of the action is wounded in the foot.

"I belive they have Drove they gratest part of our Stock away and might I think be soon overtaken I am with Due Respect your obedient servt.

"EBENEZER ZANE"

Rice's fort, about fourteen miles from Wheeling; but were repulsed by its garrison of six men, losing four of their warriors. "If the enemy," wrote Marshal to Irvine, on the 15th, "continue to advance in one body, the matter will become serious, and perhaps require our whole strength to repel them. But, if it can possibly be avoided, I could wish not to call upon a man that is going on the expedition against Sandusky." But the savages advanced no farther into the settlements. It was their last inroad, in force, east of the Ohio during the war.

The place appointed by Irvine for the rendezvous, preparatory to marching against Sandusky, was Fort McIntosh; the time, September 20th. But, notwithstanding the preparations of the borderers, and of the State and general government—the latter had gone so far as to fully mature a plan for the expedition, Irvine being appointed to command—the assembling never took place.

"I have this moment received dispatches from the Secretary of War," is the language of Irvine, on the 18th of September, to the lieutenants of Westmoreland and Washington counties, "informing me that some regular troops are ordered from below, to assist us in our intended expedition. I am, therefore, to beg you will immediately countermand the march of the volunteers and others of your counties until further orders. As soon as I am positively assured of the time the troops will be here, I shall give you the earliest notice. I hope the good people of your counties will not think hard to be stopped, as the measure is designed for the best, and to insure success if possible." But the regulars never came; for the war of the Revolution was drawing rapidly to its close. "Peace is talked of," Irvine was informed by the Secretary of War, by letter dated the 2d September; "how far we may depend on it I am at a loss to say." He wrote again, on the 27th: "From late accounts, forwarded by his Excellency, General Washington, we learn that the Indians are all called in."

"I received your letter by Sergeant Porter," was the response of Irvine to Cook, on the 18th of October, "and one last night from Colonel Marshal, which is full of despondency. Indeed, by all the accounts I can collect, it would be vain to insist on bringing the few willing people to the general rendezvous, as there is not the most distant prospect that half sufficient would assemble. Under the cirumstances, I think it will be most advisable to give up the matter at once, and direct the provisions and other articles be restored to the owners." The Secretary of War wrote to Irvine, on the 30th, that the expedition against Sandusky was laid aside. The lieutenants of Westmoreland and Washington counties were thereupon officially informed, by the commandant at Fort Pitt, of the abandonment of the enterprise by the government. Depredations, however, continued a long time afterward to afflict the border.

As late as April 16, 1783, Irvine wrote Lincoln: "Savages have lately killed and taken a number of families, at nearly the same time, in many different places of the country, as well on the frontiers of Virginia as Pennsylvania. Not less than seventeen persons are said to be killed and scalped in a small settlement on Wheeling creek." And this too, notwithstanding negotiations for peace had long been in progress, and, about this time, was publicly proclaimed! The nation at large was joyous; but the western border continued to be the theater of savage murders for many months.

"The most glorious news of peace," wrote Irvine to General Washington, from Carlisle, where he was then visiting his family, "arrived two days ago—honorable for America! On this happy occasion, I pray your Excellency may be pleased to accept my sincere congratulations. That you may long live to enjoy the well-earned fruits of your labors, is my ardent wish."[11] "The happy event of a general peace," replied Washington, "diffuses very general satisfaction. With great sincerity I return you my congratulations."[12]

---

[11] A copy of this letter, in the handwriting of Irvine, is before me. It has no date. The reply of Washington, which is in my possession, shows it to have been written on the 28th of March.

[12] Washington to Irvine, 16th April, 1783; MS. letter.

CHAPTER XIV.

PERSONAL INCIDENTS AND SKETCHES.

THAT there should have been the deepest feeling prevailing in all the humble dwellings of those who had sent forth one or more of their number to the wilderness, when it became known that the expedition against Sandusky had returned to the Ohio, is not a matter of wonder. Nor is it to be presumed the excitement was lessened by a knowledge of its failure; as then the most intense anxiety prevailed to learn who were killed, wounded, or missing.

Great was the joy upon the return of a volunteer. He was immediately surrounded by anxious neighbors who were still in terrible suspense as to the fate of relatives or friends. A thousand questions were asked. Some could report a father, brother, or son killed—the relator, perchance, had assisted at his burial. Some were wounded—several were missing when the Ohio was recrossed, as already related. Among those who were never heard of may be named William Huston, Captain Hoagland, William Johnston, and William Nimmons.

Among the numerous forts dotting the wilderness at this time was that of Wolfe's, standing about five miles west of Catfish, and inclosing Jacob Wolfe's house—

hence its name. A writer[1] speaks of the excitement caused by the report of the death of two of the volunteers in the army just returned: "We remained in Mr. Wolfe's house until February, 1782, while my father was preparing his cabin, into which we finally entered, but not to rest. In fifteen or twenty days after entrance into our log cabin, Martin Jolly came running, breathless, to tell us that a savage murder had been committed but ten miles distant. In two hours we were in Wolfe's fort. From the fort my parents removed to *Catfish* (Washington), and spent the residue of 1782, and to April, 1783, on the farm of Alexander Reynolds, recently owned by Dr. F. J. Lemoyne. On this farm we were living when . . . the militia army were defeated under Colonel William Crawford. . . . James and Hugh Workman were both in that expedition, and I fancy I see the two women now, when James Reynolds came running to my mother, exclaiming, 'Jamy Workman is killed!' James Workman, who was a married man, was not killed, but returned to his family and lived many years afterward. A like report came in regard to Hugh, and happily proved untrue, to the great joy of his betrothed wife, Peggy Bryson, living then with her brother-in-law, Thomas Nichol. John Campbell, of Pigeon creek, was killed in the action."

The brothers Workman were in the same company

---

[1] William Darby; see *Creigh's Hist. Wash. Co.* App., p. 56.

when the army, on its outward march, left Mingo Bottom; but when Crawford selected his company of light-horse, Hugh joined it, leaving his brother James in the ranks of the mounted infantry. James was twenty-five and Hugh twenty-three years of age when they joined the Sandusky expedition. The former applied for a pension fifty years after, and was successful. Both were then living (1833) in Amwell township, Washington county.[2]

Some of the stragglers from the army, who became separated from it on the night the retreat began, got very much confused, as might be expected, in their endeavors to find the trail of the retreating troops. A few, in despair of regaining it, and others out of abundant caution, struck directly through the wilderness, taking a due east course for the Ohio. Some became completely bewildered. Nicholas Dawson, a volunteer from Westmoreland, father of John Dawson of Fayette county, and then living about four miles from Beesontown, had become separated from his companions when the army began its homeward march, and was endeavoring to make his way eastward, when he was discovered by James Workman and a companion, going exactly *from* the Ohio and *toward* Sandusky! These men endeavored to persuade him that he was wrong; but Dawson insisted, with equal pertinacity, that he was right.

---

[2] Declaration of James Workman for a pension, March 29, 1833.

After some further attempts to convince him of his mistake, with no better success, they told him he would certainly be killed if he continued upon the course he had been traveling, and as he had better be shot by white men than be tortured to death, they would kill him to prevent him falling into the hands of the savages! This argument proved successful, and he turned about reluctantly. All arrived home in safety.

In the confusion attending the commencement of the retreat from the battle-field of Sandusky, Philip Smith, who, it will be remembered, was wounded in the elbow during the action, became separated from his company. With him was a companion named Rankin. Smith was a young man—born in Frederick county, Maryland, in February, 1761—then residing near Beesontown (Uniontown), in Westmoreland county (in that part which soon after became Fayette), at the time of volunteering for the expedition. Concerning the previous history of Rankin, nothing is known.

Both had lost their horses. They had their rifles and ammunition with them, but were without provisions. Their guns were of little service, as they did not dare to shoot for fear of Indians. They were compelled, therefore, to a very scanty diet, as a general thing, of berries, roots, and young birds (when these could be caught). They traveled usually by night, wisely avoiding all trails. After awhile, they came across an Indian pony which they resolved to kill for food. As they were afraid to shoot it, Smith determined to dispatch the animal with his tomahawk. This, however, proved no slight affair. It dodged all blows aimed at its head. Finally, Rankin held his hat over the pony's eyes, which enabled Smith to deal a blow that felled it to the ground. The animal was then killed, cut open, and its liver taken out, which, after being broiled, was, to the two hungry men, a savory dish indeed!

About the third night of their retreat, two men on horseback overtook them, and they then all traveled on together until a stream was reached having high banks, where the party fell into an ambuscade of savages, who had doubtless followed them from the Plains. There were four of the enemy. The two men on horseback were shot dead—their bodies falling into the stream.

When the firing took place, Smith was in the act of drinking—he had just stooped down to the water. A ball passed very near his head; he was, however, unhurt. Seizing the gun of one of the men who had been shot, he ran up the bank, and turned around to fire at the Indians; but the savages were too quick for him and dodged behind trees.

In the meantime, Rankin, who was also unharmed, was running for life. Smith threw aside his gun and ran after his companion; the latter mistook him for an enemy and three times turned to shoot him; but Smith saved himself each time by "treeing." Rankin finally discovered who it was so eagerly pursuing him; when he slackened his pace and was soon joined by Smith. The two now ran on together and escaped the savages. The men who were killed had been with them but a few hours, and their names they did not learn.

The two did not halt the next morning as daylight appeared, but continued their journey, fearing pursuit by the Indians. They came soon after upon a deserted Indian camp, which, it appeared from the signs, a number of savages had just left. A man lay there scalped and dead, but his body was still warm. He had drawn his hand over the scalp-wound several times and smeared himself with blood from it, showing that he had been scalped while still alive! He had been shot apparently while on horseback. It was the opinion of both Smith and Rankin that he was not one of the volunteers, as he rode a shod horse, and none to their knowledge in the expedition had shoes on. The Indians, after killing him, had immediately fled, for what cause was of course unknown. Their fires were yet burning, over which corn (hominy) was cooking. This the two half-famished men tasted, but did not eat, for fear of its being poisoned;—the temptation was great, as may be imagined.

After leaving this camp, no more Indians were seen; but that night, as Rankin was making himself a pair of moccasins from the skin of a horse they had found (his moccasins being worn out), savages were heard at a great distance, whereupon the two extinguished their fire and pursued their journey. They reached home in ten days from the time of their leaving the battle-ground—foot-sore, nearly naked, and well-nigh perishing with hunger.[3]

The volunteers who had been fortunate in not losing their horses, found their animals very much jaded and reduced in flesh upon their return to the settlements. Their progress homeward was, therefore, as a general thing, very slow. Some came singly, others in squads; not a few were on foot. No discharges had been given; none were expected. Quite a number came on together as far as Catfish, dispersing thence to their homes. John Sherrard left his companions at this point, to visit a cousin, Hugh Sherrard, on Miller's run. He found his relative in mourning for a son who had been killed by the Indians, in April previous—the same sad

---

[3] Philip Smith was one of the pioneer settlers of Ohio; he crossed the river into the territory now constituting the State, in 1784; built a cabin on the stream, but was driven away by the Indians. He returned in 1799, and settled near Steubenville, Jefferson county, where he continued to live until April, 1812, when he removed to Wayne county, in the same State, which he reached on the 27th of that month. Here he resided until his death, which took place on the 27th of March, 1838, in East Union township, of that county. There are now (1873) four children of Mr. Smith living: John P. Smith, of Centreville, Indiana; Jacob P. Smith, Cass county, Indiana; N. W. Smith, Wooster, Ohio; and Mrs. Agnes McFadden, West Salem, Ohio.

story, so often repeated upon the border; in this instance, intensified by the fact of a young wife being left a widow.

The home of Sherrard was with the widowed mother of James Paull, in what is now Dunbar township, Fayette county—where he soon after arrived, but could give no intelligence of the widow's son. The last time he had seen James, was on the night of the commencement of the retreat, when, just as the army was about to start, he was observed fast asleep. Sherrard gave him a shake, calling to him: " Up, James, and let us be off; they are all starting, and we shall soon be left behind!" He saw him spring to his feet, but immediately lost sight of him in the darkness, and had not seen him since or heard of him. The disconsolate mother had now the most fearful forebodings. She was a woman regarded as a sincere Christian. As her son's companions returned to the neighborhood, she would immediately send a messenger to inquire whether James had been seen or heard of. But no intelligence came. Sherrard vainly endeavored to console her with the assurance that her son would undoubtedly be home in a short time; but, like Rachel of old, she would not be comforted, because he was not.[4]

But of all those who suffered from hope deferred until the heart grew sick indeed, and then, when the facts were known, from a recital of them, none was

---

[4] Communicated by Robert A. Sherrard.

more to be commiserated than the wife of the commander of the expedition. Hannah Crawford had parted with her husband with a heavy heart. As the volunteers, one after another, returned to her neighborhood, with what anxiety did she make inquiries of them concerning her companion! But no one could give the disconsolate wife a word of information concerning him. Her lonely cabin by the Youghiogheny was a house of mourning now. After three weeks of dreadful suspense she learned the sad news of her husband's death in the wilderness.[5]

The widow was left in embarrassment as to property. Crawford's private affairs had come to be in a very unsettled condition on account of his military and other duties having called him so frequently from home; his absence, sometimes, being greatly prolonged. The excitements and vicissitudes of the later years of his life had called his attention from them necessarily. The result was that his estate was swept away, most of it, by a flood of claims, some having doubtless no just foundation. For losses sustained upon the expedition, the State afterward reimbursed his estate.

Hannah Crawford afterward drew a pension from the State on account of the military services of her husband. On the 28th of November, 1804, she applied to Congress for relief.[6] It is not known, however, that

---

[5] From what source is not now known.

[6] The original petition is in my possession. It recites that her hus-

she ever received any aid from the general government. She lived at her old home until 1817, when she died, at the advanced age of ninety-three years and eleven months.⁷ "I well recollect," says Uriah Springer,

band, William Crawford, was, at the time of his death, on the Continental establishment as colonel of the Virginia line; that in the spring of the year, 1782, in the hour of imminent danger and the defenseless situation of the western frontier, by the directions and under the instructions of General William Irvine, who then had the command of the militia and Continental troops in the western country he took the command as colonel of, and marched with, a detachment of western militia volunteers and some Continental officers against the savage enemy—the Indians; and that, in the month of June of that year, he was defeated by the savages and fell in defense of his country. The prayer of the petition is, in view of the fact that the petitioner is aged, infirm, and indigent; that "your honorable body will grant such relief and support as, in your wisdom, justice, and discretion, for the services and loss of her said husband, your petitioner may be justly entitled to."

⁷ "The log-house where the widow Crawford lived, which had been built by her husband, and in which she had resided, at the time of her death, for nearly fifty years, stood about one hundred yards from an old stone-house erected by Daniel Rodgers, but nearer the river and more opposite Gibson's stone-mill, in the borough, as already explained, of New Haven, Fayette county, Pennsylvania, opposite Connellsville. It was built on a round knoll, near where a large locust tree now stands. It was a small house, as originally built, of only one room; but afterward there was a shed-roof addition built to it; but the latter was finally taken away. It has not been many years since this interesting relic was torn down. Of some of the logs, walking-sticks were made and sold to the curious."—*Recollections*

"when I was a little boy, my grandmother Crawford took me behind her on horseback, rode across the Youghiogheny, passed the 'John Rice farm,' turned to the left into the woods, when we both alighted by an old, moss-covered, white-oak log. 'Here,' said my grandmother, as she sat down upon the log and cried as though her heart would break, 'here I parted with your grandfather!'"[8]

Sherrard, whom we left at his home at the widow Paull's, as soon as he had obtained a little rest, started for Beesontown to return the pack-saddle to the wife of Daniel Harbaugh, which, it will be remembered, he had taken from his dead companion's horse, on the banks of the Sandusky. The story of the tragic death of his comrade was a most heart-rending one to the distracted wife. There was, nevertheless, this consolation in her deep sorrow: she *knew* he was dead, and knew, too, the particulars of his last moments. It was not with her as with a few who never after heard of their loved ones—not a fearful uncertainty, until death itself would have been a relief.

Nearly all those who had become separated from the main body of the army, had, upon their return, the

---

of David A. C. Sherrard: *communicated to his brother, Robert A. Sherrard, February,* 1872; *and by the latter to the author.*

[8] Communicated by Robert A. Sherrard. The father of Uriah Springer—Uriah Springer, Sen.—was the second husband of Crawford's eldest daughter, Sally.

same story to tell of suffering from hunger; as only a few were fortunate enough to have preserved a sufficient supply of provisions. Several had lost either their guns or ammunition; they could not therefore rely upon killing any game on the way. It is related of one volunteer who reached home nearly famished that he cut up in small pieces his buckskin breeches and ate them with a relish. Many saved their lives by eating serviceberries, which at that season of the year were ripe, and in some places found in abundance. That some may have died in the wilderness of starvation, is not improbable, though the number must have been small.

As might be expected, those on horseback were the first usually to reach their homes. Some had been compelled to leave their horses in the wilderness and pursue their way, as best they could, on foot. Thomas Mills met with this mishap. His animal gave out at a spot near where St. Clairsville, county-seat of Belmont county, Ohio, now stands, and whither he had wandered in his endeavors to reach the Ohio. He left his horse at what was known as the "Indian Spring," about nine miles from the river; then in the wilderness of course, now on the National Road. Mills soon after reached Wheeling in safety. He then proceeded to Van Metre's fort; when, after a day or two of rest, he began to think of returning for his horse. At this time there was at the fort the famous hunter and Indian fighter, Lewis Wetzel. Mills applied to Wetzel to accompany him in search of his horse. The cautious backwoodsman discouraged the attempt and cautioned him of the danger. But Mills was determined to recover his animal at every hazard; and Wetzel was not the one to refuse help because of peril, however imminent it might be. So the two started.

Rapidly, but cautiously, they made their way into the wilderness. Approaching the spring, they discovered the horse, not however as he had been left, *but tied to a tree.* Wetzel at once comprehended the danger, signaled his companion, and then turned and ran for life. Mills, however, rushed up to unfasten his animal, when instantly a discharge of rifles followed, and the unfortunate man, after having escaped all the dangers of the Sandusky campaign, fell mortally wounded. The volley did not slacken the speed of Wetzel, who plunged through the enemy's ambuscade, followed now by four fleet savages, whooping in proud exultation of soon overtaking their intended victim.

After a chase of half a mile, one of the most active of his pursuers approached so close that Wetzel was afraid he might throw his tomahawk, and suddenly wheeling, shot the savage dead in his tracks. It was now that the habit he had acquired, of loading his gun while in full run, was put in requisition. Keeping in advance of the Indians for another half-mile, a second one came up so close to him that he was again compelled to turn at bay. But the savage this time was so near him as to catch the end of his gun, and for a time the contest was doubtful. At one moment, the Indian, by his great strength and dexterity, brought Wetzel to his knee, and had nearly wrenched the rifle from the grasp of his antagonist, when the latter, by a renewed effort, drew the weapon from the savage, and thrusting the muzzle against the side of his neck, pulled the trigger, killing him instantly.

By this time the two other Indians had nearly overtaken Wetzel; but by leaping forward he eluded their pursuit until his unerring rifle was a third time loaded. Anxious to have done with this kind of sport, he slackened his pace, and even stopped once or twice to give his pursuers an opportunity to face him. Every time he looked around, however, the Indians "treed," unwilling any longer to encounter his destructive weapon. After running some distance further, in this manner, he reached an open piece of ground, and turning quickly around, the foremost Indian jumped behind a tree; but, as this did not screen the savage, Wetzel fired and mortally wounded him. The remaining Indian thereupon made an immediate retreat, and the intrepid backwoodsman soon after reached the settlements in safety, to relate his daring exploit.[9]

---

[9] Compare *Doddridge's Notes*, 274, 299, 300; and *De Hass' Hist. Ind. Wars West Va.*, p. 349. The Indians who ambuscaded Mills were not of those engaged, at Sandusky, against Crawford. That the tracks of some of the straggling parties were followed near to the Mus-

Shortly after the army had recrossed the Ohio, John Crawford arrived at his mother's home upon the Youghiogheny, but could give no tidings of his father; of his cousin, young William Crawford; or of William Harrison, his brother-in-law. He had seen neither after the night when the retreat began, nor had he heard a word of them.

It has been previously stated that the homestead taken up by Colonel Crawford, upon the Youghiogheny, was in his son's name. On the 27th of November, 1786, John Crawford sold this land to Edward Cook, who obtained a patent for it on the 11th of January, 1787, from the State of Pennsylvania—including what was generally known as "Stewart's Crossings," now in Fayette county. Cook afterward conveyed the tract to Isaac Meason, who had already obtained an interest in it by purchase at a judicial sale, and, in 1796, laid out upon it the town of New Haven.[10]

John Crawford afterward emigrated to the State of

---

kingum is certain; but that "for several days after the retreat of our army, the Indians were spread over the whole country, from the Sandusky to the Muskingum," as related by Doddridge (*Notes*, 274) "in pursuit of the straggling parties, most of whom were killed on the spot," is a mistake. "They even pursued them," adds the writer, "almost to the Ohio." I find no confirmation of this. On the contrary, subsequent movements of the Indians, at Sandusky and the Shawanese towns, render it altogether improbable.

[10] A considerable part of the tract is still (1873) owned by some of Isaac Meason's descendants.

Ohio, settling upon land bequeathed to him by his father, at the mouth of Brush creek, on the Ohio river bottom, in Adams county, where he died, leaving two sons, about the year 1816.[11]

Upon the breaking up of the army, on the 14th of June, Williamson immediately returned to his home in Washington county, and was soon after sent by Marshal, with a squad of men, to guard the frontier along the Ohio. In after years he was elected sheriff of his county, and was very popular with the people. He was, however, unsuccessful in business and died in poverty. The other field officers also dispersed to their several places of abode: Gaddis to that part of Westmoreland soon to become Fayette, near Uniontown; Brinton and Leet to Washington county; Zane returned to Wheeling, where he afterward died, leaving large landed possessions; Rose made his way to Fort Pitt, and reported for duty to General Irvine.

That the salvation of the army, on its retreat from Sandusky, was largely due to the skill and exertions of Rose, has already been mentioned.[12] He remained at

---

[11] It has been generally supposed that John Crawford was tortured to death in the wilderness; but the "young Crawford" who perished, was his cousin, as presently shown.

[12] "I furnished the party with ammunition, and sent written instructions to the commander, and also sent two Continental officers—Major Rose, my own aid-de-camp, and Doctor Knight, surgeon of one of the regiments under my command—to assist Colonel Crawford. After the

Fort Pitt, as aid to General Irvine, until the close of the war. His intelligence, gentlemanly bearing, and strict integrity made him a great favorite with the officers as well as the rank and file. Before leaving Pittsburg he was intrusted with the payment of the troops garrisoned there, which shows clearly the confidence reposed in his honesty. In rendering his accounts to the government he was very particular, even to a nicety that was sometimes amusing. Upon one occasion he found it necessary to charge himself with a half-pint of whisky. The charge was accompanied with this explanation: "The half-pint of whisky was used to wash the back of my portmanteau horse, which was much hurt!"

Rose was Secretary to the Council of Censors of Pennsylvania in the fall of 1783. This board had been provided for by the constitution of the State adopted in July, 1776. The Council was elected by the people on the second Tuesday of October, 1783. It was their duty to inquire if the constitution had been preserved inviolate; whether the different branches of the government had performed their duties faithfully; and whether the taxes had been justly laid; and

---

defeat, the second in command [Williamson] and others informed me that it was owing, in a great degree, to the bravery and good conduct of Major Rose that the retreat was so well effected."—*Irvine to Hannah Crawford: MS. certificate.* It may be mentioned that the chivalric young foreigner was generally known as "Major Rose."

the like duties. That Rose was elected secretary of this body, is a clear evidence that his fame had gone beyond the military post at Pittsburg. The Council met in November, 1783; and when it became known that it would adjourn to June, 1784, Rose, having resolved to return to his native country, resigned, on the 21st of February of that year, his office of secretary.

During the winter, his brother officers employed him to look after their interests in the Pennsylvania Legislature. As an American lobbyist he proved himself an expert. On the 21st of February, 1784, he wrote to General Irvine, who was then at his home in Carlisle: "The military gentlemen of our line have awakened from their slumbers; and the walls of the City Tavern have been twice the silent witnesses of our loud deliberations." They were lobbying for the redemption of their commutations. Many pretentious English scholars have written with far less accuracy and fluency.

Rose was also at the same time exerting himself to arrange the accounts of General Irvine with the government. He had already informed him of his determination to return to Europe in the spring. "I find," said he, in a letter to his friend and benefactor, "at the office of the Commissioners of Account, that no credit has been given you for the clothing delivered the different officers, in garrison, formerly, at Fort Pitt."[13] In such ways did he further the interests and return the kindness of his general. Finally, in a letter to Irvine from Philadelphia, dated the 2d of April, 1784, he informed him that he expected to sail for Amsterdam in the course of the next week. "The final accounts," he adds, "of your Continental settlement I have properly adjusted." The magnanimous and gallant soldier,— the firm and appreciative friend,—the accomplished and sensitive gentleman,—was now ready to depart the shores of America. "I shall do myself the honor," is the postscript to his letter, "to write you again before I sail."

Not long after, General Irvine received a letter at Carlisle, post-marked New York, superscribed in the beautiful and well-known hand of his old-time aid. It expressed his warm gratitude and attachment to his benefactor and his family;—declaring, however, his sorrow for having abstained so long from making known *his true history*. He then stated that his name was not *John Rose*, but *Gustavus H. de Rosenthal*, of Livonia, Russia—a Baron of the Empire! He then explained why he had left his country:

In an encounter with a nobleman, within the precincts of the palace at St. Petersburg, he had killed his

---

[13] Rose to Irvine, 21st February, 1784. All the letters of Rose, referred to in this chapter, are in the Irvine collection.

antagonist, in a duel, brought on by a blow which the other had inflicted upon an aged uncle in his presence. He then fled to England, whence, learning of the American war, he had sailed immediately for this country, to draw his sword in behalf of the struggling colonies. And now he was about to sail for home, having received, through the mediation of his family, permission to return, from the Emperor Alexander.

The first link, then, in that bright chain of friendship which has ever since bound, in such cordial relations, the Russian Empire to the United States, was forged by *John Rose*—Baron Rosenthal, of Livonia—the hero of the retreat of Crawford's army from the Plains of Sandusky!

Baron Rosenthal left the shores of America with a full determination to return and make this country his future home; but that resolution was not carried out. He kept up a correspondence, however, with General Irvine, until the death of the latter, and afterward with his son, Callender Irvine, father of William A. Irvine. After his return to Russia, he was made Grand Marshal of Livonia. He married an early love, and became the father of five children, all of whom he outlived. His letters are full of interest. In one, he quaintly observes: "I love above all things enjoying independency in the midst of my family, on a healthy spot of ground, with a clever, sensible set of men around me."[14] In all his correspondence after he had learned of the death of General Irvine, there are the most tender expressions of respect for the memory of his benefactor. Upon this subject, in a letter to Callender Irvine, he says: "I fled to America for refuge; was graciously received by your venerated father, and cherished by him as a son. My obligations can not be told. The power of language can not express all that I feel." Baron Rosenthal died in 1830. He was the only Russian, so far as is known, who served on the American side during the war of the Revolution.[15]

So successfully had Irvine conducted the affairs at Fort Pitt and vicinity, and so satisfactory had been his administration to both the State and general government and to the people on the frontiers generally, that Washington would not consent, although solicited by the commander of the Western Department, to his quitting his command, even on the arrival of the preliminary articles of peace from Europe. And, although some of the garrison were furloughed, *he* was enjoined still to remain.

---

[14] This letter is dated, St. Petersburg, Midsummer Day, 1804, and directed to General Irvine.

[15] In consideration of his long and valuable services, the general government granted him bounty lands in Ohio, and he received from Pennsylvania two tracts of donation lands, in the northwest part of the State. What became of his interest in the Ohio lands is unknown; but that he saved his other tracts is certain;—they are situated on Oil creek, and have become very valuable.

"It is probable," wrote Washington, on the 16th of April, 1783, to Irvine, then at Carlisle, "that a dissolution of the army is not far distant; but, as it is uncertain when the proclamation of peace and cessation of hostilities will be ordered by Congress, and as it is of much importance that you should be present at your post previous to, and at the taking place of that event, I have to desire that you will proceed immediately to Fort Pitt, where your influence and prudence may be much needed."

It has already been fully explained how Irvine became so closely identified with the expedition against Sandusky, and what the motives were which induced him to authorize, to help organize, and, finally, to issue instructions for its guidance. It had been encouraged by him because he believed it might prove a success; and if so, that "ease and safety to the inhabitants" of the border would be the result. In this, no one could impugn his motives. In its failure, no one saw reason to charge him with a lack of military sagacity.

On the 13th of September, the citizens of Pittsburg presented Irvine, on the occasion of his final departure from Fort Pitt, with a highly gratulatory address:

"The inhabitants of Pittsburg, having just learned that you intend to retire from this command to-morrow, would do injustice to their own feelings if they did not express their thanks to you, and their sense of your merit as an officer. During your command in this department, you have demonstrated that, amidst the tumults of war, the laws may be enforced, and civil liberty and society protected. Your attention to the order and discipline of the regular troops under your command, as well as to the militia; your regard for the civil rights of the inhabitants; the care you have taken of the public property, and your economy in the expenditure of the public money;—we have all witnessed; and this conduct, we assure you, has given general satisfaction to a people who, before your time, were, unfortunately for them, much divided, but now united.

"As you are now about to quit the military life, in which your ability and integrity have been so conspicuous, we wish you all possible happiness, and that your fellow-citizens may long enjoy your usefulness in civil life, in which, we doubt not, you will deserve their utmost confidence."

Irvine returned to his home in Carlisle, with health much impaired by exposures in the service. Pennsylvania was not slow to acknowledge its gratitude for his services, as the proceedings of its Supreme Executive Council clearly show. The State afterward presented him with Montour's (now Neville) Island, in the Ohio river, about six miles long, beginning about four miles below Pittsburg, in recognition of his labors—the title to which, however, he subsequently lost on account of the claim of another person, who held under a prior grant from Virginia. But the Legislature of Pennsylvania afterward remunerated him for his loss, by the donation of a valuable tract of land in another part of the State.[16]

Irvine was a member of the Council of Censors in 1783 and 1784, and on the 26th of March, 1785, was appointed agent, by the Supreme Executive Council of his State, to direct the mode of distributing the donation lands promised to the troops by the Commonwealth. Among the provisions made by Pennsylvania for the better remuneration of the army was this grant of a large tract of land, situate on the western side of the Ohio and Allegheny, and bordering on these rivers. As, however, few large tracts are uniformly good, so it was presumed that a portion of this was either of middling or of bad quality; and as the whole contained a surplusage, beyond what would be sufficient for the soldiers, the government, in the liberal spirit of the grant, created an agency for exploring and characterizing the different parts of the tract, to the end that what they *did* give should be what the law intended—a *bounty* to the receiver, and not merely a surface of barren and measured acres. It was this agency that Irvine, at the instance of the troops, was called upon to fill. He was instructed to "note the quality of the land in the several parts

---

[16] On the Allegheny river, in what is now Warren county, on which tract resides (1873) his worthy grandson, Dr. W. A. Irvine.

thereof; the hills, mountains, waters, creeks, marshes, uplands, bottom lands, etc., and such other peculiarities as may deserve notice, with their situation and distance; but particularly the parts of the land which you may deem unfit for cultivation."

Irvine promptly undertook the duties of the office to which he had been appointed; and, in November, reported the result of his mission, receiving from the executive authority its entire approbation of the course he had pursued and the opinions he had given. Among the latter of these was one which, though not immediately connected with his official duties, was so interesting to the State as to merit its particular notice. He advised the acquisition, by purchase from the United States, of a small tract of land ceded to them by the State of New York, and which, from its shape, took the name of *The Triangle*. The negotiation was opened, on Irvine's suggestion; and, having been successful, it gave to Pennsylvania a considerable front on Lake Erie. On closing the business of the land-agency, he was elected a member of Congress from the Cumberland district [1786-1788] under the Confederation.

During this time the internal improvements of the western country engaged his attention. The published correspondence between him and Washington, concerning a connection of the waters of the great lakes with the eastern rivers and the Ohio, exhibit, in a striking light, not only his thorough knowledge of the country, but his sagacity in discovering, thus early, its prospective wants."[17]

Irvine afterward served as commissioner to lay out the towns of Erie, Warren, and Franklin, Pennsylvania, and to assist in settling the disputes in the Wyoming country. In 1790, he was elected a member of the Constitutional Convention of the State, which framed the constitution adopted the 2d September of that year; having previously served as one of the Council of Censors under the old constitution. The command of the expeditions that was afterward given to Harmar and St. Clair was first offered him, but declined. The active control of all the arrangements, both as to men and material, was what he required, and, as the result showed, *wisely* too; but this it was deemed best not to give. Wayne subsequently demanded the same; it was given, and the power of the savages was forever broken in the Northwest.

It was after Irvine was a member of the old Congress that the great national account between the several States and the United States, which began with the war, and which had not hitherto been subjected to any official examination, assumed a very urgent character, from the admitted fact that the contributions made by the several members of the Confederation had been unequal— some having given much, others little or nothing. To

---

[17] See *Sparks' Writings of Washington*, ix, 326, 445.

relieve the embarrassments growing out of this circumstance, and which every additional day had a tendency to multiply and aggravate, Congress proceeded to institute a board of commissioners, with powers to examine and settle this mass of old and complicated business. Of this board General Irvine was a member; and associated with him were John Kean and Woodbury Langdon. The board accomplished the task in a short time, to the satisfaction of all parties concerned. Their labors were concluded on the 29th of June, 1793.

Irvine was now again honored, by the voters of the Cumberland district, with a seat in Congress—this time under the new constitution [1793]. He was, however, a candidate for the *first* Congress, under the same, on a *general* ticket for eight members; but the opposing candidates (Federal) were elected. The average vote in the State for the successful ticket was 8,021; for the other, 6,512.

The next year, Irvine was appointed a commissioner, with Thomas McKean as associate, to act in conjunction with three named by the United States, in an endeavor to settle the difficulties of what is known, in the history of Western Pennsylvania, as the Whisky Insurrection. Negotiations failed; and troops from Eastern Pennsylvania, New Jersey, Maryland, and Virginia, amounting to about fourteen thousand militia, marched against the insurgents. Irvine was in command of the Pennsylvania troops, under Governor Mifflin, as senior major-general; and by his military skill and local knowledge, contributed much to the facility of the march and other military operations which ended in quelling the outbreak.

The excellent discipline of the militia under his command was a subject of general remark at the time; as the men had been hastily gathered together, and unused to military control. It resulted from the good sense and firmness of the commander. On the march out, the troops had committed several outrages before reaching Bedford. Just after leaving this place, insubordination culminated in one so glaring that Irvine was determined not to shut his eyes and let it pass without punishment—a defenseless woman had been outraged.

The matter was laid before Governor Mifflin, who thought if an example was made of the perpetrators of the diabolical act, the militia would break up their camp and desert in a body. Irvine thought otherwise. "If you do not punish these miscreants," said he, "I must beg to resign my command. I can not consent to be held responsible for so great a crime." Mifflin yielded.

General Irvine called a drum-head court-martial, tried and sentenced two of the militia to one hundred lashes each. Mifflin now became alarmed, and thought it would not be policy to carry the sentence into execution; but Irvine was unyielding, and ordered out General Chambers' brigade, with two field-pieces. After the guns were loaded, the men were whipped in presence of the whole army and drummed out of camp. The result was an end to all insubordination, and a successful march to the seat of the insurrection.

In 1802, after Irvine's removal from Carlisle to Philadelphia, he was one day walking along the street near his residence, when he was accosted by a man driving an oyster-cart. "How are you, General Irvine?" asked the stranger. "You seem to know *me*," responded Irvine, "but really I can not recall *you* to my mind." "Oh," said the man, "I know *you* —— well! Don't you remember the two men you had whipped on the western expedition? I am one of them. It made a decent man of me. Now, where do you live? I have some very fine oysters here, and if you will do me the favor to accept them, I will drive to your house!" He had not far to drive.

Upon the election of Thomas Jefferson to the presidency of the United States, Irvine, who had been one of the presidential electors, was appointed by him Intendant of Military Stores—an important office, as it included the charge of the arsenals, ordnance, supplies of the army, and supervision of Indian affairs. He was afterward appointed President of the Pennsylvania Society of the Cincinnati. He died in Philadelphia of an inflammatory disorder on the 29th of July, 1804, universally respected. He was a zealous patriot, a judicious statesman, an able military commander; in a word, a careful, intelligent, and conscientious executor of all public trusts confided to his management; and was noted as a man of incorruptible integrity.

NOTE.—In the April number, 1873, of that excellent periodical, *The Historical Magazine* (p. 207–209), are published, for the first time, letters of Irvine, Williamson, Rose, and Marshal—one from each,—copied from the originals in the Irvine collection—which have been frequently cited in the previous chapters of this work. In speaking of the one written by Rose, the editor (*note*, p. 208) says: "The writer of this letter, under the assumed name of 'John Rose,' was really a young Russian nobleman—the Baron Gustavus H. Rosenthal, of Livonia—who, because of having killed another in a duel, had been obliged to fly from his own country, and seek safety, first in England and then in America. He had entered the army as a hospital steward; but General Irvine, having noticed him and become interested in his welfare, he was transferred and advanced, until, as a lieutenant, he became the aid of that officer. He served with fidelity, until the close of the war, without having revealed his true name or rank; and then, by permission, he returned to Europe; was regarded with favor by the Emperor Alexander; and became Grand Marshal of the Province of Livonia."

CHAPTER XV.

STRAGGLERS CAPTURED BY THE SAVAGES.

THE confusion attending the commencement of the retreat of the Americans from their encampment in the grove, upon the Sandusky Plains, on the evening of the 5th of June, was the cause of the separation of Crawford from his command. Just as the army moved off, he missed his son, John Crawford; his son-in-law, William Harrison; and William Crawford, his nephew;[1] and, very naturally, at once made an effort to find them. He called aloud for them, but there was no response. His aid, too, Major Rose (he was called "major" by all the volunteers, although his real rank in the regular army was lieutenant, as we have already seen), was not just then by his side; so he called out for him also.

At this moment, Dr. Knight came up and remarked to Crawford that he thought they were all ahead of them. He then said those he was looking for were

---

[1] *Knight's Narr.*, p. 7. A typographical error in the Philadelphia edition of 1783 has led at this point to much confusion. "We had not got a quarter of a mile from the field of action," is the language of the narrator, "when I heard Colonel Crawford calling for his son, John Crawford, his son-in-law, Major Harrison, Major Rose, and William Crawford, his nephews." The letter *s* in the last word is

not in front, and begged Knight not to leave him. The doctor promised him he would not. Both waited and continued calling for the absent men until the troops had all passed them. The colonel then told the doctor that his horse had almost given out; that he could not keep up with the troops, and wished some of his best friends to remain with him. He then exclaimed against the militia for riding off in such an irregular manner, and leaving some of the wounded behind, contrary to his orders. Presently there came two men riding after them,—one an old man, the other a lad. These were inquired of as to whether they had seen any of the missing men before mentioned. They answered in the negative.

By this time, there was very hot firing before them; near where the main body of the army was, as they judged. Their course was then nearly southwest. They had arrived near the cranberry marsh in which some of the volunteers were struggling, in vain endeavors to disengage their horses from the oozy soil. Crawford and his three companions now changed their course to the north, traveling in that direction about two miles. They were then in what is now Crane town-

---

an error of the printer; for no one knew better than Dr. Knight that Rose was not a relative of Crawford. . The peculiar construction of the sentence naturally led to the mistake, and hence the gallant young Russian Baron has passed, in all the current histories of these events, as a nephew of Colonel Crawford.

ship, Wyandot county, about a mile and a half northwest of the battle-ground.

At this point, judging themselves to be out of the enemy's lines, they changed their route, traveling due east, taking care to keep at a distance of fifteen or twenty yards apart, and directing themselves by the north star. They reached the Sandusky river, distant three miles, a little before midnight, crossing that stream just above the mouth of Negro run, a small affluent of the Sandusky, flowing from the eastward.

The old man who was with them often lagged behind; and, when this happened, he never failed to call for those in front to halt for him. When they were near the river, he fell one hundred yards behind, and called out, as usual, for the party to wait. While the others were preparing to reprimand him for making a noise, an Indian was heard to halloo, at a distance of about one hundred and fifty yards, as believed by Knight, from the man, and partly behind him. After this, he was not heard to call again, and they saw him no more.

They then traveled onward, soon passing into what is now Eden township, in the county last mentioned. By daylight, they had crossed into the present county of Crawford, at a point about two miles northwest of the spot where the town of Oceola, in Todd township, is now located,—only eight miles distant, in a direct line, from the battle-field. Their progress had necessarily been slow on account of the darkness, and the jaded condition of their horses; those that Crawford and the young man were riding now gave out, and they left them.

They again continued their journey—in a direction, however, more to the southeast. At two o'clock in the afternoon, they fell in with Captain Biggs, who had carried Lieutenant Ashley from the field of action, dangerously wounded. Traveling an hour longer, the heavy rain set in, which has been previously described; and they concluded it was best to encamp, as they were now incumbered with the wounded officer. It was just as they came up with Biggs and Ashley that the battle of Olentangy commenced—particulars of which have already been narrated. The battle-field was at a point in the Plains six miles distant, in a southeast direction. The place where the party made their camp was in what is now Holmes township, Crawford county, nearly two miles north of Bucyrus. They had traveled only about nine miles since daylight. They were in the woods and had been ever since midnight; the open country was two miles to the south of them.

The next morning they started on their course deviating still more to the southeast, passing through a portion of what is now the township of Liberty, in the last-mentioned county; and, after crossing the Sandusky river again, they passed into the present township of Whetstone, in the same county. They had traveled about three miles, when a deer was found which had been recently killed. The meat was sliced from the bones, and tied up in the skin; a tomahawk lay beside it. They carried all with them; and, in advancing about one mile further, espied the smoke of a fire. They immediately gave the wounded officer into the charge of the young man, desiring him to stay behind; while the residue of the company walked up as cautiously as they could toward the fire. When they came to it, they concluded, from several circumstances, that some of their own men had encamped there the previous night.

They then went about roasting the venison; afterward, just as they were about to march, a volunteer was observed coming upon their tracks. He seemed, at first, very shy; but, after being called to, came up, and told them he was the one who had killed the deer; but, upon hearing them come up, was afraid of Indians, hid it in a thicket, and made off. Upon this they gave him some bread and roasted venison, and proceeded all together on their journey.

About two o'clock they came upon the paths by which the army had gone out. They were now in the present township of Jefferson, Crawford county, a mile and a half down the Sandusky river from the present site of Leesville, and on the south side of the stream, just at the point where, on the afternoon of the 2d,— it was now the 7th of June,—the army had left its banks and bore away in a southwest direction for the Plains. Knight and Biggs did not think it safe to keep the trace made by the troops; but Crawford said the Indians would not follow the army beyond the open country, which they were then considerably past. Had they reached this point nine hours sooner, they would have marched directly into the enemy's camp!

As Lieutenant Ashley was still riding Biggs' horse, Knight now lent the latter his. Crawford and the doctor, both on foot, went about one hundred yards in front, Biggs and the wounded officer in the center, and the two young men behind. They were now traveling along the south bank of the Sandusky, and a mile and a half brought them to the point just east of Leesville, where the army, when outward bound, first struck the river. Here several Indians started up within fifteen or twenty steps of Crawford and Knight. As only three were at first discovered, the doctor got behind a large black oak, made ready his piece, and raised it to take sight, when Crawford called to him twice not to fire.

One of the Indians ran up to Crawford and took him by the hand. The colonel again told Knight not to fire, but to put down his gun, which he did. At that instant one of the Indians came up to him, whom he had formerly seen very often, calling him "doctor," and taking him by the hand. The party had fallen into an ambuscade of Delaware Indians, whose chief was Wingenund,[2] and whose camp was only half a mile away, in a northeast direction—Wingenund's camp, previously mentioned, distant twenty-eight miles in a straight line east of the battle-field. As soon as the Indians were discovered by Biggs he fired among them, but did no execution. "They then told us to call these people," says Knight, "and make them come there, else they would go and kill them, which the colonel did; but the four got off and escaped for that time. The colonel and I were then taken to the Indian camp."[3] Captives to the Delaware Indians, we will leave Crawford and Knight at this point, to follow the fortunes of other stragglers from the army on the night of the 5th of June.

---

[2] "Delaware Indians of the Wingenim tribe," is the language of Knight; but the misspelling of Indian proper names has ever been a very common occurrence.

[3] The capture of Crawford and Knight is mentioned by Heckewelder (*Hist. Ind. Nations*), immediately following a very summary disposal of the operations of the Americans upon the Sandusky Plains. After noticing their arrival in the Sandusky country, whither they had come to murder, as he says, the remnant of the Christian Indians, and depicting their disappointment in finding nothing but empty huts of the "believing Indians," he adds: "They then shaped their course toward the hostile Indian villages; where being, contrary to their expectations, furiously attacked, Williamson and his band took the advantage of a dark night and ran off, and the whole party escaped, except one Crawford and another." Veracious historian!

It will be remembered, that when the army left the grove on the evening the retreat began, three divisions, in marching around the camp of the Shawanese, struck the marsh that lay to the southwest of the battle-field, and that some of the men there lost their horses, which had stuck fast in the mire. Among those who were unfortunate in this respect were John Slover, the pilot, and James Paull. These men, with five others, all now on foot, being pressed by the savages, struck off together in a northerly direction, hoping thereby, as had Crawford and Knight, to avoid the enemy by taking a different direction from that followed by the army. Two of the party, who had been in the same company with Slover, had lost their guns in the swamp.

The men kept on their course north, until near the Tymochtee creek, when, just before day, they got into a morass, and were under the necessity of waiting until it was light to see their way through. They now, for some unaccountable reason, instead of traveling eastward, thereby avoiding, to a great extent, all trails of the savages, and, at the same time, pursuing a direction toward their homes, took a course to the southwest, and throughout the day traveled along the western edge of the Plains, gradually, however, getting more to the eastward.

At about ten o'clock in the forenoon, they sat down to eat a little. A scrap of pork to each man was all their supply. They had halted, unsuspectingly, near an

Indian trace. Soon several warriors were discovered coming on the trail. The men ran off hastily, leaving their baggage and provisions; but, fortunately, were not discovered. After skulking some time in the grass and bushes, they returned and recovered their food and other articles. The savages hallooed as they passed, and were answered by others on the flanks of the Amercans. "The foremost Indian in the file," says Paull, "halted, which brought all the others to a stop. They now all looked around and listened. After a lapse of a few moments, the one in front started off, whistling, and the rest followed." [4]

About twelve o'clock, they discovered another party of Indians in front of them; but, again skulking in the grass and bushes, they were not discovered. In the afternoon, the furious rain-storm which has been previously noticed, came on, and the party halted. The sudden change in the temperature was remarkable—"the coldest rain I ever felt," says Slover. Afterward they saw other Indians at a distance, but had the good fortune again to be passed undiscovered.

During the night they got out of the Plains, having crossed the paths made by the army in its advance, at a point about five miles east of the present site of Bucyrus. They had traversed nearly the entire

---

[4] James Paull's Recollections of Crawford's campaign; communicated to Robert A. Sherrard, in January, 1826: MS. Slover puts the number of Indians at "eight or nine;" Paull, at twenty-five.

length of the open country—about forty miles from the Tymochtee creek by the route traveled; not very rapid walking, it is true; "but we would have made much greater progress," is the conjecture of Slover, "had it not been for two of our companions who were lame: the one having his foot burnt; the other being troubled with a swelling in his knee of a rheumatic nature."

The party struck the woodland near the northeast corner of what is now Whetstone township, Crawford county, designing, very wisely, to keep north of the trail of the army, and to come in to Fort Pitt by way of Fort McIntosh—the mouth of Beaver.[5] After traveling a few miles further into the woods, in a northerly direction, they changed their course due east, leaving the present sites of Crestline and Mansfield some distance to the south of them.

During the day—the 7th of June, and the second after the retreat began—one of the company; the person affected with a rheumatic swelling, was left behind some distance in a swamp. "Waiting for him some time," is the language of Slover, "I saw him coming within one hundred yards, as I sat on the body of an old tree mending my moccasins; but, taking my eye from him, I saw him no more. He had not observed our tracks, but had gone a different way. We whistled on our

---

[5] The language of Slover is—"to come in by the Tuscarawas." By this is meant the route crossing that river *above* the mouth of Sandy creek; as all *below* that point was then known as the Muskingum.

chargers, and afterward hallooed for him, but in vain." He was fortunate, however, in missing his party, as he afterward arrived safe at Wheeling.

The party traveled on until night, having reached the streams flowing into the Mohican about noon of that day.[6] In the evening they had their second meal since the retreat began. One of their number had caught a fawn during the day, and its flesh, broiled by the fire, made them an excellent repast. They encamped for the night within the limits of what is now Ashland county.

It has been mentioned that one of the party was lame with a burnt foot. This was James Paull. The accident happened in this wise: In making preparations, on the afternoon of the 5th, for the retreat of the army, among other duties many of the men engaged in baking bread; and, in doing so, some of them had made use of a spade, which served as a kind of bake-pan for them. This had been picked up, by one of the volunteers on the march out, at the wasted Moravian town, and carried along to be used for that purpose. After the last loaf had been baked the spade was thrown aside hot, and was stepped upon by young Paull. As his moccasin was worn through on the sole, his foot was severely burnt.[7]

---

[6] "We traveled on until night, and were on the waters of the Muskingum from the middle of this day."—*Slover*. The waters of the Mohican flow into the Muskingum through the Walhonding.

[7] MS. of Robert A. Sherrard: January, 1826.

The six men started at daybreak the next morning, and at nine o'clock were within about twenty miles of the Tuscarawas, in what is now Wayne county. Here they were ambuscaded by a party of Shawanese who had followed their path all the way from the Sandusky Plains. The Indians killed two of the men at the first fire. Paull was untouched, and, notwithstanding his burnt foot, ran for life and escaped. Slover and the other two men were made prisoners. Strange to say, one of the Indians was of the party which captured Slover when a boy, in Virginia. He was recognized by him; came up and spoke to him, calling him by his Indian name — Mannucothe. He upbraided him, however, for coming to war against them.

The three prisoners were taken back to the Plains, where the Indians had some horses they had taken which had belonged to the Americans. These were found; and after the whole party had mounted, they started for the Shawanese towns upon the Mad river, in what is now Logan county.[8] On the third day after their capture, they came in sight of a small Indian village. Hitherto, the savages had treated their prisoners

---

[8] It has been asserted that Slover and his companions were taken to the Shawanese towns *on the Scioto*, in what is now Pickaway county.— *Howe's His. Coll. Ohio*, p. 404. This is erroneous; as Slover particularly mentions that the towns were *fifty miles* from the Scioto. Taylor, in his *History of Ohio*, p. 387, gives the correct location—the Shawanese towns upon the Mad river.

kindly, giving them a little meat and flour to eat, which they had found or taken from other captives. Now, however, the Indians began to look sour. The town they were approaching was not far from Wapatomica,[9] their principal village—situated just below what is now Zanesfield, in Logan county—to which the savages intended to take their prisoners. We will here leave the three unfortunate borderers, for the present, to narrate other incidents which transpired upon the Sandusky, after the enemy relinquished their pursuit of the retreating army.

NOTE 1.—I have frequently consulted the published narratives of Knight and Slover in the preparation of this and the following chapters—the one relating to James Paull (Chapter XVII) alone excepted. The original edition was printed at Philadelphia, as previously mentioned, in 1783. Copies of that date are exceedingly rare. Subsequent, but imperfect, editions have been published from time to time. A small one was printed at Nashville, in 1843, and there is a Cincinnati reprint of this, of 1867.

Bailey, the printer and publisher of the Philadelphia edition, was, at that time, the printer of *The Freeman's Journal*—a newspaper of that city. A memoir of Slover, which appears in later editions, is not in the original. In the latter, is the following address by the publisher " To the Public :"

" The two following Narratives [Knight's and Slover's] were transmitted for publication, in September last [1782]; but shortly afterward,

---

[9] Called by Slover, Wachatomakak; at least so written down by Brackenridge. See *Slover's Narr.*, p. 20. " Wapatomica was on Mad river on a farm I once owned."—*Notes to the author, by John H. James, Esq., of Urbana, O.*: 1873.

the letters from Sir Guy Carlton, to his Excellency, General Washington, informing that the savages had received orders to desist from their incursions, gave reason to hope that there would be an end to their barbarities. For this reason, it was not thought necessary to hold up to view what they had heretofore done. But as they still continue their murders on our frontier, these Narratives may be serviceable to induce our government to take some effectual steps to chastise and suppress them; as from hence, they will see that the nature of an Indian is fierce and cruel, and that an extirpation of them would be useful to the world, and honorable to those who can effect it."

Immediately following the address is this letter:

"Mr. Bailey: Enclosed are two Narratives, one of Dr. Knight, who acted as Surgeon in the expedition under Col. Crawford, the other of John Slover. That of Dr. Knight was written by himself at my request; that of Slover was taken by myself from his mouth as he related it. This man, from his childhood, lived amongst the Indians; though perfectly sensible and intelligent, yet he can not write. The character of Dr. Knight is well known to be that of a good man, of strict veracity, of a calm and deliberate mind, and using no exaggeration in his account of any matter. As a testimony in favor of the veracity of Slover, I thought proper to procure a certificate from the clergyman to whose church he belongs, and which I give below.

"These Narratives you will please publish in your useful paper or in any other way you may judge proper. I conceive the publication of them may answer a good end, in showing America what have been the sufferings of some of her citizens by the hands of the Indian allies of Britain. To these Narratives, I have subjoined some Observations which you may publish or omit as it may be convenient.

"H. Brackenridge.

"Pittsburg, *Aug.* 3, 1782."

[*Certificate of the Clergyman.*]

"I do hereby certify that John Slover has been for many years a regular member of the church under my care, and is worthy of the highest credit.

"WILLIAM RENO." (*a*)

Brackenridge, to whom the world is indebted for the narratives of Knight and Slover, was an eminent lawyer and author of Pittsburg, from 1781, until his death in 1816. The last fifteen years of his life, he was one of the judges of the Supreme Court. He was noted for his talents, learning, and eccentricity. He was the author of " Modern Chivalry," "Incidents of the Whisky Insurrection," and other works. The Observations he speaks of, in his letter to Mr. Bailey, were printed by the latter, with the narratives of Knight and Slover. They are, as the writer quaintly calls them, " Observations with regard to the animals, vulgarly styled Indians." They contain, however, nothing in relation to the expedition against Sandusky.

The narrative of Knight, up to the commencement of the retreat of the army, contains little that is not suppliable from other sources; after that event, however, his account of what he saw and suffered, is exceedingly valuable and complete.

Knight throws no light, of course, upon the retreat of the army; neither does Slover. The narrative of the latter is not as well connected as that of the former; yet, of the general truthfulness of his story, there can be no question. Both narratives, it may be premised, were written immediately after the return of these men from captivity. There was no printing done in Pittsburg until the establishment and issuing of the *Pittsburg Gazette*, in July, 1786; hence, the publication of the pamphlet in Philadelphia.

I have carefully examined all the statements I could find, either in manuscript or in print, said to have been made by Knight and Slover after their return, which are not found in their narratives, and have

---

(*a*) An Episcopalian.

noted several incidents additional to those incorporated therein. Most of these were obtained from them by western correspondents of the Philadelphia newspapers of 1782. Some have been embodied in the chapters following.

NOTE 2.—There is a tradition current in the upper portions of the Sandusky valley, that the spot where Crawford was captured, was several miles northwest of Leesville, near the Cranberry marsh, in Cranberry township, Crawford county. This has obtained currency, doubtless, from the remark of Knight (*Narr.*, p. 7), as to the course taken by his party soon after the retreat began. "Judging ourselves to be now out of the enemy's lines," says the doctor, "we took a due east course." This direction, *had it been continued*, would have brought the party to the point indicated by the tradition; but their course was soon after changed, as has been stated. Besides, Knight expressly says (p. 8) that they were captured on the trail made by the army in its outward march; and further, that the spot " was about half a mile " from the Indian camp (p. 9).

It has formerly been supposed by some that the place of Crawford's capture was farther east than Leesville—at or near what is now known as Spring Mills, in Richland county. This belief was based entirely upon the supposition (already shown to be erroneous) that the Wyandot Old Town and the winter-quarters of the Moravian Indians were located up the Sandusky river as far as the present town of Bucyrus (*Taylor's His. Ohio*, p. 381); or, at least, as far up as the mouth of the Broken Sword (*Schweinitz' Life of Zeisberger*, p. 516, *note*). Now, as the party were ambushed "about thirty three miles distant" from Sandusky, which was only eight miles below these localities, as stated by Knight (p. 9), therefore, the surprise and capture, it was reasoned, must have occurred a considerable distance from Leesville.

CHAPTER XVI.

CAPTIVES IN THE WILDERNESS — INDIAN BARBARITIES.

IT was, as before related, on the morning of the 7th of June, and just west of the site of the present town of Crestline, that the enemy fired their last shot at the retreating army under Williamson. Upon the relinquishment of the pursuit, the allied forces immediately returned to the Half King's town, distant about thirty-four miles by the Indian trace, which ran along almost due west from Wingenund's camp, passing just to the north of the spot where Leesville is now located, and along a little to the south of Bucyrus—crossing the river two miles below the latter place; leading thence through the woods to Upper Sandusky Old Town, and then eight miles further down the stream, as previously shown, to the village of the great sachem of the Wyandots.

Great were the rejoicings—wild the dances—fierce the yells—upon the return of the savages. But the British troops having accomplished the object of their march to the Sandusky—aiding their allies to repel the Americans —did not stop to join in the festivities; they immediately returned to Detroit. Leith, who had remained at Lower Sandusky awaiting the issues of the contest, now that the invaders were gone, returned with his goods to the Half King's town and again began his traffic with the Indians.

No sooner had the warriors returned from their pursuit of the Americans than the squaws and children came forth from their hiding-place to join them in their savage exultation. In the towns upon the Mad river and the Miami, intense anxiety had prevailed among the women before the result became known. When, however, the men returned with scalps and other trophies, their joy was unbounded.[1]

Among the spoils gathered up by the Indians was a number of horses—some that had given out upon the retreat; some whose riders had been shot; but principally those stuck fast in the swamp near the battle-ground of the 4th of June. Lashing-ropes,[2] halters, saddles, guns, knapsacks, cooking utensils, and other articles, were found. A *broken sword* picked up on the bank of one of the creeks, gave name to the stream.[3]

---

[1] Alder MS.: *Howe's His. Coll. Ohio*, 334, 335.

[2] The statement of Heckewelder (*Narr. Miss.* 337) is that "many bundles of ropes, and ready-made halters, to take off the plunder and horses which would fall into their hands, were collected in the prairie. It seemed that they [the Americans] calculated on taking much booty home with them; but finding themselves mistaken, they chose rather to lose their baggage, than run the risk of losing their lives." (!)

[3] Communicated by William Walker: 1872. There is a tradition lingering in the Sandusky country to the effect that Crawford was captured upon the Broken Sword creek; that, in his rage, he *broke his*

As soon as the first wild uproar and frenzy at the Half King's town had subsided, Captain Pipe and Wingenund sent a runner to the camp where Crawford and the other prisoners were held, to have them brought on to the Delaware town upon the Tymochtee. Their doom was sealed; but, as the sequel will show, all were not to suffer alike. They were, however, kept in ignorance of the fate awaiting them.[4]

As the burning of prisoners was an obsolete custom with the Wyandots, the Delawares did not dare to inflict the death penalty in that manner upon their territory without obtaining permission from the Half King (the Delawares were tenants at will in the Sandusky country, under the Wyandots). But the question in the minds of The Pipe and Wingenund was, how can the consent of Pomoacan be obtained? The

---

sword rather than give it up; and that *this* circumstance gave name to the stream. This story, of course, is without foundation in fact.

On some of the early Ohio maps, the Broken Sword is put down as "Crooked-knife creek."—See *Hough and Bourne's Map of Ohio*: 1815.

There is yet another tradition concerning the *broken sword*, to the effect that during one of the councils held by the officers of the army, one of them struck his sword into a stump, breaking it in two pieces; and that this should have occurred upon the banks of this creek. But the army was not upon the Broken Sword at all;—and, of course, no council was held upon its banks.

[4] "*In future*," they were assured, "all prisoners taken were to be tortured."—*Irvine to Washington*, 11th *July*, 1782.

two war-chiefs had decreed that the American commander should be tortured to death.

Fearing a refusal if application direct was made to the Wyandot sachem, the two Delawares resorted to stratagem. A messenger, bearing a belt of wampum, was dispatched to the Half King with the following message: "Uncle! We, your nephews, the Lenni Lenape,[5] salute you in a spirit of kindness, love, and respect. Uncle! We have a project in view which we ardently wish to accomplish, and *can* accomplish if our uncle will not overrule us! By returning the wampum, we will have your *pledged word!*"

Pomoacan was somewhat puzzled at this mysterious message. He questioned the messenger, who, having been previously instructed by The Pipe and Wingenund, feigned ignorance. The Half King, concluding it was a contemplated expedition of a Delaware war-party intending to strike some of the white settlements, returned the belt to the bearer with the word—"Say to my nephews, they have my pledge."[6] This was a death-warrant to the unfortunate Crawford.

It was three o'clock in the afternoon of Friday, the 7th of June, that Crawford and Knight were led captives to Wingenund's camp. On Sunday evening following, five Delawares, who had posted themselves some distance on the road of the army, east, brought to

---

[5] A name sometimes applied to the Delawares.

[6] Communicated by William Walker: 1872.

the camp the scalps of Captain Biggs and Lieutenant Ashley; likewise, an Indian scalp taken by the former upon the field of battle. These Indians also brought in the horses of Knight and Biggs. The two young men who ran off when Crawford and Knight were taken, again escaped the savages.

The Delawares had nine other prisoners at their camp besides Crawford and Knight; all securely guarded, and with very little to eat. John McKinly, formerly an officer in the Thirteenth Virginia regiment, was one of the captives. Several of the Indians spoke English quite fluently. Some were personally known both to Crawford and Knight. All very soon learned that the former was the commander of the expedition—the "Big Captain" of the Americans.[7] This information had been immediately carried to The Pipe and Wingenund, at the Half King's place. Some of the Delawares at the camp were Christian Indians from the Muskingum, who, it is inferred, had gone back into heathenism. Two of these, who were personally known to Knight, brought in scalps of the volunteers.[8]

On Monday morning, the 10th of June, the prisoners were all paraded to march, as they were told, to

---

[7] The Indian tradition that the Delawares believed the "Big Captain" they had captured was none other than Williamson, is not to be credited. Crawford was well known to many of the now hostile Delawares.

[8] Irvine to Moore, 5th [4th] July, 1782.

Sandusky—the Half King's town—about thirty-three miles distant, by way of the Indian trail. There were seventeen Delawares having the captives in charge. They carried with them the scalps of four white men.

Crawford had been told that Simon Girty, who, it will be remembered, was an old acquaintance, was at the Half King's village; and being very desirous to see him, was permitted to go to the town the same night, with two warriors to guard him; the rest of the prisoners were to go no farther than Upper Sandusky Old Town that day. Crawford's guards had orders to go by the route taken by him from the battle-field, that they might, if possible, find the horses he and the young man had been compelled to leave behind, on the morning after the retreat began.[9]

The prisoners were all marched together on the trace leading west, for three miles, when Crawford and his two guards struck off to the right—in a northwest direction, while the others were taken on to the Old Town. The point where they separated was about eight miles almost due east from the present town of Bucyrus,—in what is now Jefferson township, Crawford county.

Crawford reached the Half King's town some time during the night, and had an interview with Girty. Very little has been preserved of their conversation.

---

[9] The desire to recover these horses was probably the reason why Crawford was allowed to go on to the Half King's town.

"Tom Jelloway,"[10] as he was called, a Christian Indian from the Muskingum, speaking pretty plain English and French, was near and heard what was said."[11] Enough was reported by this Indian to Captain Pipe and Wingenund, who were in the village, to convince them that Crawford had made an earnest appeal for his safety. He offered Girty a thousand dollars to save him; and the white savage promised, with no intention of keeping his word, to do everything in his power. Crawford's offer of money only made the two Delaware chiefs more determined against him.

Crawford clearly saw that the Indians, particularly The Pipe, were very much enraged against the prisoners. Girty informed the Colonel that William Harrison and young William Crawford were made prisoners by the Shawanese, but had been pardoned at their towns. This information was true as to their capture, but false as to their lives being spared. The Wyandots had a few prisoners at their town; what became of them is entirely unknown—tradition, even, is silent, concerning them. They were probably, soon after the visit of Crawford, tomahawked and their heads stuck upon poles, as was the usual custom of the Indians. It is

---

[10] In Schweinitz's Life of Zeisberger, this Indian is spoken of as Job or William Chillaway. William Walker, in a communication before me, says: "This Jelloway I remember seeing frequently at our house:" MS. letter—1872.

[11] Communicated by William Walker: 1872.

certain they were not tortured to death; as the Wyandots were more merciful, in this respect, than their allies, as has already been explained.

Knight and his nine fellow-prisoners reached the Old Town late in the afternoon, as they had to travel a distance, from Wingenund's camp, of twenty-five miles. Here they were securely guarded during the night. Early in the morning—Tuesday, June 11th, the two Delaware chiefs, Captain Pipe and Wingenund, came up the river to them, from the Half King's town; and the former, with his own hands, *painted the faces of all the prisoners black!* As he was painting Knight, he told him (the war-chief spoke very good English) he should go to the Shawanese towns and see his friends: Knight knew but too well the ominous import of these words, notwithstanding the blandness of the wily savage.

About an hour after, Crawford also arrived up the river, whither he had been brought, as he had been told, to march into the Half King's village with the other prisoners. The two Delaware chiefs, who had avoided seeing him at the town below, now came forward and greeted him: he was personally known to both. They had frequently seen each other before the disaffection of the clan to which these two Indians belonged. At the treaty of the 17th of September, 1778, at Fort Pitt, between the Delawares and the American government, Crawford and The Pipe were present, each taking part in the negotiations, and each signing the articles agreed upon.[12] The dissembling war-chief told the Colonel he was glad to see him, and that he would have him shaved—that is, adopted as an Indian—when he came to see his friends, the prisoners, at the Wyandot town; but, at the same time, he *painted him black!*

The whole party now started on the trail leading to the village of the Wyandots, eight miles below; but, as the march began, Crawford and Knight were kept back, guarded by The Pipe and Wingenund. They were soon ordered forward; but had not traveled far, before they saw four of their comrades lying by the path tomahawked and scalped; some of them were at a distance of a half a mile from the others. The Delaware chiefs guarded well their two prisoners to the springs where Upper Sandusky now stands, when, to their dismay, another trail, than the one leading to the village of the Wyandots, was taken. Their course was now to the northwest, toward the Delaware town upon the Tymochtee, instead of to the northeast in the direction of Sandusky. If any spark of hope had been kept alive in the breasts of the two captives, it must now have been extinguished. Onward they marched between their two guards, who seemed determined to make sure of their victims.

Passing out of what is now Crane township into the present township of Salem, they soon reached the

---

[12] Treaties between the United States and the Several Indian Tribes. Washington: Lang¹ree and O'Sullivan. 1837, p. 1.

Little Tymochtee creek, where they overtook the five prisoners that remained alive.[13] The Indians now caused all their captives to sit down on the ground—Crawford and Knight with the rest; the two last, however, some distance from the others. Knight was then given in charge of one of the Indians to be taken, on the morrow, to the Shawanese towns.

At the place they had halted, there were a number of squaws and boys, who now fell on the five prisoners and tomahawked them all. An old squaw cut off the head of John McKinly, and kicked it about upon the ground. The young Indian fellows came often where Crawford and Knight were, and dashed the reeking scalps in their faces.

Again the march began. They were in what is now Crawford township; they were soon met by Simon Girty and several Indians, on horseback. The former, well knowing what was to be the fate of Crawford, had come from the Half King's town across the Plains to The Pipe's village, to be present upon the arrival of the two Delaware chiefs with their prisoners, but, becoming impatient, had started out on the trail to meet the savages and their captives. He rode up to Crawford and spoke to him; but did not inform him

---

[13] Knight makes the distance from this point to the Delaware town a little over a mile. This he afterward corrects, but in such a manner as to leave it in doubt where they came up with the others. Tradition fixes the place at the Little Tymochtee creek.

of the determination of The Pipe and Wingenund. At this point the two prisoners had become separated, Crawford being about one hundred and fifty yards in advance of Knight.

Girty had promised, it will be remembered, at the meeting with Crawford the night previous at the Half King's home, to do all he could for him; but that promise, as we have seen, he did not intend to keep; for now, at his first meeting with the Delaware chiefs since parting with Crawford, he made not the slightest effort in his behalf.[14] Nor is there any reason for believing, that he could have made any impression upon either The Pipe or Wingenund, had he been inclined to make the trial.

---

[14] That Girty did not intercede with The Pipe or Wingenund to save the life of Crawford, there can be no doubt. In *The American Pioneer* (vol. ii, 283), there is a sequel, by McCutchen, given to the Wyandot tradition concerning the battle of Sandusky—relating the particulars of an intercession of this white savage in behalf of the American commander, which is as absurd as that part of the story already given. It is as follows:

" Crawford was taken by a Delaware: consequently the Delawares claimed the right, agreeably to their rules, of disposing of the prisoner. There was a council held, and the decision was to burn him. He was taken to the main Delaware town, on a considerable creek called Tymochtee, about eight miles from the mouth. Girty then supposed he could make a speculation by saving Crawford's life. He made a proposition to Captain Pipe, the head chief of the Delawares, offering three hundred and fifty dollars for Crawford. The chief received it as a great insult, and promptly said to Girty, ' Sir, do you think I am a

The two war-chiefs of the Delawares were the arch-enemies of the Americans. They had been, as we have seen, the prime movers in the alienation of their tribe from its neutral policy. They drew with them from the Muskingum the war-faction, which not only set up its lodges upon the banks of the Sandusky and Tymochtee, but also formed a close alliance with the British Indians. Besides, in the battles just fought, several of their bravest warriors had been killed. It is not surprising, therefore, that no mercy was to be shown the prisoners who had fallen into their hands.

How far a spirit of retaliation for the massacre at Gnadenhütten prompted (if at all) the barbarities inflicted upon the prisoners that were tomahawked, or caused the stern decree of a cruel death against Crawford, is the merest conjecture. "It has been said," wrote Brackenridge in July following, "that the putting to death the Moravian Indians has been the cause of the cruelties practiced upon the prisoners taken at Sandusky. But though 'this has been made an excuse by the refugees amongst the savages and by the

---

squaw? If you say one word more on the subject, I will make a stake for you, and burn you along with the white chief.' Girty, knowing the Indian character, retired and said no more on the subject. But, in the meantime, Girty had sent runners to the Mohican creek and to Lower Sandusky, where there were some white traders, to come immediately and purchase Crawford—knowing that he could make a great speculation in case he could save Crawford's life. The traders came on, but too late."

British, yet it must be well known that it has been the custom of the Indians at all times."[15]

While at Wingenund's camp, Dr. Knight was informed *by the Moravian* Delawares present, who had taken up the hatchet against the Americans, that, *in future*, not a single soul should escape torture; and gave, as a reason, the Moravian affair upon the Muskingum.[16] This fact was afterward made known to Irvine at Fort Pitt, who, supposing it to have come from

---

[15] *Slover's Narr.*, p. 30, note.

[16] Various have been the reflections upon the supposed retaliation of the Delawares. By the Moravian writers the act is generally considered in the light of—" Vengeance is mine; I will repay, saith the Lord." "It was the cry of vengeance for the Christian Delawares slaughtered at Gnadenhütten, which was raised by Pipe on the banks of the Tymochtee, drowning every appeal or suggestion of mercy for one so estimable as all cotemporary accounts represent Col. William Crawford to have been."—*James W. Taylor, Hist. Ohio*, p. 388. "It has been regarded as an inscrutable act of Providence, that Crawford should fall into the hands of the savages, exasperated by the murder of the Moravians, and suffer tortures unheard of in the annals of men, as a consequence of Williamson's wickedness and ferocity."—*Chas. Whittlesey, in Amer. Pioneer*, vol. ii, p. 425. "But the disastrous result [of the expedition] was a terrible example of retribution, where the white man forgetting mercy, became himself the victim of savage vengeance."—*Early Hist. of West. Penn., Pittsburg, Pa.*, 1846, p. 209. "In it [the expedition] may be seen something marvellously like a retributive dispensation of Divine justice, except that the most guilty of the Moravian marauders escaped, while the innocent were falling in their places."—*J. R. Dodge, Red Men of the Ohio Valley*, p. 285.

the "heathen" Delawares, communicated it to Washington by letters of the 5th (4th) and 11th of July. "No other than the extremest tortures that could be inflicted by savages," replied the commander-in-chief, "I think, could have been expected by those who were unhappy enough to fall into their hands; especially under the present exasperation of their minds for the treatment given their Moravian friends. For this reason no persons, I think, should, at this time, submit themselves to fall alive into the hands of the Indians."[17]

  The Pipe and Wingenund, who alone are to be held responsible for the cruelties practiced upon the prisoners by the hostile Delaware Indians, gave no reasons, *at the time*, for their conduct. The words of Knight, in recording what Crawford told him immediately upon the return of the latter up the river from the Half King's town, imply causes other than the affair at Muskingum as prompting the two chiefs to their acts of cruelty; at least as influencing the mind of The Pipe. "Crawford told me the Indians were very much enraged against the prisoners; particularly Captain Pipe, one of the chiefs," is the language of the doctor.[18] The indifference almost invariably shown by The Pipe to his Moravian brethren precludes the idea that the Gnadenhütten massacre was *now* working so powerfully

---

[17] Washington to Irvine, August 5, 1782.
[18] *Knight's Narr.*, p. 9.

upon his mind as to cause such barbarities against the prisoners. That both these chiefs should *afterward* assign it as a reason, when these cruelties had made them odious at Detroit, is not at all a matter of surprise. And Wingenund was so bold as to deny complicity, on *his* part, in any cruelties inflicted upon the prisoners.[19]

As the party moved along toward the Tymochtee, almost every Indian the prisoners met, struck them with sticks or their fists. Girty waited until Knight was brought up, and asked, " Was that the doctor?" Knight answered him in the affirmative, and went toward him, reaching out his hand; but the savage bid him begone, calling him a damned rascal; upon which the Indian having him in charge pulled him along. Girty rode up after him, telling him he was to go to the Shawanese towns.

A short distance further brought them near to the Tymochtee, and another halt was made. They had now arrived within three-quarters of a mile of the Delaware village, which was further down the creek. Just here— a memorable locality—when the afternoon was well advanced, we will leave the unfortunate Crawford, to relate the incidents which afterward befell Knight, who, for over two hours before leaving the place, drank to the dregs, it may be premised, a cup of inexpressible

---

[19] *Heckewelder's Ind. Nations*, 281-284.

horror![20] He was then taken to Captain Pipe's house, at the Delaware village, where he lay bound all night.

The next morning, the 12th of June, Knight was unied by the savage who had him in charge—a Delaware Indian, whose name was Tutelu, a rough looking fellow[21]—*and again painted black!* They then started for the Shawanese towns, which the Indian said was somewhat less than forty miles away. Tutelu was on horseback, and drove Knight before him. The latter pretended he was ignorant of the death he was to die, affected as cheerful a countenance as possible, and asked the savage if they were not to live together as brothers in one house when they should get to the town. Tutelu seemed well pleased, and said, "Yes." He then asked Knight if he could make a wigwam. Knight told him he could. He then seemed more friendly.

---

[20] The redoubtable Wingenund some time afterward, while at Detroit, related to the Moravian Heckewelder a story, if we are to believe the credulous missionary, to the effect that Crawford sent for him upon his arrival at the Tymochtee, to ask for an intercession in his behalf—the colonel having called to mind that Wingenund had been entertained by him several times at his house upon the Youghiogheny ; that he came, recognized Crawford, lectured him upon joining himself to that execrable man, Williamson, and his party—and much other fine talk: all of which, under the magic touch of the Moravian's rhetoric, certainly out-logans Logan ! See *Heckewelder's Ind. Nations*, 281–284 ; *Howe's Hist. Coll. of Ohio*, 546, 547 ; *Schweinitz's Zeisberger*, 567–571 ; *Memoirs Hist. Soc. Penn*, 1826, p. 270.

[21] *Heckewelder's Narr.*, p. 341.

The route taken by the Delaware was the Indian trace leading from the Delaware town to Wapatomica. It led off in a direction partly southwest. They traveled, as near as Knight could judge, the first day about twenty-five miles. The doctor was then informed by Tutelu, that they would reach the town the next day a little before the sun was on the meridian. The prisoner was again tied, and both laid down to rest. Knight attempted very often to untie himself, but the Indian was extremely vigilant and scarce ever shut his eyes. At daybreak he got up and untied his captive.

Tutelu now began to mend up the fire; and, as the gnats were troublesome, Knight asked him if he should make a smoke behind him. He said, "Yes." The doctor took the end of a dogwood fork, which had been burnt down to about eighteen inches in length. It was the longest stick he could find, yet too small for the purpose he had in view. He then took up another small stick, and taking a coal of fire between them, went behind the savage; when, turning suddenly about, he struck the Indian on the head with all his force. This so stunned the savage that he fell forward with both his hands in the fire. He soon recovered and got up, but ran off howling in a most fearful manner. Knight seized his gun and followed him, with a determination to shoot him down; but by pulling back the cock with too great violence, broke the mainspring, as he believed. The Indian continued to run, still followed by Knight, who was vainly endeavoring to fire his gun. The doctor, however, soon gave up the chase and returned to the fire, where we will leave him for the present, to narrate what befell Slover and his two companions in captivity, whom we left just approaching, on the 11th of June, the upper Shawanese town, in what is now Logan county.

The inhabitants of the village, which they were nearing, came out with clubs and tomahawks—struck, beat, and abused the three captives greatly. They seized one of Slover's companions, the oldest one, stripped him naked, and with coal and water *painted him black!* The man seemed to surmise that this was the sign that he was to be burnt, and shed tears. He asked Slover the meaning of his being blacked; but the Indians, in their own language, forbade him telling the man what was intended. They assured the latter, speaking English to him, that he was not to be hurt.

A warrior had been sent to Wapatomica, to acquaint them with the arrival of the prisoners, and prepare them for the frolic; and, on the approach of the captives, the inhabitants came out with guns, clubs, and tomahawks. The three were told they had to run to the council-house, about three hundred yards distant. The man who was painted black was about twenty yards in advance of the other two in running the gauntlet. They made him their principal object; men, women, and children beating him, and those who had guns firing loads of powder into his flesh as he ran naked, putting the muzzles of their guns up to his body; shouting, hallooing, and beating their drums in the meantime.

The unhappy man had reached the door of the council-house, beaten and wounded in a shocking manner. Slover and his companion having already arrived there, had a full view of the spectacle—a most horrid one! They had cut him with their tomahawks, shot his body black, and burnt it into holes with loads of powder blown into it. A large wadding had made a wound in his shoulder whence the blood gushed very freely.

The unfortunate man, agreeable to the declarations of the savages when he first set out, had reason to think himself secure when the door of the council-house was reached. This seemed to be his hope; for, coming up with great struggling and endeavor, he laid hold of the door, but was pulled back and drawn away by the enemy. Finding now that no mercy was intended, he attempted several times to snatch or lay hold of some of their tomahawks; but being weak, could not effect it.

Slover saw him borne off; and the Indians were a long time beating, wounding, pursuing, and killing him! The same evening, Slover saw the dead body close by the council-house. It was cruelly mangled;

the blood mingled with the powder was rendered black. He saw, also, the same evening, the body after it had been cut into pieces,—the limbs and head about two hundred yards on the outside of the town, stuck on poles!

The same evening Slover also saw the bodies of three others at Wapatomica, in the same black and mangled condition. These, he was told, had been put to death the same day, and just before his arrival. Their bodies, as they lay, were black, bloody,—burnt with powder. One of these was William Harrison, the son-in-law of Crawford; another, young William Crawford, a nephew.[22] Slover recognized the visage of Harrison, and saw his clothing and that of young Crawford, at the town. The Indians brought two horses to him, and asked him if he knew them. He said they were those of Harrison and Crawford. The savages replied they were.

The third body, Slover could not recognize, but he believed it to be Major John McClelland, fourth in command of the expedition.[23] The next day, the

---

[22] Brackenridge took it for granted that Slover meant by "young Crawford," the *son* of Colonel Crawford instead of his nephew; and so stated in a foot-note to Slover's Narrative. This mistake has caused it to be extensively published that John Crawford never returned from the Sandusky.

[23] Slover mentions McClelland as *third* in command; but Rose is better authority on *that* point. Slover was doubtless correct in his belief of its being McClelland.

bodies of these men were dragged to the outside of the town, and their corpses given to the dogs, except their limbs and heads, which were stuck on poles! Such were the awful results of the wild orgies at Wapatomica. What a gorge of infernal revelry did these unfortunate prisoners afford the infuriated savages!

William Harrison, one of the men recognized by Slover, was the husband of Sarah Crawford, and had his home near his father-in-law's, upon the banks of the Youghiogheny, in Westmoreland—in that part which soon after became Fayette county. He was the son of Lawrence Harrison, one of the first settlers in the valley. He was a Virginian by birth, and a man of much note;—indeed, "one of the first men in the western country. He had been greatly active on many occasions, in devising measures for the defense of the frontiers; and his character as a citizen was, in every way, though a young man, distinguished and respectable."[24]

He was a lawyer by profession—high-minded and well educated. His manners were grave and sedate; his conduct, prudent; his good sense and public spirit, duly appreciated by all who knew him. He had been a sheriff of Yohogania county,[25] Virginia, and one of its members in the House of Delegates. He was

---

[24] Brackenridge in Slover's Narr., p 23, *note*.

[25] Set off by Virginia, 8th November, 1776; but, as claimed by Pennsylvania, it was a part of Westmoreland county.

also familiar with the duties of a soldier. He had been a Major and Lieutenant-Colonel of a militia regiment under McIntosh, in the expedition of the latter into the Indian country west of the Ohio, at the building of Forts McIntosh and Laurens, in the autumn of 1778.[26]

It came to the ears of the widow Harrison afterward, that her husband had been pardoned at the Shawanese towns;[27] she was, therefore, for a long time buoyed up with the hope of his return.[28] It was circulated that he had been taken a prisoner to Canada. When all hope had vanished, the widow laid aside her weeds and married again. Her second husband was Uriah Springer, as has been already mentioned.

The surviving companion of Slover, shortly after,

---

[26] MS. Order-Book of General McIntosh: Irvine Collection.

[27] She had heard the story of Slover, it is true, but she also had been informed of what had been told Crawford at the Half King's town concerning the pardon of her husband.

[28] Slover, it seems, did not give to Brackenridge the full particulars of the death of Harrison. In *The Pennsylvania Journal and Weekly Advertiser*, 27th July, 1782, I find this additional—as coming from him: "Colonel Harrison was tied to a stake, when the savages fired powder at him until he died; they then quartered him, and left the quarters hanging on four poles." I find, also, the following statement from a Westmoreland correspondent of *The Pennsylvania Packet*, published on the 13th of that month: "The Delawares applied to the Monseys for Colonel William Harrison (son-in-law to Crawford), who, being given up, was tortured in the most cruel manner; they

was sent to another town, to be, as the latter presumed, either burnt or executed in the same manner as the other comrade had been. In the evening, the Indians assembled in the council-house. It was a large building about fifty yards in length, and about twenty-five yards wide. Its height was about sixteen feet. It was built with split poles covered with bark. The first thing done upon the assembling of the savages was to examine Slover. This was done in their own tongue; as he spoke the Miamis, Shawanese, and Delaware languages, especially the first two, with fluency. They interrogated him concerning the situation of his country; its provisions; the number of its inhabitants; the state of the war between it and Great Britain. He informed them Cornwallis had been taken.

The next day Captain Matthew Elliot, with James Girty, came to the council. The latter was a brother of Simon Girty and an adopted Shawanese. The former assured the Indians that Slover had lied; that Cornwallis was not taken; and the Indians seemed to give full credit to his declaration. Hitherto, Slover had been treated with some appearance of kindness, but now the savages began to alter their behavior toward him. Girty had informed them that when he asked him how he liked to live there, he had said that he had

---

having bound him to a stake, fired powder through every part of his skin for an hour, after which they cut him in quarters and hung them on stakes."

intended to take the first opportunity to take a scalp and run off. It was, to be sure, very probable that if he had had such intention, he would have communicated it to him!

Another man came to him and told him a story of his having lived on the south side of the Potomac, in Virginia; and, having three brothers there, he pretended he wanted to get away; but Slover suspected his design, and said nothing. Nevertheless, he reported that he had consented to go with him. In the meantime, he was not tied, and could have escaped; but having nothing to put on his feet, he waited some time longer to provide for the contingency. He was invited every night to the war-dance, which was usually continued until almost day; but he always declined participating in these revelries.

The council at Wapatomica lasted fifteen days; from fifty to one hundred warriors being usually present, and sometimes more. Every warrior was admitted, but only the chiefs or head warriors had the privilege of speaking—these being accounted such, from the number of scalps and prisoners they had taken. The third day Alexander McKee was in council, and afterward was generally present. He spoke little. He asked Slover no questions; indeed, did not speak to him at all. He then lived about two miles out of the town; had a house built of square logs, with a shingle roof.

He was dressed in gold-laced clothes. He was seen by Slover at the town the latter had first passed through.

Slover saw Tutelu, the Delaware Indian, coming into Wapatomica.[29] He said that the prisoner he was bringing to be burnt, and who he said was a doctor, had made his escape from him. Slover knew this must have been Dr. Knight, who went as surgeon of the expedition. The Indian had a wound four inches long in his head, which he acknowledged the doctor had given him; he was cut to the skull. His story was, that he had untied the doctor, being asked by him to do so, Knight promising that he would not go away; that while he was employed in kindling a fire, the doctor snatched up the gun, came up behind him, and struck him; that he then made a stroke at Knight with his knife, which the latter laid hold of, and his fingers were cut almost off, the knife being drawn through his hand; that he gave the doctor two stabs—one in the back, the other in the belly. He said Knight was a big, tall, strong man! Slover contradicted the doughty Delaware. He told the warriors that he knew the doctor, and that he was a weak, little man; at which they laughed immoderately, and did not credit the brave Tutelu!

---

[29] Tutelu should have reached Wapatomica the day after Slover arrived there—June 12th. In the narrative of the latter, the time is put some days after. He may have tarried for a while at the first town.

On the last day of the council, save one, a "speech" came from Detroit, brought by a warrior who had been counseling with De Peyster, the commanding officer at that place. The "speech" had long been expected, and was in answer to one sent some time previous to Detroit. It was in a belt of wampum, and began with the address—"My Children:" and inquired why the Indians continued to take prisoners. "Provisions are scarce; when prisoners are brought in we are obliged to maintain them; and some of them run away and carry tidings of our affairs. When any of your people fall into the hands of the rebels, they show no mercy; why then should you take prisoners? Take no more prisoners, my children, of any sort—man, woman, or child."

Two days after, all the tribes that were near, being collected in council—Ottawas, Chippewas, Wyandots, Mingoes, Delawares, Shawanese, Monseys, and a part of the Cherokees—it was determined to take no more prisoners; and in the event of any tribes not present, taking any, the others would rise against them, take away the captives, and put them to death. Slover understood perfectly what was said in these deliberations. They laid plans also against the settlements of Kentucky, the Falls (Louisville), and toward Wheeling. There was one council held at which Slover was not present. The warriors had sent for him as usual, but the squaw with whom he lived would not suffer him to go, but hid him under a large quantity of skins. It may have been done that Slover might not hear the determination she feared would be arrived at, to burn him. About this time, twelve men were brought in from Kentucky, three of whom were burnt in Wapatomica; the remainder were distributed to other towns, and shared, as Slover was informed by the Indians, the same fate.

The day after the last-mentioned council, about forty warriors, accompanied by George Girty, an adopted Delaware, a brother of Simon and James Girty, came early in the morning round the house where Slover was. He was sitting before the door. The squaw gave him up. They put a rope around his neck, tied his arms behind his back, stripped him naked, and blacked him in the usual manner. Girty, as soon as he was tied, cursed him, telling him he would get what he had many years deserved. Slover was led to a town about five miles away, to which a messenger had been dispatched to desire them to prepare to receive him. Arriving at the town, he was beaten with clubs and the pipe ends of their tomahawks, and was kept for some time tied to a tree before a house door. In the meantime, the inhabitants set out for another town about two miles distant, where Slover was to be burnt, and where he arrived about three o'clock in the afternoon. They were now at Mac-a-chack, not far from the present site of West Liberty, in Logan county.[30]

At Mac-a-chack there was a council-house also, as at Wapatomica; but part only of it was covered. In the part without a roof was a post about sixteen feet in height. Around this, at a distance of four feet, were three piles of wood about three feet high. Slover was brought to the post, his arms again tied behind him, and the thong or cord with which they were bound was fastened to it. A rope was also put about his neck, and tied to the post about four feet above his head. While they were tying him, the wood was kindled and began to flame. Just then the wind began to blow, and in a very short time, the rain fell violently. The fire which, by this time, had began to blaze considerably, was instantly extinguished. The rain lasted about a quarter of an hour.

When it was over, the savages stood amazed, and were a long time silent. At last, one said they would let him alone till morning, and have a whole day's frolic in burning him. The sun at this time was about three hours high. The rope about his neck was untied; and making him sit down, they began to dance around him. This they continued until eleven o'clock at

---

[30] Slover does not give the name of the town; but that it was Mac-a-chack, frequently written Mac-a-cheek, there can be no doubt. See *Taylor's His. Ohio*, 529; *Howe's His. Coll. of Ohio*, 299, 309

night; in the meantime, beating, kicking, and wounding him with their tomahawks and clubs.

At last, one of the warriors, the Half Moon, asked him if he was sleepy. Slover answered, "Yes." The head warrior then chose out three men to take care of him. These took him to a block-house. They tied his arms until the cord was hid in the flesh; once around the wrist and once above the elbows. A rope was fastened about his neck and tied to a beam of the house, but permitting him to lie down on a board. The three warriors constantly harassed him, saying: "How will you like to eat fire to-morrow? You will kill no more Indians now." Slover was in expectation of their going to sleep, when at length, about an hour before daybreak, two laid down; but the third smoked a pipe, and talked to the captive, asking him the same painful questions. About half an hour after, he also laid down. Slover heard him begin to snore. Instantly he went to work; and as his arms were perfectly benumbed, he laid himself down on his right one, which was behind his back. With his fingers, which still had some life and strength, he slipped the cord from his left arm over his elbow and wrist.

One of the warriors now got up and stirred the fire. Slover was apprehensive that he would be examined, and thought it was all over with him; but the Indian laid down again, and his hopes revived. He then attempted to unloose the rope about his neck; tried to gnaw it, but all in vain, as it was as thick as his thumb and very hard, being made of a buffalo hide. He wrought with it a long time; finally gave it up; and could see no relief. It was now daybreak. Again he made an attempt—almost without hope, pulling the rope by putting his fingers between it and his neck,—when, to his great surprise, it came easily untied. It was a noose, with two or three knots tied over it.

Slover now stepped over the warriors as they lay; and having got out of the house, looked back to see if there was any disturbance. He then ran through the town into a corn-field. In the way, he saw four or five children and a squaw lying asleep under a tree. Going a different way into the field, he untied his arm, which was greatly swollen and turned black. Having observed a number of horses in a glade he had run through, he went back to catch one. On his way he found a piece of an old rug or quilt hanging on a fence, which he took with him. Catching the horse,—the rope with which he had been tied serving as a halter,—he mounted the animal and rode rapidly off.

NOTE.—The pretended colloquy between Crawford and Wingenund recorded by Heckewelder (*His. Ind. Nat.*, heretofore referred to, see p. 342, *note*), which, upon its first appearance, was generally pronounced apocryphal by the critics, is now seen to be wholly fictitious; nevertheless, the following paragraph concerning it, from Howe (*His. Coll. Ohio*, p. 546), has, perhaps, tended to restore confidence in it, in the minds of readers of western history. He says: "Some doubts have been expressed of its truth, as the historian Heckewelder has often been accused of being fond of *romancing;* but Col. Johnston (good authority here) expresses the opinion that 'it is doubtless in the main correct.'" Nevertheless (though it can hardly be necessary *now* to affirm it), I make bold to assert that the whole conversation, when viewed in the clear light of historic research, vanishes "into thin air." Concerning the pretended *friendship* of Wingenund for Crawford, nothing need be said. Bearing in mind that this war-chief, along with The Pipe, guarded the unfortunate commander to the spot where Heckewelder, for the first time, brings them face to face; that these two Delawares had previously determined that he should be tortured to death, and had cheated the Half King into giving his consent for its accomplishment on Wyandot territory—the reader will be prepared fully to appreciate the absurdity of the following narration:

"While preparations were making for the execution of this dreadful sentence, the unfortunate Crawford recollected that the Delaware chief, Wingenund, had been his friend in happier times. He had several times entertained him at his home, and showed him those marks of attention which are so grateful to the poor despised Indians. A ray of hope darted through his soul, and he requested that Wingenund, who lived at some distance from the village [thirty-five miles], might be sent for. His request was granted, and a messenger was dispatched for the chief, who reluctantly, indeed, but without hesitation, obeyed the summons, and immediately came to the fated spot.

"This great and good man was not only one of the bravest and most celebrated warriors, but one of the most amiable men of the Delaware nation. To a firm, undaunted mind, he joined humanity, kindness, and universal benevolence; the excellent qualities of his heart had obtained for him the name of *Wingenund*, which, in the Lenape language, signifies *the well-beloved*.

"He had kept away from the tragical scene about to be acted, to mourn in silence and solitude over the fate of his guilty friend, which he well knew it was not in his power to prevent. He was now called upon to act a painful as well as difficult part: the eyes of his enraged countrymen were fixed upon him; he was an Indian and a Delaware; he was a leader of that nation, whose defenseless members had been so cruelly murdered without distinction of age or sex, and whose innocent blood called aloud for the most signal revenge.

"Could he take the part of the chief of the base murderers? Could he forget altogether the feelings of ancient fellowship, and give way exclusively to those of the Indian and the patriot? Fully sensible that in the situation in which he was placed, the latter must, in appearance, at least, predominate, he summoned to his aid the firmness and dignity of an Indian warrior, approached Colonel Crawford, and awaited in silence for the communications he had to make. The following dialogue now took place between them.

"'Do you recollect me, Wingenund?' began Crawford.

"'I believe I do. Are you not Colonel Crawford?'

"'I am. How do you do? I am glad to see you, Captain.'

"'Ah!' replied Wingenund, with much embarrassment. "Yes, indeed!'

"'Do you recollect the friendship that always existed between us, and that we were always glad to see each other?'

"'I recollect all this. I remember that we have drunk many a bowl of punch together. I remember also other acts of kindness that you have done me.'

"'Then I hope the same friendship still exists between us.'

"'It would of course be the same, were you in your proper place and not here.'

"'And why not here, Captain? I hope you would not desert a friend in time of need. Now is the time for you to exert yourself in my behalf, as I should do for you were you in my place.'

"'Colonel Crawford, you have placed yourself in a situation which puts it out of my power and that of others of your friends to do anything for you.'

"'How so, Captain Wingenund?'

"'By joining yourself to that execrable man, Williamson, and his party; the man who but the other day murdered such a number of the Moravian Indians, knowing them to be friends; knowing that he ran no risk in murdering a people who would not fight, and whose only business was praying.'

"'Wingenund, I assure you that had I been with him at the time, this would not have happened; not I alone, but all your friends and all good men, wherever they are, reprobate acts of this kind.'

"'That may be; yet these friends, these good men, did not prevent him from going out again to kill the remainder of these inoffensive, yet *foolish* Moravian Indians! I say *foolish*, because they believed the whites in preference to us. We had often told them that they would be one day so treated by those people who called themselves their friends! We told them that there was no faith to be placed in what the white men said; that their fair promises were only intended to allure us, that they might the more easily kill us, as they have done many Indians before they killed these Moravians.'

"'I am sorry to hear you speak thus: as to Williamson's going out again, when it was known that he was determined on it, I went out with him to prevent him from committing fresh murders.'

"'This, Colonel, the Indians would not believe were even I to tell them so.'

"'And why would they not believe it?'

"'Because it would have been out of your power to prevent his doing what he pleased.'

"'Out of my power! Have any Moravian Indians been killed or hurt since we came out?'

"'None; but you went first to their town, and finding it empty and deserted, you turned on the path toward us. If you had been in search of warriors only, you would not have gone thither. Our spies watched you closely. They saw you while you were embodying yourselves on the other side of the Ohio; they saw you cross that river; they saw you where you encamped at night; they saw you turn off from the path to the deserted Moravian town; they knew you were going out of your way; your steps were constantly watched, and you were suffered quietly to proceed until you reached the spot where you were attacked.'

"'What do they intend to do with me? Can you tell me?'

"'I tell you with grief, Colonel. As Williamson and his whole cowardly host ran off in the night at the whistling of our warriors' balls, being satisfied that now he had no Moravians to deal with, but men who could fight, and with such he did not wish to have anything to do; I say, as he escaped, and they have taken you, they will take revenge on you in his stead.'

"'And is there no possibility of preventing this? Can you devise no way to get me off? You shall, my friend, be well rewarded if you are instrumental in saving my life.'

"'Had Williamson been taken with you, I and some friends, by making use of what you have told me, might perhaps have succeeded in saving you; but, as the matter now stands, no man would dare to interfere in your behalf. The King of England himself, were he to come to this spot, with all his wealth and treasures, could not effect this purpose. The blood of the innocent Moravians, more than half of them women and children, cruelly and wantonly murdered, calls aloud for *revenge*. The relatives of the slain, who are among us, cry out and stand ready for *revenge*. The nation to which they belonged will have *revenge*. The Shawanese, our grandchildren, have asked for your fellow-prisoner; on him they will take *revenge*. All the nations connected with us cry out, *Revenge! revenge!* The Moravians whom they went to destroy having fled, instead of avenging their brethren, the offense is become national, and the nation itself is bound to take *revenge!*'

"'Then it seems my fate is decided, and I must prepare to meet death in its worst form?'

"'Yes, Colonel!—I am sorry for it; but can not do anything for you. Had you attended to the Indian principle, that as good and evil can not dwell together in the same heart, so a good man ought not to go into evil company, you would not be in this lamentable situation. You see, now when it is too late, after Williamson has deserted you, what a bad man he must be! Nothing now remains for you but to meet your fate like a brave man. Farewell, Colonel Crawford,—they are coming!' (*a*)

"The people were at that moment advancing with shouts and yells, to torture and put him to death.

"I have been assured by respectable Indians that at the close of this conversation, which was related to me by Wingenund himself as well as by others, both he and Crawford burst into a flood of tears; they then took an affectionate leave of each other, and the chief immediately *hid himself in the bushes*, as the Indians express it, or, in his own language, retired to a solitary spot.

"He never afterward spoke of the fate of his unfortunate friend without strong emotions of grief, which I have several times witnessed."

(*a*) It will not do to attempt to screen Heckewelder behind the statement—as has so frequently been done—that what he here relates is from the lips of Wingenund and that he is not to be held responsible for the misstatements of the latter. The truth is, there is unmistakable evidence in the composition itself, that it is, to a great extent, the work of the Moravian alone. That the learned author of the *Life of Zeisberger*, should for a moment believe that this conversation was taken, *word for word*, from Wingenund, passeth all understanding! See *Schweinitz's Zeisberger*, p. 571, *note*. For an ingenious attempt to shift the whole responsibility of this fabrication to the shoulders of Wingenund, consult *Mem. His. Soc. Pa.*, 1826, p. 270.

CHAPTER XVII.

JAMES PAULL—HIS ESCAPE FROM DEATH—HIS SUBSEQUENT CAREER.

JAMES PAULL was born in Frederick (now Berkeley) county, Virginia, on the 17th of September, 1760. He was the son of George Paull, who removed into that part of Westmoreland which afterward became Fayette county, Pennsylvania, with his family, in 1768, and settled in the Gist neighborhood, in what is now Dunbar township, on the land where his son James afterward resided until his death.[1]

James Paull's early life evinced qualities of mind and heart calculated to render him conspicuous; added to which was a physical constitution of the hardiest kind. He loved enterprise and adventure as he loved his friends, and shunned no service or dangers to which they called him. He came to manhood just when such men were needed. His military services began before he was eighteen years of age. About the 1st of August, 1778, he was drafted to serve a month's duty in guarding the Continental stores at Redstone (Brownsville, Fayette county); an easy service—consisting in fishing and swimming during the day, and taking turns in standing sentry at night.

---

[1] And where *his* son, Joseph Paull, still lives [1872]—near Dunbar Station, on the Uniontown Branch Railroad from Connellsville, about four miles from the latter place.

About the 1st of May, 1781, he began recruiting in his county, then Westmoreland, for the projected campaign of that year against Detroit, under the auspices of George Rogers Clark. He had gone frequently, before that time, on brief tours of service to the frontier. He then held a commission as first lieutenant, from Thomas Jefferson, governor of Virginia. A company was raised, which, taking boats on the Monongahela, floated down to Pittsburg. Paull's company from thence found its way down the Ohio to the Falls (Louisville), in the month of August, and went into garrison at that point. The requisite forces for the expedition having failed to assemble, it was abandoned, as has already been mentioned. Paull returned home in the company of about one hundred others, through the wilderness of Kentucky and Virginia, after more than two months of privations and hardships.

Early in April, 1782, he was again drafted for a month's frontier duty; which was no sooner ended than he resolved, as the expedition against Sandusky was then projected, to volunteer for that campaign. His parting with his widowed mother just before marching to Mingo Bottom; his mishap at "Battle Island," on the Sandusky Plains; and his retreat, in company with John Slover and other companions, to within twenty miles of the Tuscarawas, where they fell into an ambuscade—have all been related. We left him, at nine o'clock, on the 8th day of June, in what is now Wayne county, Ohio, running for his life.

Paull had, the day after the retreat began, picked up a piece of an Indian blanket. This was of especial service to him. By tearing off a strip and wrapping it around his burnt foot, which by this time had all the skin off the sole, he was much relieved. He continued, as fast as one bandage was worn, to replace it by a new strip from the blanket, which he carried along for that purpose.

When fired upon by the savages, from their hiding place, Paull ran, as has before been related; but his gait was a lame, hobbling one. Two warriors started in pursuit. This nerved him to mend his pace. He now felt, for the first time during the campaign, that his life was at stake. His burnt foot was forgotten. He ran faster than his pursuers, who, observing it, fired at him, but without effect. These shots only served to increase his speed. Coming soon to a steep, bluff bank of a creek, he leaped down, gun in hand, without injury. The savages did not choose to follow, and relinquished the chase. Paull, as soon as he discovered he was no longer pursued, slackened his gait. In the descent of the precipice he hurt his burnt foot severely; and, to bandage it, was obliged to tear a strip from the ragged extremities of his pantaloons. In his flight he had thrown away the piece of blanket which had served him so good a purpose. Fearing further pursuit, he occasionally walked upon fallen logs, and would sometimes cross his own trail; he, however, escaped further molestation. The first night he slept in the hollow of a fallen tree. Early the next morning he started again, but it was with the greatest difficulty he could walk, his foot was so much swollen and so very painful. He had no provisions, and was afraid to shoot any game, for fear the report of his gun would be heard by Indians. He was fortunate, however, in catching a young blackbird, which he ate raw. He found also some service-berries, which were now ripe; so that he did not suffer very much from hunger. It was very *fresh* fare, Paull used afterward to say, but wholesome! He was, nevertheless, very weak as well as lame. The second night he slept under a shelving rock, upon some leaves, and rose the next morning much refreshed.

Paull had traveled down Sugar creek, a stream flowing into the Muskingum—as it was then called—from the northwest, in what is now Tuscarawas county. Being now very hungry, and seeing a deer, he shot it; but having lost his knife, the only device he could adopt was to open the skin with his gun-flint and get some of the flesh. Some of this he ate raw. Arriving at the Muskingum, he found it too deep to cross; and thereupon changed his course up that stream until a shallow place was reached, when he forded the river in safety. Here he discovered an old Indian camp, where there were a large number of empty kegs and barrels lying scattered around. It was now nearly dark; so he built a fire, the first he had ventured to kindle since his escape from the ambuscade, and cooked some of his venison; the smoke, as he lay down to rest for the night, protecting him from the gnats and mosquitoes, which were very troublesome.

He had passed out of what is now Wayne county, through the southwest corner of Stark, into Tuscarawas. His course lay in a southeast direction, through the present counties of Harrison and Belmont, to strike the Ohio opposite Wheeling. He made the distance in two days, reaching the river a little above the latter place. Traveling up the stream, he succeeded in crossing it on a rude raft made for the purpose. Once on the Virginia side of the Ohio, and he felt himself out of danger. Upon the river bottom he found a number of horses feeding; one, an old mare, he succeeded in catching after much trouble—having previously provided himself with a rude halter made of bark.

Paull finally reached a fort near Short creek, where he found the inhabitants of the vicinity had collected, upon hearing the news of the return of the expedition and its failure. He also found here some who, like himself, had just escaped the perils of the wilderness— some of his companions in arms. Resting a day at this point, he procured a horse and proceeded on to the vicinity of Catfish (Washington), in Washington county, where he had some relatives. Here his foot was doctored, which had become very badly inflamed, and he was furnished some clothes. Remaining with his relatives until he had gained considerable strength, he again started—a boy and a horse having been kindly sent to help him home. His meeting with his widowed mother can better be imagined than described!

The military services of James Paull did not end here. He took an active part in the Indian war which followed the Western Border War of the Revolution. He served with honor in Harmar's campaign against the Indians, at the head of the Maumee river, in what is now the State of Indiana, in the year 1790, as major of Pennsylvania militia.[2] History and tradition accord to Major Paull, on the perilous march, and in the encounters which followed, the character of a brave and good officer.

In after life, Paull was elected colonel of a regiment on the peace establishment. Having married, he settled down to the pursuits of agricultural life, in which he was eminently successful. He was sheriff of his county (Fayette) from 1793 to 1796, during the "Whisky Rebellion;" and had to administer the extreme penalty of the law to John McFall for the murder of John Chadwick.

---

[2] *McBride's Pion. Biog.*, vol. i, 116, 123; *Brice's Hist. Fort Wayne*, 124.

Colonel Paull had a family of seven sons and one daughter,[3] all of whom, as well as of his more remote descendants, who are numerous, are worthy their parentage. He was a man of commanding appearance, fully six feet in height, muscular and active; having a large frame, but not fleshy, with a massive head and a most manly face. In his youth and prime he was fond of athletic exercises, and always devoted to his friends, who were many. He was a man of most heroic and generous impulses. He was also a man of the strictest integrity. These qualities he evinced by many deeds and few words. He died on the 9th of July, 1841, aged nearly eighty-one years.

NOTE.—I have had occasion to consult, in the preparation of this chapter, a sketch of James Paull, to be found in the printed sheets of *The Monongahela of Old*, by James Veech; also, the Application of Paull for a pension, 15th January, 1833; and the Recollections by the latter of the Sandusky Expedition, as written down from his dictation in January, 1826, by Robert A. Sherrard: MS. The substance of these Recollections is to be found in a pamphlet entitled, "*A Narrative of the Wonderful Escape and Dreadful Sufferings of Colonel James Paul. By Robert A. Sherrard.* Cincinnati: 1869."

---

[3] His daughter, Mrs. William Walker, and one son, Joseph Paull, both of Fayette county, still survive—1872. Another son, George, was a distinguished army officer, in the regular service. He was in the war of 1812, under Gen. Wm. Henry Harrison. Two others resided for many years at Wheeling, Virginia, where they died, leaving children.

CHAPTER XVIII.

DR. JOHN KNIGHT'S ESCAPE THROUGH THE OHIO WILDERNESS.
13TH JUNE—4TH JULY, 1782.

THE spot where Knight so effectively belabored the valorous Tutelu with his dogwood fork, on the morning of the 13th of June, was near the Scioto, in what is now Hardin county, a short distance down the river from Kenton, its county-seat. He and his Indian guard had traveled, during the previous day, out of what is now Wyandot county, across the northwest corner of Marion, into Hardin—following an Indian trace leading from Pipe's town up the Tymochtee and across the Scioto to Wapatomica and other Indian towns upon or near the upper waters of Mad river, then known as the Shawanese towns, as already frequently mentioned.

Immediately upon Knight's return to the fire from the pursuit of the Indian who had had him in charge, he made preparations for a march homeward through the wilderness. He took the blanket of the Delaware, a pair of new moccasins, his "hoppes," powder-horn, bullet-bag,—together with the Indian's gun,—and started on his journey in a direction a little north of east.[1] At about half an hour before sunset, he came

---

[1] " Directing my course by the five o'clock mark," is Knight's lan-

to the Plains, when he laid down in a thicket until dark. He had traveled some distance into what is now Marion county.

Taking the north star as a guide, he again proceeded on, crossing the Plains in nearly a northeast direction. He was of opinion the open country extended about sixteen miles. He got into the woods, in the present county of Crawford, before daylight. His course then was near where the town of Galion now stands; thence onward into Richland county, striking the paths by which the troops had gone out, near the site of Spring Mills, in what is now Springfield township, Richland county, at noon, on the second day of his escape. These paths, at this point, lead in nearly an east and west course. Knight, we may be assured, saw no reason to change his mind as to the danger of returning by the route taken by the army. Fresh in his recollection were the scenes which transpired in the afternoon of the 7th, soon after he and Biggs gave Crawford their opinion upon that subject!

To avoid the enemy, he went due north all the afternoon, reaching a point not very far south of what is now the northern boundary line of Richland county. In the evening he began to be very faint. He had been six days a prisoner before his escape; the last two

---

guage. It is a singular circumstance that Knight makes no mention of what became of the horse which his guard was riding at the commencement of the journey.

he had not tasted a mouthful of food, and but very little the first four. There were wild gooseberries in abundance in the woods, but being unripe, required mastication, which, at that time, he was unable to perform, on account of a blow he had received from an Indian on the jaw with the back of a tomahawk. There was a weed that grew plentifully where he had stopped for the night, the juice of which he knew to be grateful and nourishing. He gathered a bundle, took up his lodging under a large, spreading beech-tree, and having sucked a quantity of the juice of the herb, went to sleep.

The next day, Knight made a due east course. Afterward, at times, he bore more to the southward. He often imagined his gun was only wood-bound, and tried every method he could devise to unscrew the lock, but could not effect it, having no knife or anything fitting for the purpose. He had now the satisfaction to find his jaw began to mend; and in four or five days, he could chew any vegetable proper for nourishment. He finally left his gun, as he found it a useless burden.

He had no apparatus for making fire to sleep by, so that he could get but little rest, the gnats and mosquitoes were so troublesome.

He was now traveling on a beech ridge where there were a great many swamps, which occasioned him much inconvenience. The ridge upon which he was traveling he judged to be about twenty miles broad, the ground in general very level and rich, and free from shrubs and brush. There were, however, very few springs; yet wells, he believed, might easily be dug in all parts. The timber was very lofty; and he found it no easy matter to make a straight course, as the moss grew as high upon the south side of the trees as upon the north. It is not surprising, therefore, that he should have deviated considerably from the course intended.

He observed that there were a great many white oaks, ash, and hickory trees growing among the beech timber; there were, likewise, some places on the ridge, perhaps for three or four continued miles, where there was little or no beech; and, in such spots, black and white oak, ash, and hickory were seen in abundance. Sugar-maple also grew there to a very great bulk. The ground was generally a little ascending and descending, with some small rivulets.

When he got off the beech ridge and nearer the Muskingum—for he had now gone a considerable way south—the lands were more broken, but equally rich with those just mentioned, and abounded with brooks and springs of water. In all parts of the country through which he passed, game was very plenty—deer, turkeys, and pheasants. He also saw vestiges of bears, and some of elks. He crossed the Muskingum just above the mouth of the Conotten, an eastern tributary, in what is now Tuscarawas county.² All this time his food had been gooseberries, young nettles, the juice of herbs, a few service-berries, and some mandrakes; likewise, two young blackbirds and a terrapin, which he devoured raw. When food sat heavily on his stomach, he would eat a little wild ginger.

He now aimed for the Ohio river direct, crossing all paths, and striking that stream about five miles below Fort McIntosh, mouth of Beaver, in the evening of the twentieth day after the one on which he had escaped. On the morning of the next day, July 4th, at about seven o'clock, he arrived safe at Fort Pitt, very much fatigued. "This moment," wrote Irvine to Moore, "Doctor Knight has arrived, the surgeon I sent with the volunteers to Sandusky. He was several days in the hands of the Indians, but fortunately made his escape from his keeper, who was conducting him to another settlement to be burnt."³

Dr. Knight afterward performed the duties of Surgeon to the Seventh Virginia regiment—Colonel John Gibson's, remaining at Fort Pitt until the close of the war. On the 14th of October, 1784, he married

---

² The words of Knight are—"About three or four miles below Fort Lawrence [Laurens]."—*Narr.*, p. 15.

³ Irvine to Moore, 5th July, 1782. This letter should have been dated July 4th; for, in a letter to Washington, from Fort Pitt, 11th July, he says: "Dr. Knight (a surgeon I sent with Crawford) returned on the 4th instant to this place." Knight, also, expressly states that his return was on the "4th day of July."—*Narr.*, p. 15.

Polly Stephenson, a daughter of Colonel Richard Stephenson, whose father was the second husband of Colonel Crawford's mother. He subsequently moved to Shelbyville, Kentucky, where he died on the 12th of March, 1838, the father of ten children. His wife died on the 31st of July, 1839.

NOTE.—Dr. Knight drew a pension from the general government. He made his application under the act of May 15, 1828. After his death, his children applied for whatever was due under the act of 1832. In this last application, the names of the children are given, as well as of some of the persons whom the daughters married.

CHAPTER XIX.

A RACE FOR LIFE—ESCAPE OF JOHN SLOVER FROM MAC-A-CHACK.

THE horse Slover had mounted, the morning after his providential escape from the old council-house at Mac-a-chack, was a strong and swift one. His course lay a little north of east, to the Scioto, distant nearly fifty miles. He rode for life! The woods were open; the country level. *He was entirely naked*, and had only a rope halter to guide his horse. On he rode—on, on! By ten o'clock he had reached and crossed the Scioto! He had already passed out of what is now Logan county, through Union, and far into Delaware; still he urged his animal onward, well knowing that he would be pursued, and rapidly too, by the savages thirsting for his blood, who now, by his escape, were made—

"Fierce as ten furies; terrible as hell!"

By three o'clock in the afternoon, he had left the Scioto full twenty-five miles behind him, when his horse failed; it could go no longer, not even on a trot. He instantly sprang off its back, left the animal, and ran ahead at the top of his speed; nor did he relax his efforts as evening came on. *Hearing hallooing behind him*, he pressed forward; and not until ten o'clock did he halt, when, sitting down, he became extremely sick and vomited.

The moon rose about midnight, and Slover again traveled on until day. During the night he had followed a path; but in the morning he judged it prudent to forsake the trail, and take a ridge running north, for the distance of fifteen miles, in a line at right angles to his previous course.[1] As he walked on, he put back the weeds bent by his feet, with a stick carried along for that purpose, lest he should be tracked by the enemy.

The next night he lay upon the waters of the Muskingum. The nettles had been troublesome to him ever since crossing the Scioto; and he had nothing to protect himself with but the piece of rug which he had brought from the Indian town, and which he had used under him while riding. The briers and thorns were now painful also, preventing him from traveling in the night until the moon appeared. In the meantime, he was hindered from sleeping by the mosquitoes, which were very troublesome—so much so, indeed, that even in the daytime he was under the necessity of carrying a handful of bushes to brush them from his naked body.

On the third day, about three o'clock, he found and ate a few raspberries, the first food he had taken into

---

[1] Slover does not say he went north; but he would hardly have taken an opposite direction, as that would have increased the difficulties of his route.

his stomach since the morning previous to his escape. He did not feel very hungry, but was extremely weak. He had then reached Newcomer's town, in what is now Tuscarawas county.[2] He swam the Muskingum some distance further up the stream, at a point where it was about two hundred yards wide.[3] Having reached the opposite bank he sat down, looked across the river, and thought he had the start of the Indians, if any had pursued him. That evening he traveled about five miles farther.

The next day he came to the Stillwater, an eastern affluent of the Muskingum, in a branch of which he obtained two small crawfish which he ate. The next night he lay within five miles of Wheeling. He had not slept a wink during the whole time, so troublesome had been the gnats and mosquitoes. He reached the Ohio opposite the island in the river at the post just named, where, seeing a man across the channel, he called to him. He had, however, great difficulty in persuading him to come to his relief. After telling him his name, and asking for particular persons who had been out in the expedition, the man was finally in-

---

[2] "The second night," says Slover, "I reached Cushakim; next day came to Newcomer's town."—*Narr.*, p. 30. I have been unable to locate the former place.

[3] "I swam the Muskingum," is Slover's language, "at Oldcomer's town." This is another locality I have not been able to fix with any degree of certainty.

duced to come over and take him across, in his canoe, to Wheeling.

"A certain Mr. Slover," wrote Irvine, from Fort Pitt, in his letter to Washington, of the 11th of July, "came in yesterday, who was under sentence of death at the Shawanese towns." No other arrival was afterward chronicled by the commander of the Western Department. Slover, who, as one of the pilots, had led, on the morning of the 25th of May, the volunteers into the woods from Mingo Bottom, returned to Fort Pitt on the 10th of July—the last of all to reach the settlements.

NOTE 1.—I have seen one or two very brief published accounts of escapes of stragglers from the army, that are not mentioned in these sketches; but these are unreliable. It is pretty extensively circulated that Dunlevy, the night of the beginning of the retreat, having been on the extreme western flank, engaged in conflict with the Indians, was left, with one or two more, to make his way home as best he could. But that volunteer, in his application for a pension, disproves the statement.

NOTE 2.—It will be remembered that Slover left the field at Sandusky, on the night the retreat began, without any knowledge of the presence of the British from Detroit. (See p. 267.) This is accounted for, from the fact that he was posted as sentry in the high grass on the *southwest* side of the grove during the afternoon of the 5th, while the Rangers were located to the *northeast;* and he was not withdrawn from the outpost until after dark.

CHAPTER XX.

AWFUL DEATH OF CRAWFORD BY TORTURE—11TH JUNE, 1782.

IN the capture of Crawford, the Delawares had secured the "Big Captain" of the invading army—a prize they were determined should not be lost, as evinced by his being guarded, from the Sandusky to the Tymochtee, by their two war-chiefs—The Pipe and Wingenund. Common prisoners were tomahawked with little ado; but Crawford was reserved for a more terrible death.

There was a fire burning at the spot where, on the afternoon of the 11th of June, we left Crawford in charge of the Delawares, to follow the fortunes of Knight. Around that fire was a crowd of Indians—about thirty or forty men, and sixty or seventy squaws and boys.[1]

A few Wyandots were there, and Simon Girty with them, as already mentioned; also Captain Elliott, it is believed, as he did not arrive at the Shawanese towns, where Slover was held captive, until *after* this date.[2] "Dr. Knight thinks a British captain was present," wrote Irvine to Washington, on the 11th of July.

---

[1] *Knight's Narr.*, p. 11.
[2] *Slover's Narr.*, p. 23.

"He says he saw a person there who was dressed and appeared like a British officer." There, too, was Samuel Wells, the negro boy, who had been captured by the Indians, as previously stated, and who afterward stoutly affirmed to early white settlers in the Sandusky country that his employment, at the time, was the holding of Girty's horse. A spectator, likewise, but an unwilling and horrified one, was Dr. Knight, who stood at a short distance from the fire, securely bound and guarded by the rough-visaged Tutelu.

Within hearing distance at least, if not in the crowd around the fire, was Christian Fast, a boy seventeen years of age, who, the year previous, having enlisted in that part of Westmoreland which soon after became Fayette county, as a member of the expedition from Western Pennsylvania that descended the Ohio river in aid of George Rogers Clark, was captured when near the Falls (Louisville) and taken to Sandusky. Fast, it seems, saw Crawford either at the Half King's town or at Wingenund's camp, and had a conversation with him, the particulars of which are unknown.[3]

Crawford was stripped naked and ordered to sit down. It is a tradition seemingly well authenticated that his clothes, especially his hat, which was made of leather, were long after in the keeping of the Delawares. The

---

[3] *Knapp's Hist. Ashland County*, pp. 507, 508. The particulars of the capture and final escape of young Fast are interesting. They are given in full in Mr. Knapp's history.

Indians now beat him with sticks and their fists;[4] and, presently after, Knight was treated in the same manner. The fatal stake—a post about fifteen feet high—had been set firmly in the ground. Crawford's hands were bound behind his back, and a rope fastened—one end to the foot of the post, and the other to the ligature between his wrists.[5] The rope was long enough for him to sit

---

[4] A Wyandot tradition runneth to the contrary of this; but, in addition to the positive assertion of Knight, there is the fact that such treatment always preceded the torturing to death of prisoners by the savages. Knight's swollen jaw afterward fully attested the severity of *his* beating.

[5] Whether Heckewelder's statement (*Narr. Miss.* 338, 339) of what transpired just before Crawford " was tied to the stake," is the result of his being imposed upon by Indians, or of an unwonted zeal, or both, it is now impossible to determine; certain it is, however, that all of it is fictitious. He says :

"'Where is Williamson, the head murderer?' was the call of the Indians from every quarter. They being told that he had been one of the first who fled from the ground, they cried out, 'Revenge! revenge! on those we have in our power for the murder of the Christian Indians on the Muskingum, and our friends at Pittsburg!'

"'These (said they to one another) have come out on a similar expedition, and with the *same* men who committed that atrocious murder on our friends and relatives, to do the same to us; they are all alike!—they want our country from us, and knew no better way of obtaining it, than by killing us first! for this very reason they killed the believing Indians at Pittsburg!'

" They called aloud for the surviving Christian Indians to come forward and take revenge on these prisoners; but they having removed,

down, or walk around the post once or twice and return the same way. Crawford then called to Girty and asked if they intended to burn him. Girty answered, "Yes." He then replied he would take it all patiently. Upon this, Captain Pipe made a speech to the Indians, who, at its conclusion, yelled a hideous and hearty assent to what had been said.[6]

---

their savage relations stepped forward in their stead. The fire was kindled, and poor Crawford was tied to the stake."

[6] In this crowd was Wingenund. That this chief should have attempted afterward to shift the responsibility of all participation in the torture of Crawford upon others, or that he should have endeavored to excuse the deed as justifiable on the ground that the Americans had shown no quarter to Moravian Indians upon the Muskingum, is not at all incredible; that he did both is quite probable; but it was not so done by him until he had discovered that the act was odious in the sight of the British at Detroit. In recording the conversation and describing the feelings of this Delaware concerning the matter, Heckewelder has so drawn upon his own imagination, that it is extremely difficult (indeed, quite impossible) to say how much of it is from Wingenund, or how much from his own fertile brain. From whichever source it may have proceeded, its absurdity is palpable:

"Once (it was the first time he [Wingenund] came into Detroit after Crawford's sufferings) I heard him censured in his own presence by some gentlemen who were standing together, for not having saved the life of so valuable a man, who was always his particular friend, as he had often told them. He listened calmly to their censure, and first turning to me said in his own language: 'These men talk like fools,' then turning to them, he replied in English: 'If King George himself—if your King—had been on the spot with all his ships laden

The spot where Crawford was now to be immolated to satisfy the revengeful thirst of the Delawares for the blood of the borderers, was in what is now Crawford

with goods and treasures, he could not have ransomed my friend, nor saved his life from the rage of a *justly* exasperated multitude.'

" He made no further allusion to the act that had been the cause of Crawford's death [the Gnadenhütten massacre, as Heckewelder will have it], and it was easy to perceive that on this melancholy subject grief was the feeling that predominated in his mind. He felt much hurt, however, at this unjust accusation, from men who, perhaps, he might think, would have acted very differently in his place.

" For, let us consider in what a situation he found himself, at that trying and critical moment. He was a Delaware Indian and a highly distinguished character among his nation. The offense was national and of the most atrocious kind, as it was wanton and altogether unprovoked [the Gnadenhütten massacre is again referred to]. He might have been expected to partake with all the rest of his countrymen, in the strong desire which they felt for *revenge*. He had been Crawford's friend, it is true, and various acts of sociability and friendship had been interchanged between them. But no doubt, at that time, he believed him, at least, not to be an enemy;—he might have expected him to be, like himself, a fair, open, generous foe.

" But when he finds him enlisted with those who are waging a war of extermination against the Indian race, murdering in cold blood, and without distinction of age or sex, even those who had united their fate to that of the whites, and had said to the Christians—' Your people shall be *our* people, and your God *our* God ' (Ruth i, 16), was there not enough here to make him disbelieve all the former professions of such a man [Crawford], and to turn his abused friendship into the most violent enmity and the bitterest rage ?

"Instead of this, we see him persevering to the last in his attachment to a person, who, to say the least, had ceased to be deserving of

township, Wyandot county—a short distance northeast from the present town of Crawfordsville.[7]

Colonel John Johnston describes the place as "a few miles west of Upper Sandusky, on the old trace leading to the Big Spring Wyandot town. It was on the right hand of the trace going west, on a low bottom on the east bank of the Tymochtee creek."[8]

"I have been on the ground often," is the testimony of a resident of that part of Crawford which soon after

---

it. We see him, in the face of his enraged countrymen, avow that friendship, careless of the jealousy he might excite. We see him not only abstain from participating in the national revenge, but deserting his post, as it were, seeking a solitary spot to bewail the death of him, whom, in spite of all, he still loved, and felt not ashamed to call his *friend*.

"It is impossible for friendship to be put to a severer test, and the example of Wingenund proves how deep a root this sentiment can take in the mind of an Indian, whenever such circumstances as those under which the chief found himself, fail to extinguish it."

[7] It was somewhere on what is now the south half of section twenty-six, of township one south, of range thirteen east, of the government survey; the *precise* spot I do not attempt to locate.

[8] *Howe's His. Coll. Ohio*, p. 546. It should be remembered, however, that the "Big Spring Wyandot town" was not in existence until long after the year 1782.

Howe, in 1847, thought he had found the *exact* spot. He then wrote: "The precise spot is now owned by the heirs of Daniel Hodge, and is a beautiful green, with some fine oak trees in its vicinity."

"The locality is on the Tyamoherty, about four miles above its junction with the Sandusky."—*The Forest Rangers. By Andrew Coffinberry.* p. 100, *note* 9.

became Wyandot county; "it is near to the creek bank, [Tymochtee] on the east side. This land is now [1844] owned by Daniel Hodge; and, in place of a bare piece of ground, as is reported, and that there will no grass grow on the spot, it is a beautiful grove, and some fine, healthy white-oak trees growing near, which the now occupant, Mr. William Richey, promises to preserve for future generations."[9]

"The spot is on the southeast bank of the Tymochtee," writes an old-time resident in the vicinity, "on lands owned by the heirs of Daniel Hodge, in Crawford township, about five miles from the mouth of the creek." "This information," continues the writer, "I obtained from the Wyandots living here when I came to the country in 1821, and from two negroes, Jonathan Pointer and Samuel Wells, captured by the Indians when small boys. They were intelligent and spoke good English."[10]

The following is from an early settler[11] in Crawford township: "From all I could learn when I came to the vicinity in 1823, the spot was then owned by Daniel Hodge—afterward belonging to his heirs."

---

[9] Joseph McCutchen.—*The American Pioneer*, vol. ii, p. 284.

[10] Jonathan Kear—*Notes to the author:* 1872. I am informed by William Walker that Pointer was at Brownstown, on the Detroit river, when Crawford was brought to the Tymochtee; *his* information, therefore, must have been derived from others. For a sketch of Pointer, see *His. Wyandot Miss.*, p. 78.

[11] Hon. John Carey, of Carey, Wyandot county, Ohio.—*Notes to the author:* 1872.

"When the Wyandots resided in what was then known as western Crawford, now Wyandot county," writes William Walker, "the precise spot was pointed out to many inquirers and early white settlers, by the Indians. The place is about seven miles northwest from Upper Sandusky, near Carey, but nearer to Crawfordsville, and near to the east bank of the Tymochtee creek."

"Find a brick house," continues the writer, "built in early times by Daniel Hodge, who died a few years afterward, leaving an only daughter; she married William Richey. They inherited the farm. From this house proceed, I think, a little north of west, nearly a quarter of a mile to a piece of rising ground, near the east bank of the Tymochtee creek. If not cleared, fenced, and cultivated, the spot is surrounded with (or was then) a grove of young white-oaks.

"When I first visited the place in the spring of 1814, there was no grass or weeds growing on the spot; but, on disturbing the surface, ashes and charcoal appeared. The spot was pointed out to me by a Wyandot of high respectability who was present when Crawford was tied to the stake, and was in the engagement at Battle Island, where he was wounded in the mouth, injuring the tongue and shattering the left jaw. This Wyandot died in Michigan, about the year 1827, aged over ninety years."[12]

---

[12] Original communication: 1872. It is suggested that the fact of

That the stake was planted in the immediate vicinity, so abundantly described, there can be no doubt. Besides, we have the positive statement of Knight that the place was three-quarters of a mile from "Captain Pipe's house"[13]—the Delaware village upon the Tymochtee. Here, then, at about four o'clock in the afternoon, of Tuesday, June 11, 1782, the torture began."[14]

The Indian men took up their guns and shot powder into Crawford's naked body from his feet as far up as his neck. It was the opinion of Knight that not less than seventy loads were discharged upon him! They then crowded about him, and, to the best of Knight's observation, cut off both his ears; for when the throng had dispersed, he saw the blood running from both sides of his head!"[15]

Walker's finding the spot *bare* as late as 1814, may prove of interest to those who have always put confidence in the report that no grass would grow where Crawford was tortured.

[13] *Knight's Narr.*, p. 12.

[14] The legislature of Ohio, finding this particular locality within the limits of one of the new counties erected in 1820 out of the New Purchase, very appropriately gave that one the name of *Crawford*. Afterward, on the 3d of February, 1845, the county of Wyandot was set off from western Crawford, when the spot fell within the limits of the new county.

[15] The reader will not fail to appreciate the absurdity of the following account of the torture by Heckewelder (*Narr.*, p. 342): "The torture Crawford had to endure was a double one, during which he

The fire was about six or seven yards from the post to which Crawford was tied.[16] It was made of small hickory poles burnt quite through in the middle, each end of the poles remaining about six feet in length. Three or four Indians by turns would take up, individually, one of these burning pieces of wood, and apply it to his naked body, already burnt black with powder.

was often mockingly asked how he felt; and whether they did as well to him, as he had done to the believing Indians;—they adding, ' We have to learn barbarities of you white people!' "

Equally as absurd is his account of the events transpiring from the time Crawford and his men found nothing but "empty Moravian huts" upon their reaching the Sandusky, to the close of the campaign. It is as follows: " They [Crawford and his men] shaped their course toward the hostile Indian villages, where being, contrary to their expectations, furiously attacked, Williamson and his band took the advantage of a dark night and ran off; and the whole party escaped, except one Colonel Crawford, and another, who, being taken by the Indians, were carried in triumph to their village, where the former was condemned to death by torture, and the punishment was inflicted with all the cruelty which rage could invent. The latter was demanded by the Shawanese, and sent to them for punishment."—*His. Ind. Nations*, p. 216. His subsequent statement (*Narr. Miss.* 338) modifies this somewhat. He says: " In the pursuit, many were killed, and poor Colonel Crawford, together with a Dr. McKnight, had the misfortune to be taken prisoners."

[16] Crawford, it will be seen, was not "burned at the stake," in the strict sense of that term, like the martyrs of old; the savages were more refined in their modes of torture. In Slover's case, the wood, it will be remembered, was placed four feet from the post.

These tormentors presented themselves on every side of him, so that, whichever way he ran round the post, they met him with the burning fagots. Some of the squaws took broad boards, upon which they would carry a quantity of burning coals and hot embers and throw on him; so that, in a short time, he had nothing but coals of fire and hot ashes to walk on!

In the midst of these extreme tortures, Crawford called to Girty and begged of him to shoot him; but the white savage making no answer, he called again. Girty then, by way of derision, told Crawford he had no gun; at the same time turning about to an Indian who was behind him, he laughed heartily, and, by all his gestures, seemed delighted at the horrid scene![17]

Girty then came up to Knight and bade him prepare for death. He told him, however, he was not to die at

---

[17] The reason given, upon the authority of a Wyandot tradition, for the non-interference of Girty, either to save his old acquaintance or put an end to his misery, as stated by McCutchen (*Amer. Pioneer*, ii, 283), is, the rebuke he got "the day before" from Captain Pipe! "Colonel Johnston informs us," writes Howe (*Hist. Coll. Ohio*, 549), "that he has been told, by Indians present on the occasion, that Girty was among the foremost in inflicting tortures upon their victim." I am compelled, however, to the belief that Girty took no part in Crawford's torture: simply a spectator and nothing more. Greatly delighted, as stated by Knight, he undoubtedly was, at the horrid spectacle; but, along with a few Wyandots present, *only* a looker-on. The Delawares afterward, in their intercourse with the whites, sought, very naturally, to throw the odium, as much as possible, upon Girty.

that place, but was to be burnt at the Shawanese towns. He swore, with a fearful oath, that he need not expect to escape death, but should suffer it in all its extremities! He then observed that some prisoners had given him to understand, that if the Americans had him they would not hurt him. For his part, he said he did not believe it; but desired to know Knight's opinion of the matter. The latter, however, was in too great anguish and distress, on account of the torments Crawford was suffering before his eyes, as well as the expectation of undergoing the same fate in two days, to make any answer to the monster. Girty expressed a great deal of ill-will for Colonel Gibson,[18] saying he was one of his greatest enemies—and more to the same purpose; to all which Knight paid but little attention.

Crawford, at this period of his suffering, besought the Almighty to have mercy on his soul, spoke very low, and bore his torments with the most manly fortitude. He continued, in all the extremities of pain, for an hour and three-quarters or two hours longer, as near as Knight could judge; when, at last, being almost spent, he lay down upon his stomach.[19]

---

[18] Colonel John Gibson—the same who was in command of the Virginia regiment at Fort Pitt, to which Dr. Knight belonged.

[19] The Wyandot and Delaware traditions, concerning the scenes at the torture, differ in minor details from the account given by Knight. I have followed, however, the statements of the latter, with the most implicit confidence in their truthfulness.

The savages then scalped him, and repeatedly threw the scalp into the face of Knight, telling him that was his "great captain." An old squaw, whose appearance, thought Knight, every way answered the ideas people entertain of the devil, got a board, took a parcel of coals and ashes, and laid them on his back and head. He then raised himself upon his feet and began to walk around the post.

They next put burning sticks to him, as usual; but he seemed more insensible of pain than before. Knight was now taken away from the dreadful scene.

It was a tradition, long after repeated by the Delawares and Wyandots, that Crawford breathed his last just at the going down of the sun. On the following morning, when Knight started for the Shawanese towns, he was conducted to the spot where Crawford had suffered, as it was partly in the direction he and his Delaware guard were taking. He saw the bones of his commander, lying among the remains of the fire, almost burnt to ashes. The Delaware told Knight that was his "Big Captain," at the same time giving the scalp halloo.[20]

After Crawford died—so runs the tradition—the fagots were heaped together, his body placed upon

---

[20] A fearful yell, consisting of the sounds *aw* and *oh*, successively uttered; the last drawn out at great length—as long as the breath will hold, and raised about an octave higher than the first.

them, and around his charred remains danced the delighted savages for many hours.

When the news of the torture reached the Shawanese villages the exultation was very great.[21] Not so when the awful story was repeated in the settlements upon the border. A gloom was spread on every countenance. Crawford's melancholy end was lamented by all who knew him. Heart-rending was the anguish in a lonely cabin upon the banks of the Youghiogheny. There were few men on the frontiers, at that time, whose loss could have been more sensibly felt or more keenly deplored.

The language of Washington, upon this occasion, shows the depth of his feeling: " It is with the greatest sorrow and concern that I have learned the melancholy tidings of Colonel Crawford's death. He was known to me as an officer of much care and prudence; brave, experienced, and active. The manner of his death was shocking to me; and I have this day communicated to the honorable, the Congress, such papers as I have regarding it."[22] In a letter to Irvine, at Fort Pitt, written on the 6th of August, he says: "I lament the failure of the expedition against Sandusky, and am particularly affected with the disastrous death of Colonel Crawford."

---

[21] *Slover's Narr.*, p. 26.
[22] Washington to Moore, 27th July, 1782.

INDEX.

Address to Crawford, 105, 106.
Albach's *Annals of the West*, 80.
Alder MS. 328.
Alexander, Emperor of Russia, 300, 310.
Alexander, James, 247.
American Archives, 100.
American Pioneer, The, 31, 230, 231, 247, 337, 385, 389.
Amherst, General, 17.
"Armstrong's Bottom," 154, 202.
Armstrong, General John, 20.
Armstrong, Silas, 154.
Arnold, the traitor, 20.
Arundle, a trader, 192, 193.
Ashley, Lieutenant, wounded, 212; assisted by Biggs, 220; overtaken by Crawford, 314; escapes the savages, 317; killed and scalped, 331.
Augusta county, Va., 89, 124.

Bailey, Francis, 4, 323, 324, 325.
Barker, Joseph, 247.
"Battle Island," 213, 235, 363, 386.
Battle of Olentangy, 233, *et seq.*; Americans victorious, 234; their loss, *ib.*; an incident, 235, *et seq.*
Battle of Sandusky, 207; "close and hot," 208; the enemy draw back, *ib.*; incidents of the battle-field, 209, *et seq.*; killed and wounded, 212, 213.
Beall, Captain Robert, 261.
Bean, Joseph, elected captain, 76; reconnoitering adventure of, 141; shot, but recovers, 235.
Beeson, elected captain, 75.
Believing Indians, see Christian Indians.
Beesontown (Uniontown, Pa.), 67, 75, 284, 291.
Bell, Captain, 254.
Berry, Jr., Hon. Curtis, 203.
Betty, "a mulatto girl," 118.
"Billy Wyandot," 163.
"Big Captain Johnny," 211.
Big Foot, the Poes' encounter with, 270, *et seq.*
Biggs, John, elected captain, 76; takes the advance, 138; takes a scalp, 212;
aids Lieutenant Ashley, 220; overtaken by Crawford and Knight, 314; Knight lends him his horse, 316; ambushed, *ib.*; escapes, 317; his fate, 331.
Big Spring Wyandot town, 169, 384.
Boice, captured by savages, 49.
Botetourt, Lord, 93.
Boundary controversy, 12, 44, 98, 99.
Bouquet, Colonel Henry, 169, 170, 183; his *Expedition*, 83.
Brackenridge, Hugh H., cited, 4, 90, 113, 120, 324, 338, 339, 346, 347, 348; biographical sketch of, 325.
Brady, Lieutenant Samuel, 255.
Brashears, Zach. 247.
Brice's *History of Fort Wayne*, 367.
Brinton, elected field-major, 77; his character, 124; reconnoitering adventure of, 141; is wounded, 212; Major Leet takes his command, 219, 220; returns home, 296.
Brodhead, Colonel Daniel, 7, 10, 11, 254; his Muskingum expedition, 8, 9, 36, 157, 250; his expedition up the Allegheny, 129, 255; his *MS. Order Book*, 6.
Broken Sword creek, 146, 181, 326, 328, 329.
Brown, Jos., see "Jos. Brown."
Brown, Joseph, 249.
Brown's *Map Wyandot Reservation*, 205, 213.
Brown, Thomas, 249.
Brown, William, 205, 213.
Bryson, Peggy, 282.
Burdin, Charles, 248.
Butler, General Richard, killed, 197.
Butler's Rangers, 173, 174, 176, 180, 216, 228, 234, 239, 267, 327, 378.
Butler's Spring, 142.
Byrd, Colonel, 85.

Cane, Samuel, 247.
Canon, Colonel John, 254; Daniel, 139, 209, 210.
Carey, Hon. John, 385.

Carlton, Sir Guy (British), 324.
Carmichael, Major, 45.
Carpenter, John, 34, 35,·37, 38.
Carson, Alexander, 139.
Case, William, 248.
Catfish Camp (Catfish), 275.
Catfish (Washington, Pa.), 67, 253, 281, 282, 287, 366.
Cathcart, Mary, 229.
Chadwick, John, 367.
Chambers, sons of, murdered, 268.
Cherry, young, killed, 274.
Chilloway, Job or William, see "Tom Jelloway."
Christian Indians, 3, 4, 9, 36, 37, 38, 70, 78, 79, 80, 140, 152, 155, 156, 172, 177, 180, 181, 190, 194, 231, 252, 317, 331, 338, 339, 340, 359, 360.
Clark's Campaign, 108.
Clark, Colonel Geo. Rogers, 10, 11, 26, 108, 189, 363, 380.
Clark, Captain, 189.
Clark, Richard, 247.
Cleghorn, surgeon, 16.
Coffinberry's *Forest Rangers*, 384.
Cole, Lady, 16.
Colonial Records, compilation of, 78.
Connell, Anne, 117; James, *ib.*; Nancy, *ib.*; Polly, *ib.*; William, *ib.*
Connell, Zach. 247.
Cook, Edward, 28, 43, 45, 261, 279, 295.
Cook, Moses, 250.
Corbly, John, attacked by Indians, 61.
Cornwallis, Lord (British), 49, 112, 349.
Council of Censors, 297, 298, 304, 306.
Cox, Captain Isaac, 253.
CRAWORD, COLONEL WILLIAM, elected commander of the expedition against Sandusky, 77; his birth, parentage, and childhood, 81, *et seq.*; he learns the art of surveying, 83; commissioned ensign, and joins Braddock's army, *ib.*; employed afterward upon the frontier, 84; receives a captain's commission, and recruits a company, 85; presses a wagoner into service, *ib.*; marches to the reduction of Fort du Quesne, 88; remains in the army three years, and then returns home, *ib.*; examines the valley of the Youghiogheny, and locates upon that river, 89; removes his family there, 90; selects lands for Washington, 91, *et seq.*; follows and captures a murderer, 93; appointed justice of the peace for Cumberland county, 94; he is visited by Washington, *ib.*; accompanies Washington down the Ohio, 95, *et seq.*; appointed justice of the peace for Bedford county, 97; made presiding justice of Westmoreland county, *ib.*; serves as captain in Dunmore's War, 99; removed from office in Westmoreland county, 101; accepts office under Virginia, *ib.*; sides with the colonies against Great Britain, 102; recruits a regiment for Continental service, 103; receives a colonel's commission, *ib.*; serves under Washington upon the sea-board, 104; repairs to Fort Pitt, 105; takes command of a Virginia regiment, 106; builds Fort Crawford, 107; invited to join Clark's expedition to the Illinois, 108; engaged under McIntosh in the Detroit expedition, 109; he has a narrow escape, 110; leads small parties against the savages, 111; aids the abortive expedition of Clark and Gibson, 112; retires from the army, *ib.*; his children and grandchildren, 113; his pleasure at home, 114; resolves to join the Sandusky expedition, 115; prepares to leave home, 116; makes his will, 117; has an interview with Irvine at Fort Pitt, 118; arrives at Mingo Bottom, 119; Goodman's memoir of, *ib.*; Brackenridge's sketch of, 120; his expectation of being elected commander, 121; he marches for Sandusky, 136, *et seq.*; changes his course, 138; guards against surprises, *ib.*; reaches the Muskingum, 139, *et seq.*; he crosses the Killbuck, 142; reaches the Sandusky, 143, *et seq.*; arrives at the Sandusky Plains, 148; marches through them, 151; finds the Wyandot town uninhabited, 153; orders a halt, *ib.*; moves in search of Wyandot settlements, 202; calls a council of war, 203; resolves to march but a few hours longer in search of the enemy, *ib.*; discovers the savages, 205, *et seq.*; attacks the enemy, 207; fights the battle of Sandusky, 208; prepares for a final attack, 215; discovers the enemy largely reinforced, 216; resolves on a retreat, 217; commences the return march, 220; is missed by the army, 224; he is reported missing to Irvine, 243; cause

Index. 395

of his separation from the army, 311;
his wanderings homeward, 312, *et seq.*;
he is captured, 316; taken to Wingenund's camp, 317; sent for by Captain Pipe and Wingenund, 329; his
death warrant, 330; he is to march
to Sandusky, 331; goes to the Half
King's town, 332; has an interview
with Simon Girty, 333; arrives at
Upper Sandusky Old Town, 334;
painted black, 335; taken toward the
Tymochtee, 336; Girty's faithlessness
to him, 337; cause of his death sentence—query, 338, *et seq.*; beaten by
the savages, 341; reaches the Tymochtee, *ib.*; he is stripped naked, 380;
tied to a stake, 381; his resignation,
382; powder shot into his body, 387;
his ears cut off, *ib.*; fire applied to his
body, 388; he begs Girty to shoot
him, 389; scalped, 391; live coals
laid on him, *ib.*; his remains charred,
ib.; the savages dance around them,
392; exultation at the Shawanese villages, 392; gloom upon the border,
ib.; his death lamented by Washington, *ib.*
Crawford county, Ohio, erected, 144;
Sandusky river flows through, 145;
Sandusky Plains in, 149, 150; the
county named *Crawford*, why, 387.
Crawford County (Ohio) Forum, 119.
Crawford county, Pa., set off, 144.
Crawford, Effie, 90; Hannah, 90, 117,
118, 289, 290, 291, 296, 297; John,
90, 113, 115, 117, 118, 247, 249,
295, 296; Moses, 117; Richard, *ib.*;
Sarah, 90, 113, 347, 348; William,
son of John, 117; William, son of
Valentine, 118, 138, 311, 333, 346;
Valentine, 81, 118.
Crawford's Defeat, a "poem," 76, 77, 212.
"Crawford's Battle Ground," 213.
Creigh, Dr. Alfred, Notes, 81; *Hist.
Wash. Co.* 15, 50, 213, 282.
Cressap, Captain Daniel, 254; Mike, *ib.*
Crook, Colonel, 45, 265.
"Crooked Knife creek,"(Broken Sword),
329.
Crow, Captain John, 254.
Custard, John, 249.
Custis, Miss, 97.

Daniel, a "mulatto man," 117.
Darlington, William M., notice of, 146;
assistance rendered by, 147.

Darby, William, 259, 282.
Dawson, Nicholas, bewildered, 283; convinced against his will, 284; John,
283.
Dean, John, 247.
De Hass, Wills, *Hist. Ind. Wars W. Va.*,
cited and approved, 33, 92, 129, 259,
274; cited and criticised, 54, 79, 80,
121, 274, 294.
Delaware town (or village), see Pipe's
town.
Detroit, 2, 4, 5, 6, 10, 26, 27, 50, 70,
109, 112, 156, 159, 163, 164, 165,
166, 177, 180, 186, 188, 189, 190,
191, 192, 193, 201, 216, 267, 327,
352.
Dick, a "negro man," 117.
Dinwiddie, Governor, 94.
Doddridge, Rev. Jos., *Notes*, cited and
approved, 40, 54, 122, 274; cited and
criticised, 41, 57, 70, 72, 78, 79, 121,
141, 156, 159, 203, 217, 228, 229,
239, 251, 252, 274, 294, 295.
Dodge's *Red Men O. Vall.* 80, 339.
Dorman, Timothy, taken prisoner, 35.
Drake's *Dic. Amer. Biog.* 20.
Draper, Lyman C., notes of, 180.
Dry, Wm., see "Wm. Dry."
Dualls, Samuel, 247.
Dunlevy, Anthony, 252, 253; A. H.
78; Walker's Notes to 199, 201;
sees "Big Captain Johnny," 211;
Francis, 77, 211, 252-257; his declaration for a pension and MS. notes
cited, 129, 142, 143, 208, 212, 214,
223, 224, 234, 235, 239, 240; a
fiction concerning him, 378.
Dunmore, Lord, 97, 99, 101.
Duval, Lewis, 248.

Early Hist. West. Pa. 339.
Edgar, James, 45.
Edmondson, Captain, 95.
Elliott, Captain Matthew, hurries up the
Sandusky, 176; a tory, *ib.*; arrival in
the Indian country, *ib.*; taken to Detroit, 177; commissioned a captain,
ib.; his subsequent career, *ib.*; assumes
command at Sandusky, 178; holds
back the Wyandots, 206; his orders
to Captain Pipe, 207; arrives at Wapatomica, 349; believed to have been
at Crawford's torture, 379.
Elliott, Commodore, 178.
Ellis, Captain, 255.
Euler, John, 117.

Evans, John, 44, 254, 262.
Ewing, Nathaniel, communication from, 75.

Fairfax, Lord, 81.
Fast, Christian, 380.
Fayette county, Pa., erected, 89.
Ferrol, Captain, 254.
Fink, Henry, attacked by Indians, 33; John, killed, *ib.*
Finley's *Hist. Wyandot Miss.* 168, 385.
Flood, Andrew, 254.
Forbes, General, 29, 85.
Forts: Crawford, 107; Dunmore, 99; Henry, 4, 8, 23, 24, 28, 277; Laurens, 7, 109, 111, 373; McIntosh, 6, 8, 373; Pitt, 3, 5, 6, 11, 21, 29, 41, 42, 94.
Foster, Hon. Charles, assistance from, 71.
Frank, Michael, 247.
Freeman's Journal, 323.

Gaddis, Thomas, elected field-major, 77; his home, 123; biographical sketch, *ib.;* reimbursed for losses in the Sandusky expedition, 247; returns home, 296.
Galaxy, The, 134.
Gard, Jeremiah, 247.
Gibson, Chief Justice of Pennsylvania, 42; Colonel John, 7, 11, 22, 26, 28, 29, 30, 31, 32, 33, 36, 38, 39, 42, 126, 253, 254, 255, 390.
Girty, George, 183, 276, 353; James, 183, 349; Thomas, 183; Simon, 182; his birth and parentage, *ib.;* captured by the Senecas, 182; returns to the settlements, *ib.;* associates with Kenton and Crawford, *ib.;* deserts to the enemy, 184; his hostility to the Americans assured, 185; captured by the Wyandots, 186; arrives at Detroit, *ib.;* employed in the British Indian department, *ib.;* resides with the Wyandots, 187; saves the life of Kenton, 188; his wild career against the border, 188, 189; attempts the life of Zeisberger, 189, *et seq.;* his treatment of the Moravian missionaries, 190, *et seq.;* assists against Crawford, 194; his subsequent history, 195, *et seq.;* his appearance and character, 199; his savageness and ferocity, 200; his fool-hardiness, *ib.;* his fear of being captured, 201; in the advance against the Americans, 206; his conspicuity at the battle of Sandusky, 208; his voice recognized, 218; supposed by some to have chief command, 219; his presence at Fort Pitt in 1777, 254; his interview with Crawford at Half King's town, 332, *et seq.;* crosses the Plains to witness his torture, 336; speaks to him, *ib.;* fails to intercede for him, 337; Crawford begs him to shoot him, 389; his delight at the scene, *ib.;* bids Knight prepare for death, 389, 390; expresses ill-will for Colonel Gibson, 390.
Gist, Thomas, 117; neighborhood of, 362.
Gnadenhütten, 9; the "massacre" at, 38; locality of, 139.
Goodman, Alfred T., 119, 120.
Graham, Noble, 247.
Graham, Richard, 249.
Greentown, 143.
Guffee, James, 250.

Hale, Richard, 249.
Half King, 163, 170, 189, 191, 329, 330, 357.
Half King's town, see Sandusky of 1782.
Hall, Colonel William, 247.
Hall, Edward, 247.
Hall's *Rom. Wes. Hist.* 88.
Hamilton, Henry (British), 2, 4, 177, 186, 189.
Hand, Brigadier-General Edward, 5, 105, 184, 253.
Hanna, Robert, 97.
Hannah's-town, 101, 268, 269.
Harbaugh, Daniel, 225, 226, 227, 291.
Hardin, Jr., John, 248; John, father, 255.
Harmar, General Josiah, campaign of, 171, 196, 306, 367.
Harrison, Benj., Governor of Virginia, 14, 53.
Harrison, Colonel William, 94, 113, 115, 116, 117, 118, 295, 311, 333, 346, 347, 348; Lawrence, 347; Sarah (Colonel Crawford's daughter), 113, 118, 349.
Harrison, General William H. 211, 368.
Harris, S. R., information from, 274.
Hartley, Lieutenant-Colonel, 131.
Hay, Lieutenant, 24, 25, 28.
Hazard, Mr., compiler *Colonial Record,* 78.
Hazle, a Canadian, 182.
Heckewelder, John, followed by Dodd-

ridge, 70; *Hist. Ind. Nations,* cited and criticised, 72, 78, 79, 155, 156, 317, 341, 342, 356-361, 382-384, 388; *Narr. Morav. Miss.*, cited and approved, 54, 154, 173, 174, 180, 190-194; the same cited and criticised, 78, 79, 156, 211, 231, 328, 342, 381, 387, 388.
Heming, Louis, 247.
"H. H. Smith," 162.
Hickman, Charles, 248.
Hildreth's *Hist. U. S.* 79.
Hill, John, 250.
" H. Klipfer," 162.
Historical Magazine, 310.
Hoagland, elected a captain, 75; his fate uncertain, 281.
Hodge, Daniel, 384, 385, 386.
Hoge, Rev. James, 256.
Hood, Andrew, elected captain, 76.
Hoofnagle, Mr. 269.
Hopkins, Richard, 250.
Hough and Bourne's *Map of Ohio,* 143, 329.
Howe, General (British), 104.
Howe's *Hist. Coll. Ohio,* 31, 195, 199, 201, 274, 322, 328, 342, 354, 356, 357, 384, 389.
Huston, William, 259, 281.

Ingham, John, 93.
" Indian Stephen," murdered, 93.
Indian Tribes: Cherokees, 352; Chippewas, *ib.*; Delawares, 3, 5, 8, 9, 160, 161, 167, 206, 207, 214, 217, 221, 222, 316, 317, 329, 330, 331, 332, 334, 337, 339, 340, 352, 379, 380, 383; Eries, 161; Iroquois, 6, 7; Miamis, 126, 127, 153; Mingoes, 95, 164, 189, 264, 352; Monseys, 264, 348, 352; Ottawas, 352; Senecas, 184, 186; Shawanese, 3, 30, 49, 60, 127, 160, 161, 164, 169, 170, 173, 185, 187, 217, 221, 222, 226, 322, 352, 360; Wyandots, 2, 60, 80, 147, 160, 161, 162, 163, 164, 165, 166, 167, 172, 173, 174, 180, 182, 186, 187, 194, 205, 206, 207, 213, 214, 264, 329, 333, 352, 379, 386.
IRVINE, BRIGADIER-GENERAL WILLIAM, appointed to command the Western Department, 13; his birth, parentage, education, and profession, 16; emigrates to America and marries, 17; sides with the colonies against Great Britain, 18; raises and commands a Pennsylvania regiment, 19; marches into Canada, and is taken prisoner, *ib.*; exchanged and commissioned brigadier-general, 20; his military career in the east, *ib.*; repairs to Fort Pitt, and assumes command of the Western Department, 21; reforms the garrison, 22, *et seq.*; sends a militia force to Wheeling, 23, *et seq.*; attends to the condition of the country, 25; investigates a scheme against Detroit, 26, *et seq.*; prepares to visit Congress, 28; starts for Philadelphia, 29; receives instructions from Washington, 41; returns to Fort Pitt, 42; reduces refractory troops to obedience, 43; calls a convention in the Western Department, *ib.*; his exertions in protecting the frontier, 47; his attention called to a proposed expedition against Sandusky, 51; he carefully considers the proposition, 52; opposes a scheme for a new state, 53, *et seq.*; his kindness to the Moravians, 54, *et seq.*; consents to the Sandusky expedition, 58; writes to Moore concerning it, 59; notifies Washington of its assembling, 68; issues instructions to its commander, 69, *et seq.*; nominates a candidate for its first officer, 76; details two of his officers for the expedition, 77; urges Crawford to accept the command of, 115; advises with him concerning the order of marching, 118; he is notified of Crawford's election, 119; his preference for Crawford, 121; notified by Marshal of the failure of the campaign, 241; receives from Williamson and Rose an account of the expedition, 242, *et seq.*; sends an official report to Washington, 244, *et seq.*; informs the executive of Pennsylvania of the failure of the expedition, 246; importuned to organize another expedition against Sandusky, 261; considers the proposition, 263; encourages the borderers, 276; the scheme abandoned, 278, *et seq.*; his subsequent career and death, 301, *et seq.*
Irvine, Callender, 210, 300, 301; Captain Andrew, 17; Dr. Matthew, 17; Dr. William A., 210, 300, 304.
Irvine's *MS. Order-Book,* 29, 43, 132.

Jackson, Robert, 248.
James, John H., note of, 323.

Jeffers, Ewell, 165.
Jefferson's *Notes on Virginia*, 31.
Jefferson, Thomas, President of United States, 42, 309; Governor of Virginia, 363.
Jelloway, Tom, see "Tom Jelloway,"
"John Newman," 168.
"John Ricefarm," 291.
Johnson, Margaret, 229.
Johnston, William, 259, 281.
Johnston, Colonel John, 357, 384, 389.
Jolly, Martin, 282.
Jones' Spring, see Butler's Spring.
"Jos. Brown," 168.

Kean, John, 307.
Kear, Jonathan, Notes of, 167, 174, 385.
Kemp, Reuben, 247.
Kendall, Thomas, 248.
Kenton, Simon, 183, 187, 188.
"Kilbourne road," 162, 163.
Klipfer, H., see "H. Klipfer."
Knapp's *Hist. Ashland County*, 143, 380.
Knight, Dr. John, appointed surgeon, 77; spared by Irvine for Sandusky, 118; biographical sketch of, 125; solicited by Crawford to join the expedition, *ib.*; reported missing, 224, *et seq.*; accompanies Crawford after retreat commenced, 311, *et seq.*; captured by Delawares, 316; taken to Wingenund's camp, 317; marched to Upper Sandusky Old Town, 332; *painted black*, 334; guarded by Captain Pipe and Wingenund to Little Tymochtee creek, 335, *et seq.*; put in charge of an Indian to be taken to the Shawanese towns, 336; beaten by the savages, 341; meets Simon Girty, *ib.*; arrives at the Tymochtee, *ib.*; taken to Pipe's town, 342; *again painted black*, *ib.*; starts for the Shawanese towns, *ib.*; strikes for liberty, 343; his escape and return to Fort Pitt, 369, *et seq.*; remains at Pittsburg until the close of the war, 373; his marriage and death, 374; he had been pensioned, *ib.*
Knight's *Narrative*, cited, 4, 70, 77, 90, 141, 163, 167, 173, 181, 203, 217, 223, 311, 340, 369, 370, 373, 379, 387; its history, 323-326.

Langdon, Woodbury, 307.
La Salle, the adventurer, 147.
Lashley, Alexander, 250.
Leatherlips, a Wyandot chief, 186.

Leet, Daniel, elected brigade-major, 77; biographical sketch, 124, 125; his bravery, 207; commands a division, 219, 220; returns home, 296.
Leith, Geo. W. 179; John, biographical sketch of, 178, 179; Samuel, 179.
Leith's *Narrative*, 165, 175 176, 180, 235, 236, 327, 328.
Lemoyne, Dr. F. J. 282.
Lenni Lenape, 330, 357.
Leonard, Patrick, 134.
Levallie, Francis, 192.
Lewis, Colonel Andrew, 99, 100.
Lincoln, Major-General B., Secretary of War, 259, 262, 268, 274, 278, 279, 280.
"Little Eagle," 32.
Little Sandusky creek, 146, 151, 152.
Lochry, Colonel Archibald, 10, 43, 111.
Logan, the Mingo chief, 30, 31, 200.
"Log Cabin school" (Rev. Thaddeus Dodd's), 255.
Longstreet, Aaron, 231, 232.
Loskiel's *His. Miss.*, cited and criticised, 72, 78, 155, 260; cited and approved, 54, 173.
Lower Sandusky, 11, 153, 159, 165, 169, 174, 175, 191, 192, 197, 216, 235, 236, 264, 327.
Lowry, Sally, 179.
Lucas, John, 248.
Lyon, John, 72, 74, 121.

Mac-a-chack, a Shawanese town, 354, 375.
Mac-a-cheek (Mac-a-chack), 354.
Map of Crawford County, Ohio, 168.
Map of Wyandot County, Ohio, 154, 162, 174.
Marshal, James, 23, 24, 28, 44, 45, 50, 51, 57, 70, 74, 123, 124, 134, 136, 216, 241, 256, 258, 265, 275, 276, 277, 278, 279.
Martin, "a mulatto boy," 118.
McBride's *Pioneer Biography*, 10, 367.
McCaddon, John, 231.
McClelland, John, elected field-major, 77; biographical sketch, 123, 124; leads the retreat, 221; wounded, *ib.*; body recognized by Slover, 346.
McClung, John A. 232; his *Sketches of Western Adventure*, *ib.*
McCormick, Alexander, 166, 189, 191.
McCormick, Anne, 117; Effie (daughter of Colonel Crawford), 113, 117, 118; William, 113, 117.

Index. 399

McCoy, James, 247.
McCulloch, Major, 45.
McCutchen, Joseph, Notes of, in *Amer. Pioneer*, 229, 230, 337, 338, 384, 385.
McDonald, Alexander, 248.
McDonald's *Biog. Sketches*, 188.
McFadden, Mrs. Agnes, 287.
McFall, John, 367.
McGeehan, elected captain, 75.
McIntosh, Brigadier-General Lachlin, 5, 10, 106, 109, 124, 188, 254; *MS. Order-Book of*, 6, 109, 348.
McKean, Thomas, 307.
McKee, Alex. 177, 184, 189, 198, 350, 351.
McKee, Nancy, 117.
McKenzie, Dr. 125.
McKinly, John, 331, 336.
"McKnight, Dr." 388.
McMasters, Ensign, 76.
McMillan, Hon. John, 15.
Meason, Isaac, 295.
Mem. Hist. Soc. Penn. 342, 361.
Mifflin, Governor, 308.
Miller, John, elected captain, 76.
Miller, Robert, 249.
Mills, Thomas, 292, 293.
Mingo Bottom, 59, 62, 63, 133, 136, 241, 244.
Missionary establishments, see Moravian Indian villages.
Monongahela river, 24, 40, 62, 67, 84, 88, 261.
Monongalia county, Va. 14, 44, 46, 109, 262.
Monteur, Andrew, 255; John, *ib*.
Moore, Thomas, 261.
Moore, William, Governor of Pennsylvania, 14, 59, 60, 122, 172, 241, 243, 269, 331, 373, 392.
Moravian Indians, see Christian Indians.
Moravian missionaries, 3, 5, 9, 10, 36, 37, 55, 70, 152, 156, 170, 171, 189, 190, 191, 192, 193, 219.
Moravian Indian villages, 3, 9, 36, 38, 122, 137, 138, 139, 152, 156, 159, 160, 176, 179, 241.
Moravian towns, see Moravian Indian villages.
Morgan, George, 3.
Morgan, Major-General Daniel, 88.
Mountz, Providence, 116.
Munn, elected captain, 75; wounded, 212.
Munro, Andrew, 248.
Murray, Charles, 198.

Muskingum river, 3, 6, 8, 9, 37, 38, 139, 140, 152, 161, 167, 169, 170, 176, 177, 189, 240, 320, 321, 365, 372, 373, 377.

Nace, G. 213.
Neville, John, 3, 5.
Newman, John, see "John Newman."
New Schönbrun, 9, 139, 140, 160.
New State scheme, 12, 53, 54.
Nicholl, James, 247.
Nichol, Thomas, 282.
Nimmons, William, 259, 281.

Odell's lake, 147.
Ogle, elected captain, 76; killed, 212, 213.
Ohio county, Va. 14, 44, 46, 73, 74, 92, 109.
Olden Time, The, 20.
Olentangy creek, 149, 150, 233.
Orr, John, 221.

"Pan-handle, Va." 14, 41, 67.
Parisi., Joseph., 247.
Parkman, Francis, 83.
Patterson's *Hist. Backwoods*, 79.
Patrick, Peter, 247.
Paull, George, 302; George, Jr. 368; James, 66; a sorrowful parting, 67; recollections of, 76; in the advance company, 139, remembers the route from Mingo Bottom, 160; lost sight of by Sherrard, 288; separated from the army, 318; his wanderings homeward, 318, *et seq.*; a burnt foot, 321; ambushed, 322; escapes, *ib.*; a biographical sketch, 362, *et seq.*; his escape from the Indians and return home, 364, *et seq.*; his subsequent career, 367, *et seq.*; his death, 368; Recollections, MS., *ib.*; Paull, Joseph, Notes of, 66; he still survives (1872), 368.
Penn. Archives, cited, 59, 241; compiled by Hazard, 78.
Penn. Jour. and Weekly Ad. 234, 235, 259, 260, 348.
Penn. Packet, 35, 37, 269, 348.
Pentecust, Dorsey, 58, 59, 97, 101, 122, 216, 241, 243, 259.
Perkins' *Annals of the West*, 79.
Peterson, Peter, 249.
Peyster, Arentz Schuyler de, 2, 159, 173, 180, 189, 191, 192, 193, 352.
Pipe, Captain, 169; upon the Tymochtee, *ib.*; early history of, *ib.*; his

hostility, 170; his subsequent career, 171, *et seq.*; marches to aid the Wyandots, 172; his advance, 206; skillful maneuver of, 207, *et seq.*; sends for Crawford, 329; cheats the Half King, 330; enraged against the prisoners, 333; arrives at Upper Sandusky Old Town, 334; *paints the prisoners black*, *ib.*; greets Crawford, but *paints him black*, 335; guards him and Knight towards the Tymochtee, *ib.*; Girty fails to intercede with, in behalf of Crawford, 337; his barbarity accounted for, 338, 339; he and Wingenund alone responsible, 340; his subsequent excuse, 341; makes a speech at Crawford's torture, 382.
Pipe's town, 167, 168, 169, 174, 180, 194, 206, 329, 335, 336, 341, 342, 369, 387.
Pirtle, Hon. Henry, 108.
Pittsburg, 3, 10, 12, 40, 47, 94, 126, 132, 133, 157, 177, 179, 183, 184, 254, 297, 298, 302, 303, 325, 363.
Pittsburg Gazette, 325.
Plains, see Sandusky Plains.
Poe, Adam, 270–274; Andrew, 270–273.
Pointer, Jonathan, 385.
Pollock, Major, 133.
Pollock, William, 276.
Pomoacan (the Half King), 163, 190, 329.
"Pontiac's War," 169, 170, 183.
Portage between the Sandusky and Scioto, 146, 152.
Porter, Sergeant, 279.
Pratt, Captain (British), 276, 277.
Price, Miss Mary, 135.

Rankin, 284–287.
Redstone Old Fort (Brownsville), 67, 362.
Reily, John, 256.
Reno, William, 325.
Reply of Crawford, 106.
Reynolds, Alex. 282; James, *ib.*
Reynolds, spirited reply of, 195.
Rhea, Audley, 247.
Richey, William, 385, 386.
Ring hunt, 150, 151.
Ritchie, Captain Craig, 76, 135, 211, 248, 256.
Robbins, a trader, 192.
Rodgers, Daniel, 290.
Rodgers, John, 138, 237.

Rogers' *Amer. Biog.* 20, 31.
Rollins, Aaron, 248.
Rose, Lieutenant John, aid to Colonel Crawford, 77; spared by Irvine for the campaign, 118; his eulogy of Williamson, 121; his first appearance in the American army, 130; his story, *ib.*; he is appointed surgeon, *ib.*; becomes the warm friend of Irvine, 131; leaves the army and joins the navy, *ib.*; he is taken prisoner, *ib.*; exchanged, and again joins the army, 132; appointed aid to Irvine, with rank of lieutenant, *ib.*; accompanies Irvine to Pittsburg, *ib.*; arrives at Mingo Bottom, 133, *et seq.*; his gallantry in face of the enemy, 206; his martial appearance, 207; pursued by mounted Indians, 210; aids Williamson upon the retreat, 224; his good conduct at the battle of Olentangy, 234; writes to Irvine from Mingo Bottom, 242, 244; returns to Fort Pitt, 296; subsequent career in America, 297, *et seq.*; makes known to Irvine *his true history*, 299, *et seq.*; returns to Europe, 300; made Grand Marshal of Livonia, *ib.*; his death, 301; known as "Major," 311.
Rosenthal, Gustavus H. de ("Rose"), 299, 300, 301, 310.
Ross, Captain, 76, 212.
Ross, James, 75.
Ross, William, 248.

Safford's *Records Revolutionary War*, 112.
Salem, 9, 139, 140.
Sandusky Expeditions: McIntosh's expedition, 6, *et seq.*; its failure, 7, 8; Clark's, 10; its abandonment, 11; Gibson's, *ib.*; given up, *ib.*; another suggested, 51; considered by Irvine, 52; he sends out a reconnoitering party, *ib.*; its failure, 53; Irvine's precaution concerning the enterprise, *ib.*; not combined with the new state scheme, 54; Irvine's power to act concerning, 55; conditions precedent, 56; what aid he could furnish, 57; the country people clamorous, *ib.*; Irvine consents to the project, 58; arrangements agreed upon, 59; executive of Pennsylvania notified, *ib.*; the project not irruptive, 60; the necessity for the expedition, *ib.*; a stimulant unnecessary to induce volunteering for, 61; excitement concerning, 62; the place of

rendezvous, 63; precautions of the volunteers, 64; object of the expedition, 69, 70; organization of, 75, *et seq.*; a prevalent error concerning the intention of, 78; history of its march to the Sandusky, 136, *et seq.*; of the battles fought and the retreat to the Ohio, 202, *et seq.*; ending of the campaign, 244; its legality recognized, 246, *et seq.*; causes of its failure, 249, *et seq.*; the loss, 259, 260; Irvine importuned to organize a second expedition, 261, *et seq.*; considers the proposition, 261, *et seq.*; the necessity for it, 265; frontiers harassed, 268, *et seq.*; citizens of Washington county arrange for the enterprise, 275, 276; place appointed for rendezvous, 278; the scheme abandoned, 279; peace, 280.

Sandusky of 1782 (Half King's town), 162, 163, 164, 165, 166, 169, 175, 179, 180, 189, 190, 191, 194, 202, 205, 206, 326, 327, 328, 329, 331, 332, 334, 380.

Sandusky, origin of the word, 147.

Sandusky Plains, 148, 149, 150, 151, 172, 204, 205, 208, 227, 228, 230, 231, 233, 234, 235, 314, 318, 319, 363, 370.

Sandusky river, 2, 6, 60, 137, 140, 143, 144, 145, 146, 147, 150, 152, 154, 156, 157, 158, 161, 162, 167, 169, 174, 179, 180, 202, 204, 234, 313, 314, 315.

Scalp halloo, 391.

Schweinitz's *Life of Zeisberger*, cited and approved, 54, 55, 140, 141, 180; cited and criticised, 70, 71, 141, 181, 326, 333, 361.

Scioto river, 3, 127, 146, 149, 157, 161, 162, 169, 185, 194, 233, 322, 369, 375, 376.

Scott, Captain, 254.

Scott, Hon. Josiah, communication from, 225.

Scott, James, 249.

Seidel, Rev. Nathaniel, 55.

Sherman, Hon. John, courtesy of, 138.

Shearer, William, 249.

Shepherd, David, 44.

Sherrard, David A. C., 229; recollections of, 290, 291; Hugh, 287; John, 139, 209, 217, 225, 226, 227, 228, 229, 240, 287; Robt. A., notes of, 115, 138, 139, 160, 210, 219, 229, 240, 288, 291, 319, 321, 368; William, 229.

Sherrard's *Narr. of James Paul*, 368.

Slover, Abraham, 126; John, appointed pilot to the Sandusky expedition, 77; his previous history, 126, *et seq.*; familiarity with the Indian country, 128; guides the army on the march, 138; announces the Sandusky Plains near, 148; his knowledge of the Sandusky region, 153; missing, 224; loses his horse, 318; wanders around the Plains, 318, *et seq.*; reaches the woodland, 320; ambushed and captured by Shawanese, 322; starts for Shawanese towns, *ib.*; reaches the Mad river, 323; beaten at an Indian village, 344; arrives at Wapatomika, *ib.*; runs the gauntlet, 345; recognizes dead bodies of companions, 346; he is examined by the Indians, 349; designs against him, *ib.*; sees Tutelu, 351; tied, stripped naked, and blacked, 353; taken to Mac-a-chack, 354; bound to a post and fire kindled around him, *ib.*; wonderfully preserved, *ib.*; his efforts to untie himself, 355; his success, 356; his ride for life, 375; his escape and return to the border, 376, *et seq.*; his ignorance of the British being at Sandusky Plains explained, 378.

Slover's *Narrative*, cited, 4, 90, 323, 339, 346, 347, 377, 379, 392; its history, 323, 324, 325, 326.

Smilie, John, 248.

Smilie, Robert, 248.

Smith, Albert M., courtesy of, 75; Jacob, P. 287; John P. 287; N. W. 287; Philip, 75, 143, 148, 210, 212, 284, 285, 286, 287.

Smith, Devereaux, 101.

Smith's *His. Jefferson College*, 274.

Smith, H. H., see "H. H. Smith."

Smith, Moses, 247.

Smith's *Old Red Stone*, 61.

Society of the Cincinnati, the Penn., 309.

South, Jacob, 248.

Spark's *Corr. Amer. Rev.*, 55, 68, 119, 121, 133; his *Writings of Washington*, 42, 92, 98, 306.

Spencer, O. M., 199.

Spicer, William, 145.

Springer, Captain Uriah, 52, 291, 348; Uriah, Jr., 115, 290.

Springer, Lieutenant John, 254.

Sprouls, Hugh, 249.

State Hist. Soc. Wisconsin, 173, 180, 187.
St. Clair, Arthur, 97, 100, 171, 196, 306.
Steele, Captain, 254.
Steele, Lieutenant David, 253.
Stephenson, Elizabeth, 81; Hugh, 81, 90, 254; James, 81; John, 81; Marcus, 81; Polly, 374; Richard, 81; Richard, Jr. 81, 374.
Stevens, Dennis, 248.
Stewart, Lieutenant Edward, 76, 237.
Stewart, William, 91.
"Stewart's Crossings," 89, 91, 94, 96, 261, 295.
Stone, William L., 134.
Sup. Ex. Council Pennsylvania, 13, 58, 59, 124, 246, 247, 248, 249, 250, 259, 303, 304.
Swartz, Jacob, 248.

Taylor, Henry, 249.
Taylor, *His. of Ohio*, 322, 326, 339, 354.
Taylor, Robert, 250.
The Pipe, see Captain Pipe.
"The Half Moon," 355.
The Triangle, 305.
Thompson, Charles, 13.
"Tom Jelloway," 333.
Tompoh, George, 249.
Treaties of the United States (Langtree and O'Sullivan), 335.
Turvey, John, 250.
Tuscarawas river, 3, 170, 320, 322, 363.
Tutelu, 342, 343, 351, 369, 380.
"Tyamoherty" (Tymochtee), 384.
Tymochtee creek, 146, 149, 150, 167, 170, 174, 216, 320, 329, 338, 341, 342, 369, 379, 384, 385; signification of the word, 149.

Upper Sandusky, Ohio, 153, 162, 163, 167, 169, 180, 181, 203, 213; Old Town, 152, 153, 154, 155, 163, 167, 168, 173, 180, 223, 226, 235, 251, 326, 327, 332; a Wyandot town, 162.

Vallandigham, Colonel, 45.
Vance, Isaac, 225.
Vankirk, Jacob, 247.
Veech, James, Notes of, 92, 102, 184; his *Monongahela of Old*, 117, 368.
Vernon, Major Frederick, 7.

Walhonding river, 152, 170.
Wallace, George, 42.

Wallace, Mrs. Robert, 34; Robert, 33, 34, 37; Robert, Jr. 34.
Walker, Hon. Charles I., Address of, 173, 187.
Walker, Jr., Robert, 250.
Walker, Mrs., 49.
Walker, Mrs. William, 368.
Walker, Hon. William, Notes of, 146, 152, 154, 163, 166, 167, 174, 175, 180, 182, 199, 201, 236, 328, 330, 333, 385, 386, 387; his recollections, value of, 154, 155.
Wapatomica, 188, 323, 343, 344, 346, 347, 350, 351, 353, 354, 369.
Ward, John, 255.
War-dress of the volunteers, 65.
Washington county, Pennsylvania, 14, 23, 47, 50, 67, 73, 74, 275.
Washington, General George, 12, 13, 26, 27, 41, 42, 81, 82, 85, 88, 91, 92, 94, 95, 96, 97, 98, 105, 106, 120, 246, 268, 279, 280, 301, 302, 305, 324, 373, 378, 379, 392; John Augustine, 92; Lund, 92; Samuel, 92.
Watson, M. H. and J. V. B., map of, 168.
Wayne, General Anthony, 21; campaign of, 172, 196, 198.
Weems' *Life of Washington*, 82.
Wells, Samuel, 174, 175, 380, 385.
West Augusta, district of, 89.
Westmoreland county, Pennsylvania, 8, 46, 47, 50, 67, 74, 89, 99, 112, 363.
West. Res. Hist. Soc., 119.
Wetzel, Lewis, 292, 293, 294.
"Whisky Insurrection," 123, 135, 307, 367.
White, William, 35.
Whittlesey, Charles, discourse of, 31; notes in *Amer. Pioneer*, 339.
Williamson, Colonel David, marches to the Muskingum, 37; leads a second expedition to that river, 38; attends a convention at Fort Pitt, 45; proposes an expedition against Sandusky, 51; he is a candidate for commander, 76; elected a field-major, 77; his good conduct, 121; eulogized by Doddridge, 122; his proposition to attack Sandusky, doubted, 217; takes command of the army on the retreat, 224; his valor at the battle of Olentangy, 234; his good management after, 237, *et seq.*; his letter to Irvine from Mingo Bottom, 242, *et seq.*; returns home, 296; his death, *ib*.

"Williamson's trail," 138, 241.
Wisendorf, Dr., 130.
Wingenund, 168, 206, 329, 330, 331, 333, 334, 335, 337, 340, 341, 342, 356, 357–361, 379, 382, 383, 384.
Wingenund's camp, 168, 317, 327, 330, 380.
"Wm. Dry," 154.
Wolfe, General, 17.
Wolfe, Jacob, 281, 282.
Woods, James, 247.
Workman, Hugh, 78, 204, 282, 283; James, 78, 204, 282, 283.
Wright, Mary, 117.
Wyandot county, Ohio, 61, 136, 145, 149, 150, 154; set off, 387.

Wyandotte (Kan.) *Gazette*, 201.
Yohogania county, Virginia, 89, 101, 102, 109, 347.
Youghiogheny river, 40, 62, 67, 89, 92, 94, 96, 113, 116, 125, 392.

Zane, Ebenezer, 128, 277; Jonathan, pilot to the Sandusky expedition, 77; his previous history, 128; his skill in shooting, 129; guides, with Slover, the army to the Sandusky, 138, *et seq.*; advice to Crawford, 203; had been wounded, 129, 255; returns home, 296; death of, *ib.*; Silas, 128.
Zeisberger, David, 140, 180, 189, 190, 191.
Zhaus-sho-toh, 166, 172, 194, 206, 207.

www.ingramcontent.com/pod-product-compliance
Lightning Source LLC
Chambersburg PA
CBHW030604300426
44111CB00009B/1098